COMMERCE INDUSTRY AND TRANSPORT

Studies in economic change on Merseyside

COMMERCE INDUSTRY AND TRANSPORT

Studies in economic change on Merseyside

Edited by
B. L. ANDERSON and
P. J. M. STONEY

LIVERPOOL UNIVERSITY PRESS

Published by
LIVERPOOL UNIVERSITY PRESS
Press Building, Grove Street, Liverpool L7 7AF

First published 1983

British Library Cataloguing in Publication Data

Commerce, industry and transport: studies in economic change on Merseyside.
1. Merseyside—Economic conditions
I. Anderson, B. L. II. Stoney, P. J. M.
330.9'427'5083 HC257.M46

ISBN 0-85323-374-8

Typeset in Century and printed and bound
in Great Britain by Biddles Ltd, Guildford and King's Lynn

PREFACE

The studies brought together in this book reflect the variety of work in progress at the University of Liverpool and elsewhere, on different aspects of economic, social, and cultural change in Liverpool and its region. Some are designed to provide an historical perspective on major themes in the economic and social development of the port and its hinterland. Others explore the changing fortunes of the city-region in more recent times, its present position and prospects. In their different ways all the contributions are intended to reveal something of the complex texture of past history, current problems and new developments in the Merseyside economy. A book of this type cannot hope, and does not claim, to supply the need for a comprehensive study of the development of the Merseyside region, however defined, in its entirety; but some effort has been made to relate changes taking place in Liverpool and its immediate environs to those occurring in the wider region.

The subject areas of the authors are those of most immediate relevance to the study of commercial and industrial change. For the most part the authors are presently, or have been at some time, teachers and researchers in the Departments of Business Studies, Economics, Economic History and Geography, and the Marine Transport Centre of the University of Liverpool. In collecting some of the products of their research in one place it is hoped that they will stimulate wider interest in the past and future development of one of the country's oldest and largest conurbations. Many publications devoted to different topics in the economic and social life of Liverpool and Merseyside have appeared over the years and because opportunities to review and distil their findings are rare, where it has seemed appropriate the authors have attempted to indicate the extent of published work in their fields of interest.

The study by Langton serves to emphasize that Liverpool experienced considerable industrial decline in the late eighteenth century at the same time as its overseas trades and internal communications were coming to exert some of their strongest influences on the local economy in its entire history. Chapter two charts the growth of the city's banking and insurance institutions which helped to give it such an important place in the national and international economy during its Victorian heyday. Murray's study shows how an old-established port industry, sugar-refining, was being transformed during the nineteenth century by new entrepreneurs applying technical change to a traditional industry of the region. The importance of service employment throughout Merseyside's modern history is reflected in the two chapters, four and ten, devoted to tracing its changing character. The one shows the significance of domestic service before 1914, while the other shows how dependent the regional economy had become on the service sector between the wars and the problems associated with restimulating its expansion.

The study by Bean of industrial relations in the dock industry shows how important were many of the changes in the framework and environment of bargaining between the wars for the fortunes of the port in recent years. The interaction between the port of Liverpool and the industry of its hinterland is the theme of Stoney's work on the regional economy and Lister's study is concerned with evaluating the impact of government regional policies on industry in the area. Finally in chapters eight and nine the far-reaching changes that have taken place in transport and communications in the last decades are examined in respect of the port and its trade, and with regard to their impact within the region and between it and the rest of the country. Such academic work is evidence, the editors believe, of a continuing interest and dedication on the part of scholars in the University and elsewhere, towards the economic and social life of Merseyside, past and present.

The editors are conscious of a pressing need for greater understanding of the processes of economic and social change at all levels within, as well as beyond, the region. This has relevance not only for those undergoing full-time study in schools, where the subject matter of this book has not always easily found a place in the curriculum, but in institutions of further and higher education as well. A higher level of awareness of the factors influencing the growth and decline of industries, and of environmental change and urban renewal, in regions such as Merseyside appears more necessary today than ever before. The speed and degree of success with which problems of change have been resolved in the distant and immediate past have depended greatly on how far common perceptions of commerce and industry have accurately reflected the complex realities of the business world. A recurring theme of the contributions to this book is that in a region whose growth has depended on its ability to forge and maintain strong links with outside in trade, industry and ideas, the challenges of change have invariably been least tractable where ignorance and inaccuracy have prevailed.

The editors and the University Press wish to make grateful acknowledgement to the following organizations for financial help towards publication of this book: Mast Laboratories; E. A. Clare & Son Ltd.; Mersey Docks and Harbour Company; Shell UK Ltd.; Capper-Neill Ltd.; Higson's Brewery Ltd.; I.C.I. Mond Division; Pilkington Bros. Ltd.; Dista Products Ltd.; Unilever Merseyside Committee; Plessey Telecommunications Ltd.; Ford of Britain Trust; British Nuclear Fuels Ltd; and the Confederation of British Industry.

B. L. ANDERSON
P. J. M. STONEY

CONTENTS

LIST OF FIGURES

LIST OF TABLES

1

Liverpool and its hinterland in the late eighteenth century

J. LANGTON

During the late eighteenth century, Liverpool grew as quickly as at any other time in its history and as any other city in Europe.[1] It is reputed already to have been 'an *emporium*, a warehouse for produce from countries beyond the seas. The lifeblood and wealth of Liverpool flowed in from abroad, from those distant countries where England, mistress of the seas, was already establishing her commercial supremacy'.[2] This view was expressed by people living in and writing about Liverpool at the time: Enfield explained in the 1770s that 'the History of a place which chiefly subsists by foreign Commerce, cannot be expected to furnish many materials on the head of Manufactures'[3] and according to the *Liverpool Guide* of 1801, what industries there were 'are chiefly confined to what is necessary to the construction and equipment of ships'.[4] Considerable alarm was caused by government intervention in the slave trade in the late 1780s. The consequent fall in the number of slave ships using the port (from 92 vessels in 1786 to 66 in 1789) was carefully calculated to have caused nearly 1500 craftsmen to be laid off, considerable outmigration, and an increase of over 800 paupers; furthermore, 'the number of distressed families, who struggle with their Difficulties without Parish Relief are great indeed. Had a scarcity of provisions been added to the reduction of African commerce the confusion must have been great indeed'.[5]

This strong impression that Liverpool's mercurial growth in the late eighteenth century was based upon its function as an Atlantic entrepôt shines on vividly in recent authoritative histories of the city,[6] and it is reinforced by the most commonly consulted and reprinted statistics of trade.[7] But Liverpool was not built on a pontoon anchored out in the Irish Sea, penetrated by nothing except Atlantic shipping and influences emanating from it. In fact, the

Notes and references begin on page 20.

number of coasting vessels using the port almost equalled the number of ships involved in all foreign trade to and from the Mersey in, for example, 1791; and the tonnage bound for Ireland and the Isle of Man accounted for one-third of all the shipping engaged in foreign trade to and from Liverpool between 1788 and 1791. This was more than double the share of the West Indies trade and considerably more than the Africa, North America, and West Indies trades combined.[8] Nor did Liverpool look only outwards, down the Mersey. The author of the *Liverpool Guide* resisted any temptation to explain the explosive growth of the city in terms of exotic contracts with the Guinea Coast, Jamaica, and Virginia. Eschewing an opening sentence of this kind, one which would undoubtedly have gripped the attention of the stranger for whom his work was intended, he began as follows:

> The advantages the town possesses in its near connexion and ready communication by internal rivers and canals, with . . . Manchester . . . Wigan . . . Staffordshire; the exclusive export of salt; its central situation on the western coast of the Kingdom, thereby communicating readily with Dublin, and the northern parts of Ireland; and finally the goodness of the Harbour, and the very superior accommodation for Shipping; have all conspired to force it into a vortex, that has nearly swallowed up the foreign trade of Bristol and the other western ports of the Kingdom.[9]

A great deal is now known about the speed with which this vortex swallowed up the Atlantic trade, and about the alimentary processes that followed its ingestion.[10] Detailed accounts of dock construction are available,[11] and the progress of the salt trade and its impact on the port have been revealed by Barker and Willan.[12] However, relatively little has yet been discovered about the inland waterway trade in general or about the Irish trade, and the bias in research effort due to 'the obvious attractiveness of the astonishing growth of Liverpool's shipping and commerce' has, if anything, increased even further since it was lamented by Harris in 1970.[13] Although no work on eighteenth-century Liverpool would now neglect local traffic and manufacturing industry completely, this heavy and cumulating concentration on the slave and cotton trades, on privateering, and on the emergence of the great ocean shipping companies, on their impact on the commercial development of the port, and the moulding of attitudes, policies, and factions within it, tends to deflect attention away from the more mundane short-distance traffic which actually brought the vortex into being. This emphasis automatically bolsters the impression that Liverpool functioned purely and simply as an entrepôt: that the vortex had, as it were, an economic void at its centre.

The purpose of this essay is simply to direct a little attention upstream along the Mersey and the waterways intersecting with it: to discover the progress of trade along the river and canal navigations around Liverpool in the late eighteenth century and the kinds of commodities that moved along them. This survey will be followed by an assessment of the ways in which the rate of growth and changing nature of inland waterway traffic affected the functioning of a city which, it will transpire, was a far more variegated economic organism in the late eighteenth century than the entrepôt that it later became.

I

Perhaps it is the attractiveness of symmetry which usually leads to a grouping of the ports of London, Bristol, Hull, and Liverpool, the outlets of the four great estuaries of England which became the pivots of the canal system in the nineteenth century. Such a grouping masks a considerable difference between Liverpool and the other three before the late eighteenth century. The Thames, the Severn, the Trent, the Ouse, and many of their tributaries, were navigable for long distances, but the Mersey was penetrable only as far as Warrington. Naturally, Liverpool 'was the worst supplied with the means of internal transport than any other port in England', which meant that the cost of passage to Liverpool from inland was about four times as much per mile as the cost to other ports.[14] Overland access was difficult anyway across the steep, bog-capped, sandstone ridge which encircled the creek on which the port grew. The development of the city was very closely paralleled by improvements in these execrable natural links with its hinterland.

The chronology of the construction of routeways to Liverpool is described fully in a number of easily accessible publications and will be dealt with briefly here.[15] The first clutch of new routeways was opened between 1732 and 1742: a turnpike was built to Prescot, where the main road from Liverpool branched northwards to Wigan and southwards to Warrington to intercept the major line of north to south communication west of the Pennines; the Mersey and Irwell were made navigable from Warrington to Manchester; the Weaver was opened from Frodsham on the Mersey estuary into central Cheshire, and the Douglas was deepened and locked to link Wigan with the Ribble estuary below Tarleton and thence by sea to Liverpool. Activity then slowed down. The turnpike was extended from Prescot to the north road at Warrington and Ashton-in-Makerfield, just south of Wigan, by 1760, and, symbolic of the natural disadvantages of the area, the first major English canal was built along the line of the Sankey Brook in 1757 to link the Mersey

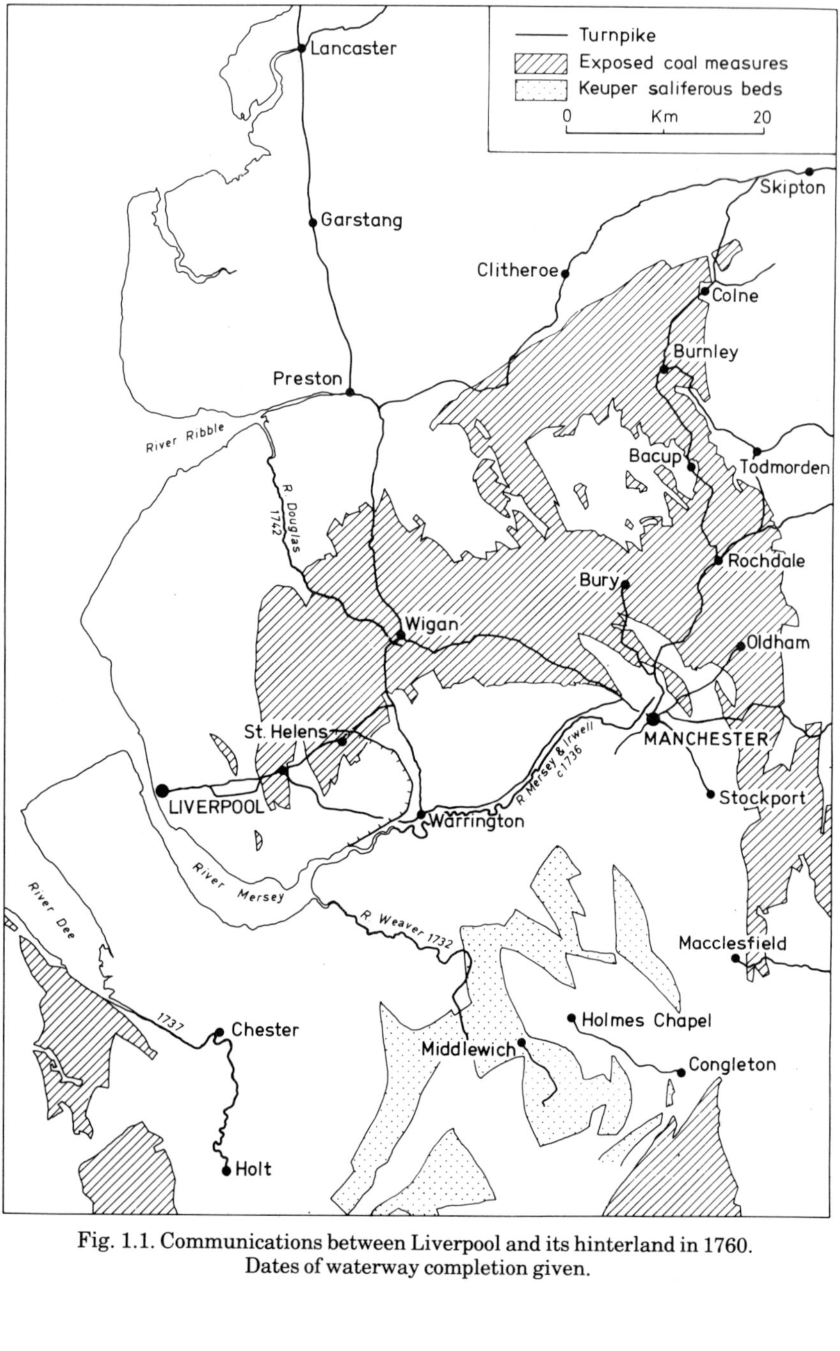

Fig. 1.1. Communications between Liverpool and its hinterland in 1760. Dates of waterway completion given.

below Warrington with what became St Helens on the Lancashire coalfield.

The pattern of links between Liverpool and its hinterland in 1760 is shown on fig. 1.1. They were still few and tenuous. The growing manufacturing areas were beyond Prescot: a line between Preston, Wigan, and Warrington, with a salient along the turnpike towards Liverpool, marked the western border of the region where population and industry were increasing most rapidly inland. Liverpool depended for connection with this region and places beyond it upon the turnpike through Prescot and the estuarine length of the Mersey below Warrington. Both were bad. Even though the road was continually repaired, widened, and flattened-out after its completion, it was never adequate comfortably to accommodate the traffic which moved along it, and physical barriers to trade were supplemented by high tolls on manufactured goods.[16] Most of the traffic between the head of the estuary and Liverpool still used the river after the completion of the turnpike, and this channel, too, was far from perfect.[17] The fitful activities of the proprietors of the Mersey and Irwell navigation failed to remove the shallows and shifting sand-banks from the upper arm of the estuary, which reduced shipping to less than one-half of what it would have been without them.[18] Access to both the Sankey Canal and the Mersey and Irwell was thus severely blocked, and although the Weaver opened into the estuary below the troublesome stretch above Runcorn, it was itself very imperfect until large-scale improvements were made under powers granted by an Act of 1760.

Apart from a few new lengths of turnpike, work on the Weaver, and a partial by-passing of the upper estuarine shallows by an extension of the Sankey, little improvement was made in Liverpool's links with its hinterland during the 1760s and early 1770s. Still, 'owing to the smallness of those streams the inland navigation from Liverpool did not extend more than thirty miles in any one direction, nor more than a hundred miles in the whole'.[19] It is noteworthy that the rapid subsequent acceleration in the growth-rate of the city came at the same time as the swift and comprehensive removal of these constrictions, and its population continued to climb through the late 1770s and early 1780s despite the interruption of North Atlantic shipping.[20] The Mersey shallows were not cut through until 1802 nor completely by-passed by the Sankey until 1830, but the Bridgewater Canal, linking Manchester through North Cheshire to the Mersey at Runcorn, was opened in 1773. The link from the Bridgewater at Preston Brook along the Trent and Mersey through the Potteries to the Trent, and thence to the Severn by the Staffordshire and Worcestershire Canal, was completed before the end of the 1770s, and by the end of the next decade continuous passage through the West Midland system to the Thames was

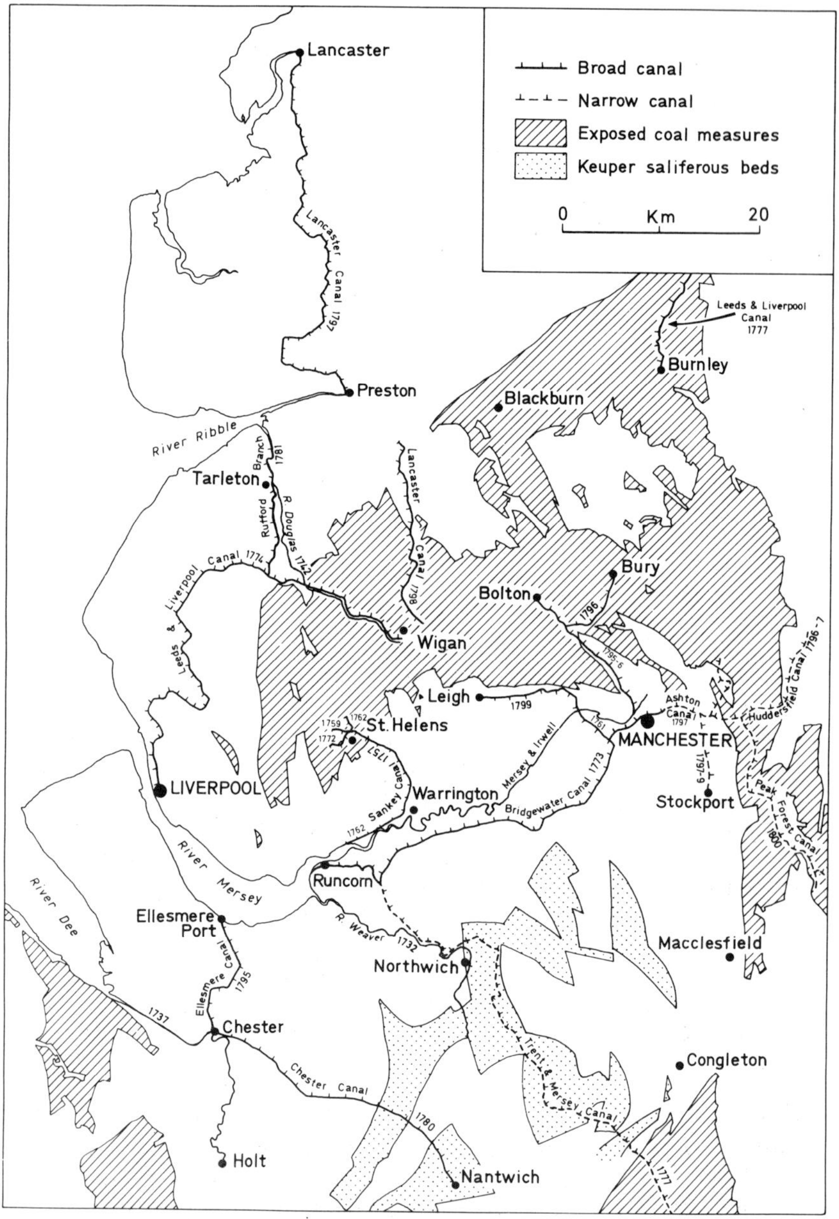

Fig. 1.2. Waterways in North-West England in 1800. Dates of completion given.

possible along a number of waterways. The Leeds and Liverpool Canal was opened from its basin high above the shore on the northern outskirts of the port to intersect with a much improved Douglas Navigation at Newburgh in 1774, and the river up to Wigan and down to Tarleton was supplemented by deadwater cuts in 1780 and 1781. In 1795, the Wirral Line of the Ellesmere Canal linked Chester with the Mersey and, after improvement of the connecting Chester Canal, it provided a third route from the Mersey into the Cheshire saltfield before the end of the eighteenth century.

The turn of the nineteenth century marked an interesting stage in the development of the waterway network in the North-West (see fig. 1.2). The Leeds and Liverpool, Sankey, Mersey and Irwell, Bridgewater, Trent and Mersey, and Ellesmere all funnelled towards the Mersey estuary. The Severn and the Trent and therefore almost the whole of England, could be reached through the Trent and Mersey, and the Bridgewater and Mersey and Irwell gave access to a fan of lines radiating up the valleys of Rossendale and the Pennines. All these routes except for the last group and the Ellesmere, built in the 1790s, were opened to Liverpool before 1780. Manchester, in contrast, was as yet badly served. It was merely a terminal apex from which short cul-de-sac routes pushed out from the Bridgewater and Mersey and Irwell, with only circuitous access southwards through the Trent and Mersey at the western-end of the Bridgewater. Furthermore, most of these routes to Manchester had been open for only a few years in 1800. Until the Bridgewater was extended from Leigh to Wigan and joined there to the Leeds and Liverpool, and through it to the southern-end of the Lancaster Canal; until the Leeds and Liverpool, the Rochdale, and the Ashton and Huddersfield canals crossed the Pennines, and until Manchester was linked southwards through the Peak Forest and Macclesfield canals, Liverpool had by far the best location on the waterway network of the North West.[21] It was the only pivotal point where traffic could be directly syphoned off from a network which defined an enormous and rapidly growing hinterland.[22] In 1800, Liverpool was the best connected port in England, whereas in 1770 it was still probably the worst. What 'advantages' accrued from this position?

II

I will deal first with the volume of traffic and the rate at which it grew, then with the nature of the goods carried. It must be emphasized at the outset that neither of these programmes can be accomplished with the degree of precision that is ideally desirable. Full accounts have survived only for the Weaver Navigation;[23] some summary accounts, in varying degrees of completeness, are available

Table 1.1. *Estimates of traffic to and from Liverpool and inland waterways, 1771–99, in 000s of tons.*[1].

	1771	*1783*	*1788*	*1791*	*1799*
A. Mersey and Irwell[2]	45·9[3]	23·0[4]	33·8	37·8[5]	44·6[6]
B. Weaver[7]	94·0	110·2	107·9	133·5	162·7
C. Sankey[8]	45·6[9]	?	57·9[10]	?	?
D. Bridgewater		77·2	120·1	117·2	105·3
E. Leeds and Liverpool		88·1	147·9	197·8[11]	274·9[11]
F. Ellesmere					68·4[12]
Total[13]	185·4	(344·1)	467·5	(544·1)	(713·7)

1. Based on sources given in notes 23–7. Numbers rounded after completion of calculations.
2. Calculated from the number of boats at work. In the early nineteenth century, each boat carried an average of 32·5 tons from Liverpool to Manchester and about 5 tons on the return journey (Hadfield and Biddle, op. cit., p. 102). In the late eighteenth century, each boat made an average of 36 trips a year along the navigation, so the number of boats at work in a year was multiplied by 1350 to get an estimate of the tonnage carried.
3. In 1772.
4. In 1781.
5. In 1790.
6. Average of 36 boats in 1796 and 32 in 1801.
7. Coal tonnages, which moved up the Weaver from the Sankey and were unconnected with Liverpool, have been omitted.
8. Excludes traffic from the Sankey to Warrington and the Weaver (see table 3).
9. Coal only.
10. Total tonnage was 115,828. It has been assumed that one half was to and from Liverpool, as in 1771.
11. Only coal tonnages are available. They have been increased in the ratio of 81:100, the ratio of coal to total tonnage in 1788.
12. This is the least satisfactory of the estimates. It was calculated from total receipts in 1805, minus income from rents, multiplied by the quotient of receipts and total tonnage on the Bridgewater, 1803–5. It thus incorporates assumptions that the two canals had similar structures of tolls and cargoes.
13. Bracketed totals include Sankey figures for the nearest earlier year.

in manuscript for the Leeds and Liverpool during the last twenty years of the eighteenth century and for its Douglas Navigation arm for a few years;[24] a breakdown of traffic on the Bridgewater in 1791 for the early nineteenth century has been published,[25] and enumerations of boats on this canal and on the Mersey and Irwell were printed in a number of contemporary directories.[26] This information can be supplemented from manuscripts in the Liverpool and Public record offices,[27] but the total accumulation is far less than would be necessary to reconstruct the pattern of waterway traffic-flows properly (the Sankey and Ellesmere are particularly badly documented). To get comparative data for the various lines requires considerable juggling of facts about vessels, tonnages, and receipts in different years, and only the boldest features of the sketchy outline presented below can be considered as reliable representations of reality.

Table 1.2. *Estimates of waterway traffic between Liverpool and inland towns in about 1791, in 000s of tons.*[1]

Town	*A*	*B*	*C*	*D*	*E*	*F*	*total*	*per cent*
Manchester	31·1			59·7			90·8	17
Middlewich[2]				12·0			12·0	2
Northwich		113·6					113·6	21
Potteries and beyond[3]				34·0			34·0	6
Runcorn &c.[4]				11·5			11·5	2
St Helens[5]			57·9				57·9	11
Warrington[6]	6·8						6·8	1
Wigan					197·8		197·8	36
Winsford		19·9					19·9	4
Totals	37·8	133·5	57·9	117·2	197·8		544·1	100

Note: Waterway letters refer to table 1.1.

1. Based on sources given in notes 23–7 and methods of calculation given on table 1.1. Numbers rounded after completion of calculations.
2. Rock salt via Trent and Mersey only.
3. Tonnage on Trent and Mersey to Liverpool minus rock salt.
4. Includes goods loaded and unloaded between Runcorn and Manchester.
5. 1788 tonnage on Sankey, assuming one-half of it went to Liverpool as in 1771.
6. Scheduled Mersey and Irwell boats only, assuming 36 trips a year and tonnages per vessel as to and from Manchester. This may therefore be an underestimate.

The notes to table 1.1 show just how much juggling with figures is required to estimate traffic on some of the waterways, and provide an indication of the ways in which the estimates may err. The calculated tonnages cannot be unacceptably far from the truth; if any consistent bias is present it is probably towards under-counting because of the inclusion of anachronistic figures for the Sankey in three of the totals. Even so, the numbers in the bottom row of the table are higher than those of ocean going shipping using the port in the same years and their growth-rate is much faster.[28] Trade grew at different rates on different waterways. It declined on the Mersey and Irwell and the Weaver after the competing lines of the Bridgewater and Trent and Mersey were opened, but the new canal carried a more than compensating amount and traffic on both the older waterways eventually recovered; pre-Bridgewater tonnages were soon far surpassed on the Weaver, and parity with them was reached by 1799 on the Mersey and Irwell, which followed almost exactly the same line as the Bridgewater Canal. The largest tonnages and the fastest growth-rate seems to have been on the Leeds and Liverpool Canal, although the figures of table 1.1 might be somewhat misleading in this respect because traffic increased very quickly on the Sankey, too, during the short period in the 1780s for which data are available.[29] By the 1790s, traffic was growing quickly on all waterways except the Bridgewater.[30]

It is possible to reconstruct a reasonably accurate picture of the

Table 1.3. *Non-Liverpool traffic on North-Western waterways in about 1790.*[1]

Between	*000s of tons*
St Helens and Northwich (1788)[2]	35·5
St Helens and Winsford (1788)[2]	7·9
St Helens and Warrington (1788)[3]	14·5
Wigan and Tarleton (1791)[2]	20·6
Manchester and Trent and Mersey (1791)	36·5
Worsley and Manchester (1791)[4]	76·3
Total	191·3

1. Based on sources given in notes 23–7.
2. Coal only.
3. It was assumed that half of the total Sankey traffic was to and from Liverpool and the other half to and from Warrington and Cheshire, and that only coal moved between St Helens and Cheshire.
4. Coal and limestone only.

origins and destinations of most of this inland shipping, as shown in table 1.2. Again, the notes beneath the table explain the derivation of the figures and their possible inaccuracies, but again a pattern emerges which is so clear that its accuracy could not seriously be questioned even if the maximum possible errors in the figures all conspired against it. More than one-third of all the inland waterway traffic moved between Liverpool and Wigan;[31] Northwich and Manchester accounted for just over and just under one-half as much, respectively, and St Helens for about one-third as much as Wigan. The relative size of these flows to Liverpool can be gauged by comparing them with tonnages carried between other destinations on the routes concerned (see table 1.3). It is apparent that about three-quarters of all the traffic on the North-Western canal system in about 1790 passed into or out of Liverpool, whilst less than one-third of it moved through Manchester.

Flows were not equal in both directions between Liverpool and these destinations. As note 2 on table 1.1 indicates, only two-thirteenths as much tonnage moved from Manchester to Liverpool as in the opposite direction along the Mersey and Irwell, whilst on the Bridgewater the imbalance was even greater (see table 1.4). There was a marked contrast on the Leeds and Liverpool, which carried equally imbalanced flows in opposite directions (see table 1.4). In tonnage terms, therefore, Liverpool had a large balance of trade deficit with Wigan, but large surpluses with places on the Mersey and Irwell, Bridgewater, and Trent and Mersey, especially with Manchester. The reasons for this pattern of surpluses and deficits lie in the nature of the goods carried on the different waterways, to which attention will now be turned.

Unfortunately, it is even more difficult to discover what was

Table 1.4. *Balances of trade on some North-Western canals in about 1790, in 000s of tons.*[1]

	To Liverpool	*From Liverpool*
Manchester (1791)	5·8	53·9
Runcorn &c. (1791)	0·9	10·6
Potteries and beyond (1791)	14·7	19·3
Wigan (1786–8 average)[2]	103·3	17·3

1. Based on sources given in notes 23–7.
2. Excludes timber, of which an average of 16,326ft per year were taken from Wigan to Liverpool and 169,159ft in the opposite direction.

traded along the rivers and canals than it is to discover how much of it there was. The few surviving accounts only distinguish between categories of goods which were charged different rates of toll, and some of these categories subsume a great variety. This is particularly true of 'merchant goods' or 'merchandise', which usually seems to have comprised the residual left after the individual assessment of cargoes which attracted a preferential tariff because of their high bulk to value ratio (such as coal, bricks, limestone, manure, timber, building stone, and so on). Thus manufactured goods bound for export, imports distributed from Liverpool, and foodstuffs, were indistinguishably lumped together in most accounts and only low value bulk cargoes can be separated out from them.

It is quite clear from other sources of information that the waterways were used to send manufactured goods to Liverpool for export, redistribution, and consumption in exchange for the raw materials needed to make them, and that foodstuffs flowed in considerable quantities from an ever-widening area. The Mersey and Irwell was probably concerned almost exclusively with these kinds of trade: 'Meat, Grain, Rum, Wine and Spirits; Italian and Baltic produce are sent up—Manufactured goods from Manchester and from all parts of Yorkshire are returned'.[32] Food travelled downstream as well: cattle were assembled for slaughter in Warrington from a wide area, their carcasses sent on to Liverpool by water, and between thirty- and forty-thousand bushels of potatoes a year were shipped from Bank Quay in Warrington in the 1790s.[33] The Trent and Mersey sent 'Groceries and West India produce to every part of this Island, and return loaded with products and manufactories of almost all the country on the South of the Humber, Mersey, &c.'[34]

The Warrington sail cloth industry (which supplied one-half of the Navy's demands in the late eighteenth century) was provided with hemp and flax from Russia through Liverpool and along the Mersey,[35] and Wigan's iron industry obtained its metal and ore via the port and the Leeds and Liverpool Canal.[36] At least some finished ironware and machinery, bound for North America and the

Caribbean and including such things as steam engines and sugar mills, left Wigan in the same way.[37] This sort of relationship with Liverpool along the waterways was repeated on a larger scale by the Potteries, importing clay and flints and exporting finished earthenware through the port via the Trent and Mersey,[38] and, on a larger scale again, by Manchester, importing cotton and exporting textiles along the Mersey and Irwell and the Bridgewater Canal.[39] Perhaps somewhat paradoxically, it was at St Helens, the other 'Merseyside town', where manufacturers were least dependent on Liverpool, with copper ore moving directly from Anglesey and Cheshire without the need for intercession by the port.

Thus, a good proportion of Liverpool's inland trade was in foodstuffs or of the archetypal entrepôt kind, sending in raw materials and consumption goods to specialist manufacturing towns in its hinterland and channelling out their exports in exchange. However, it is easy to get carried away by the variety of such links, and by the complex economic geography they signify, to an over-estimation of their importance. Even if the exchange of imported raw materials and consumer goods for manufactures bound for export was the dominant aspect of trade on the Mersey and Irwell, the Bridgewater, and the Trent and Mersey (and Liverpool's balance of trade surplus in tonnage terms with Manchester and the Potteries suggest that this was so), it must be remembered that these three lines together accounted for only one-quarter of the total waterway tonnage (see table 1.1), and the pattern along other canals was quite different. The crude categorizations of cargo available for the Weaver and the Leeds and Liverpool Canal allow the relative importance of different commodities to be measured. 'Merchandise' was spectacularly unimportant on both these waterways and, what is more, as total tonnages grew its proportion shrank (see table 1.5).[40] Traffic on these waterways and on the Sankey was dominated by flows of the opposite kind from those on the Mersey and Irwell, Bridgewater and Trent and Mersey: bulky raw materials flowed into Liverpool in vastly greater quantities than they and merchandise flowed out, hence the large negative balances of trade between Liverpool and destinations on these lines.

Of course, even on these shorter connections, not all raw material flows were directed towards Liverpool. Coal from the Mersey to Chester was probably the main cargo on the Wirral Line of the Ellesmere Canal,[41] and many of the numerous bulky commodities distinguished in the Weaver Navigation accounts must have moved up the river. Coal, which normally accounted for between twenty and thirty per cent of Weaver tonnages, went down the Sankey from St Helens before entering the river, and stone, bricks, metals, and, until the trade was captured by the Trent and Mersey, clay and flints were shipped from Liverpool into Cheshire. However, such

Table 1.5. *Cargoes on the Weaver, 1760–99 and the Leeds and Liverpool, 1783–5 and 1788.*[1]

	average annual total in 000s of tons	*per cent*				
		white salt	*rock salt*	*coal*	*merchant goods*	*other goods*
Weaver, 1760–9	77·8	31·7	34·6	22·2	5·3	6·1
Weaver, 1770–9	112·9	31·9	35·8	21·5	5·2	5·6
Weaver, 1780–9	135·8	34·4	34·7	26·1	3·1	1·8
Weaver, 1790–9	197·1	43·8	22·3	30·0	2·7	1·2
Leeds and Liverpool, 1783–8	107·3			79·5	5·4	15·1

1. Based on sources given in note 40.

miscellaneous heavy materials rarely comprised even as much as merchant goods on the Weaver, and traffic between Liverpool and Cheshire was dominated by the movement of salt down to the port (see table 1.5). White refined salt and raw rock salt between them made up two-thirds of the total tonnage shipped on the Weaver, and although the rock salt proportion fell it must be remembered that the Trent and Mersey was augmenting supplies by 12,000 tons a year by the early 1790s.[42] A significant portion of the rock salt was bound for refineries at Liverpool, Frodsham, Dungeon, and Garston on the Mersey estuary.[43]

Trade on the Leeds and Liverpool Canal was also dominated by the haulage of one kind of bulky commodity, in this case coal (see table 1.5). Ten times more general merchandise moved from Liverpool to Wigan than in the opposite direction, but the total merchant goods tonnage was negligible compared with that of coal, and so was the tonnage of lime, limestone, manure, bricks, stone, and timber which comprised 'other goods' on this canal. Leeds and Liverpool coal traffic rapidly expanded right through the 1780s and 1790s, with a sizeable hiccough in 1793, much faster than that bound from St Helens for the Weaver (see fig. 1.3);[44] it was the fastest growing of all the canal borne trades. Even in the absence of accounts, there is no doubt that coal was similarly dominant on the Sankey, 'which also supplies abundance of coals to Liverpool',[45] whilst along the Ellesmere Canal 'we receive Lead, Iron, and Timber from Wales'.[46]

The inland waterway trades to and from Liverpool were quite distinctively patterned. The longer distance links to Manchester and the Potteries carried out raw materials imported through Liverpool and brought back manufactured goods, whilst the shorter distance links to Wigan, Chester, St Helens, and Northwich brought in bulky raw materials and carried out relatively negligible quantities of imported merchandise, bricks, lime, manure, and so on. The hinterland of Liverpool comprised a series of three 'rings':

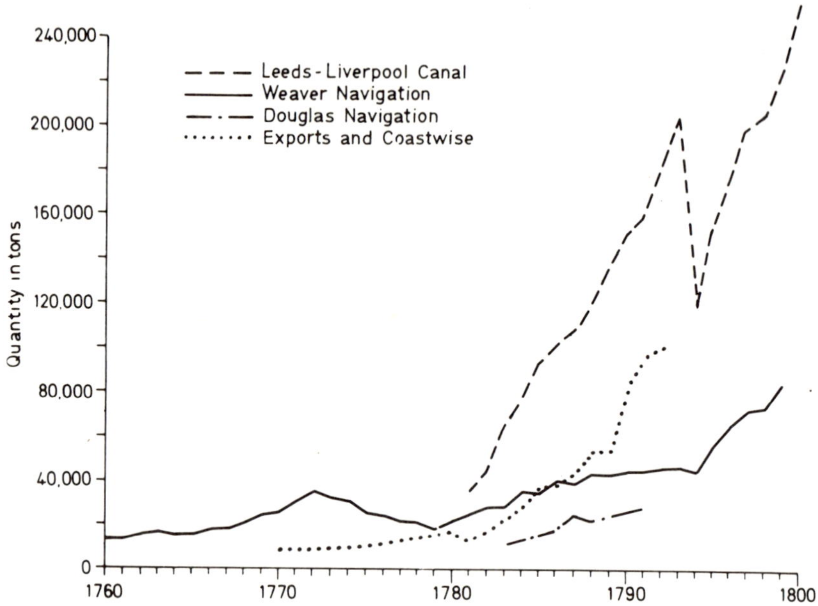

Fig. 1.3. Coal tonnages hauled on the waterways of South-West Lancashire and exported from Liverpool 1760–1800.

the outer one, beyond Manchester and the Potteries, sent and received only small quantities of high value manufactured goods and imports; the middle one, comprising destinations along the Bridgewater, Trent and Mersey and Irwell, imported raw materials and sent out goods from specialist manufacturing centres in large quantities, and the innermost ring, defined by the termini of the Leeds and Liverpool, Sankey, Weaver and Ellesmere, took imported consumer goods and some raw materials from Liverpool but mainly pumped raw materials into the port.

The last series of flows accounted for a very large proportion of the total tonnages carried along the waterways; indeed, the inner ring of its hinterland, served by the turnpike to Prescot as well as four waterways, and the coastal and overseas trades together poured a cascade of raw materials into Liverpool. Coal was chief amongst them in volume. About 350,000 tons a year were being hauled into Liverpool by the late 1790s from Wigan, St Helens, and Prescot, which was more than one-quarter of the total imported into London at the same time, nearly six times as much as the Bridgewater Canal carried to Manchester, and over one-half of the whole output of the South-West Lancashire pits.[47] Almost every type of coal was represented, including excellent furnace and steam coal, cannel (the choicest house coal), smith's and ordinary house coal. With the salt, lead and iron from other waterways, potting clay, flints, and copper ore from the coasting trade, grain and timber from both these sources, and tobacco, sugar, cotton, hemp, flax, iron, and timber from overseas added to its supplies of coal, Liverpool appears to have been a cornucopia of industrial resources in the late eighteenth century.

These raw materials were not only varied and abundant, but also cheap. Of course, all of them must have been more expensive in the port than at their sources, but on the other hand the cost of any particular bundle of raw materials necessary in manufacturing must have been at least as low in Liverpool as anywhere else. Certainly, copper ore must have been cheaper in Liverpool than in St Helens, cotton than in Manchester, iron than in Wigan, hemp and flax than in Warrington, clay and flints than in the Potteries, and although coal was dearer than on the coalfield it was still remarkably cheap in Liverpool compared with elsewhere in the country. According to Arthur Young, 'firing' cost less in Liverpool than in coalfield towns such as Newcastle-on-Tyne, Leeds, and Wakefield in 1770,[48] and in the early 1790s one cwt of best house coal cost 5*d.* at the pithead in Oldham, the source of 'vast quantities' sent to Manchester,[49] where it must have cost even more, but only 4½*d.* in Liverpool itself. Supplies were so lavish that the price remained constant in Liverpool for about a quarter of a century after the early 1770s (see fig. 1.4).

Most of the traffic between Liverpool and the 'outer' and 'intermediate' rings of its hinterland in the late eighteenth century was of the kind usually associated with an entrepôt: the city acted as a mart where cargoes were simply exchanged without any value being added to them through transformation in manufacturing. However, such flows as these only amounted, at a generous estimate, to about one-quarter of all the inland trade. What happened to the bulky, low-value goods which poured in from the 'inner ring' of Liverpool's hinterland; did they, too, simply pass through the port *en route* for other destinations?

Most of the refined salt did: indeed, it was Liverpool's principal export.[50] So, too, did considerable quantities of rock salt, although sufficient found its way into the city's one saltworks to give it a refined rock salt output more than half as big as that of Northwich in the early 1790s.[51] This situation was repeated in many of the other raw material flows passing through the port; enough was retained to give Liverpool a sizeable manufacturing capacity. Its most important industry of this kind was brewing. Thirty-nine public breweries produced nearly 50,000 hogsheads of ale a year in the 1780s, besides sixty-nine brewers of table beer and a large porter brewery built in 1789.[52] Eight sugar houses refined 6000 hogsheads a year; numerous limekilns and brickfields produced an excess for

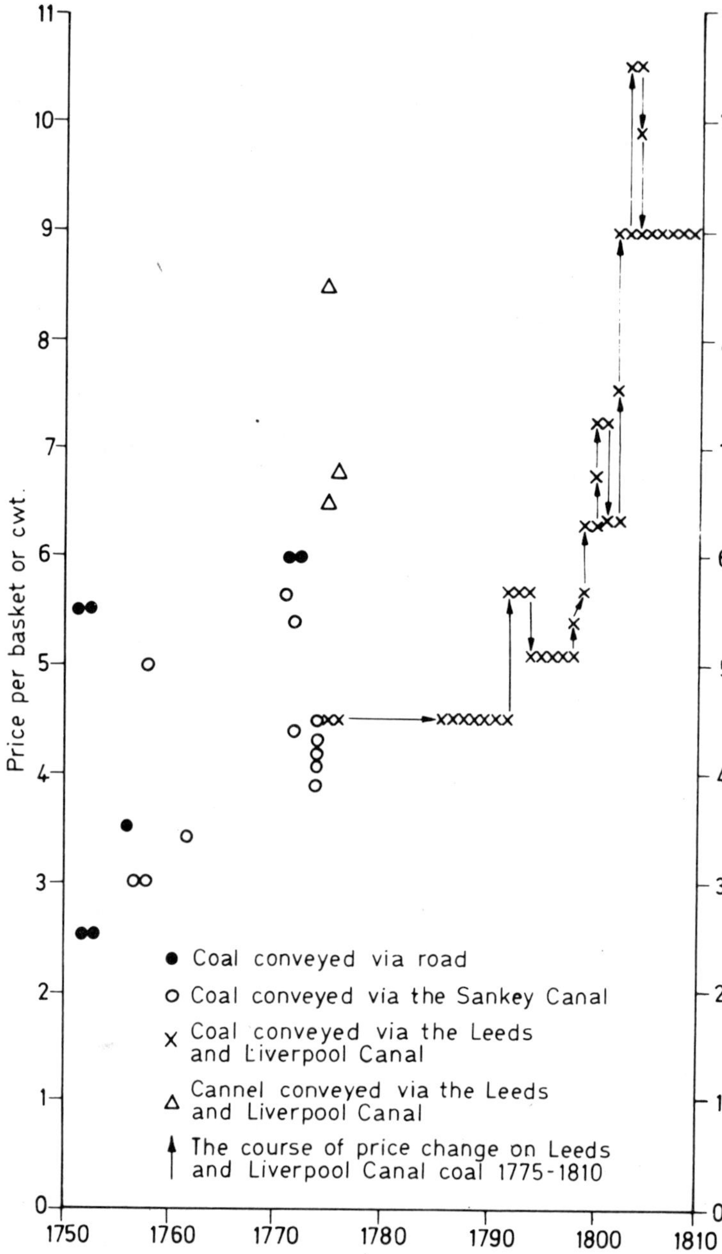

Fig. 1.4. Coal prices in Liverpool, 1750–1810.

distribution through the canal system beyond what was needed to build the houses, warehouses, and docks of the rapidly growing city. There were three glassworks, four iron foundries, one of which was run by the Coalbrookdale Company, and several potteries, including delft and porcelain works, seven tobacco-pipe manufacturers, and the famous Herculaneum Pottery. Liverpool copperworks had thirty-nine furnaces and consumed 10–12,000 tons of coal a year. Red and white herring, snuff, and tobacco-curing houses; copperas and other dye and colour works; a vitriol (sulphuric acid) plant with a capital of £8000, built in the early 1790s; a stocking manufactory built in the 1780s, and four cotton mills opened in 1790 and 1791 added further variety to an industrial complex which contained, by the early 1790s, far more than the largest watch and watch-tool manufacture in the world, and the roperies, anchorsmithies, shipyards, block-making shops, and cooperages which directly supplied the needs of overseas shipping. There was ample justification for Gore's observation in 1794 that 'now in the town and its vicinity, are numerous erection for most of the manufactures hitherto carried on in the inland towns . . . which give a new character and spirit to the place.'[53] According to Gore, this had only occurred 'of late', and it is not difficult to recognize a reason for this efflorescence of large-scale boiling, melting, roasting, smelting, and steam powered industries in the cheap high-quality coal supplies which poured into the port after the completion of the Sankey in 1757 and, especially, after the Leeds and Liverpool Canal was opened in 1774.

But a worm was already in the flower while Gore was admiring its freshness. As the 1790s progressed, many of these new industries closed down.[54] The potteries were 'in decline' then and most of the delft and porcelain works were shut. The saltworks closed and moved up-river in 1798. The public breweries were proving inadequate; ever increasing quantities of ale had to be imported from the surrounding area, and the porter works closed in 1799, its buildings sold for £17,000 in 1802. The copperworks ceased production in 1794, one year after the Coalbrookdale Company left Liverpool; none of the other foundries expanded very much and all the textile ventures were short lived. The vitriol works closed in 1799, and even the shipbuilding industry declined through the last decade of the eighteenth century. It seems clear that the industrial efflorescence was as brief as it was spectacular and that Liverpool was in 1800 set fair on the course which led to the status of entrepôt.

It would be foolish to attempt fully to explain this situation without reference to the war and consequential convulsions of the overseas trade of the port which were happening at the time. Nonetheless, what must have been potent partial causes are apparent in the changes which began to occur in Liverpool's relations with its hinterland in the 1790s, changes which continued to move even more strongly in the same directions through the early nineteenth century. It was already becoming apparent that Liverpool manufactures could not compete with those of the specialized complexes growing at the source of one of the heavy raw materials they used along the banks of the inland waterways. The external economies of scale available to the potters of Staffordshire; the copper and glass smelters of St Helens; the iron smelters and engineers of Wigan; the salt producers of Cheshire, and the textile manufacturers of Manchester and South-East Lancashire, were denied to their Liverpool counterparts, who operated in a much more disparate if initially much larger local industrial matrix. The waterways created an integrated industrial system in North-West England, and the rationalization of patterns of production through competition between manufacturers in different parts of it consistently disadvantaged industry in Liverpool, which increasingly became a specialized place of exchange serving the whole of the region.

Flows of resources as well as competing finished goods are required for the development of a regional industrial complex of this kind. Bulky raw materials moved along the canals to the places where they could most profitably be transformed, and non-material resources such as capital, expertize and labour flowed along intangible channels within the system to the same purpose. Indeed, it has been argued that the decline of industry in Liverpool was due largely to the movement of industrial capital out to hinterland locations where it could be invested more profitably.[55] The Cheshire salt industry and the collieries which supplied its fuel were financed from Liverpool, but it is easy to exaggerate the importance of this flow of funds. No other manufacturing industry besides salt refining was financed in this way, and most of the money invested from Liverpool in the hinterland went into the construction of turnpikes, canals, and collieries in the 'inner ring' to provide raw materials for the industries of the city.

Workmen and their skills flowed in directions which disadvantaged industry in Liverpool. The rate of migration into the city was not sufficient to produce low wages, nor to prevent wages from rising by between fifty and sixty per cent in different industrial trades during the last thirty years of the eighteenth century.[56] It was probably not just in quantity that labour flows were unconducive to thriving industry in Liverpool. Harris has demonstrated the importance of labour skills in early industrialization; workers did not only provide muscle-power, but also the knowledge and expertize necessary to put new industrial techniques into effective practice.[57] Most labour movement was over short distances during the industrial revolution, and an abundance of opportunities was available in the hinterland for putative migrants from the villages and small towns of the North-West who were already familiar with industrial work.

Liverpool cannot have exerted a strong attraction on such recruits; many of its migrants came from the west, from North Wales and Ireland, and they possessed neither industrial skills nor, frequently, the linguistic ability to learn them after they arrived.[58] Thus, attractions nearer home for industrially trained migrants, plus abundant opportunities for unskilled work in house-building and dock construction in Liverpool, generated cumulating flows of labour which denied the external economies provided by an industrially skilled labour pool to manufacturers in the city.[59]

The biggest re-orientation of resource flows, and the one which occurred as suddenly as the decline of manufacturing industry early in Liverpool, was that of coal supplies. For twenty years before the early 1790s the city had abundant, cheap, and expanding provisions of coal. This was due to its sole access to supplies from Prescot along the turnpike, and from Wigan along the Leeds and Liverpool Canal, and to its command of a large share from the pits alongside the Sankey. Henceforth continually increasing quantities were diverted. One of the main diversionary channels was exports (see fig. 1.3). Wigan coal was of excellent quality and found a ready market in Ireland, North America, and the West Indies. The steep rise of the graph of exports up to the early 1790s shown on fig. 1.3 probably continued; in about 1792 it was feared that 'the export of this useful article from this Port, which is now considerable, may prove prejudicial to the town',[60] and shipments were running so high by 1801 that Liverpool 'may be called a coal port'.[61] Another increasing fraction of supplies was usurped by industries growing quickly at places which had initially developed as points of coal production for Liverpool, especially on the Sankey after the early 1770s.[62] Rapid expansion of the output of Cheshire salt refineries after about 1780 (see table 1.5) drew off further quantities of Sankey coal, and the road link to Prescot could provide no amelioration because it was already used to capacity by the early 1790s.[63] The growth of the iron industry at Wigan, and later steam-powered textiles production, put pressure on supplies from the Leeds and Liverpool Canal, and the waterway network as a whole developed in such a way that Liverpool's position inexorably worsened after the halcyon days before the early 1790s. The Ellesmere Canal drew off supplies from the Mersey to Chester after 1795;[64] high-grade coal and cannel moved northwards from Wigan along the southern end of the Lancaster Canal after 1799,[65] and the sole purpose of linking Wigan to the Bridgewater at Leigh was to give Manchester access to what had been a coalfield preserve of Liverpool.

The loss of a near monopoly held by Liverpool on the coal output of much of South-West Lancashire was at first a gradual, then by the early 1790s a perceptible, then almost a runaway process. The first prick was felt in 1792, when the copperworks 'on account of the scarceness and dearness of this great Article of Consumption . . . are under contemplation of being removed'.[66] In the same year, the price of coal from the Leeds and Liverpool moved upwards for the first time in over twenty years when 1*d.* was added to the customary 4½*d.* per cwt. There was a consequent fall in demand and shipments, and the price was lowered, but four years later a giddy spiral began which carried the price to 10½*d.* a cwt by 1803 (see fig. 1.4).[67] The level of shipments on the Leeds and Liverpool in 1801 was not reached again until the 1820s; more and more Sankey coal stayed in St Helens or went to Northwich and Chester, and the turnpike was at breaking point. Surely, we can see in these circumstances a potent cause of contraction in the industrial base of Liverpool after the early 1790s?

III

In the late eighteenth century Liverpool was not simply an entrepôt and its economic fortunes and rate of expansion then cannot be understood solely with reference to the Atlantic shipping trades. Its rapid accelerating expansion after about 1770 accompanied developments in the inland waterway network which quickly made the city the supreme transportation node of the North-West and created a focus of routeways superior to those serving all other English ports. For nearly a quarter of a century, the shape of the waterway network and the newness of industrialization upon it ensured that Liverpool had a near monopoly hold over raw materials, particularly coal, from the 'inner ring' of its hinterland. As the hinterland evolved; as growing industries sorted themselves out along the waterways into patterns that were economically rational on a large scale; as resources began to flow along profitable paths which led them away from Liverpool, and as the 'inner ring' of its hinterland was broken open to other markets by new canals, so Liverpool's advantageous position was continually, and by the late 1790s, significantly eroded. That Liverpool became an entrepôt was due to its changing links with its hinterland as well as to the profitability of Atlantic shipping.

NOTES AND REFERENCES

1. Contemporary estimates of Liverpool's population were made as follows: 25,787 in 1766; 34,107 in 1777; 41,600 in 1786; 55,732 in 1790, and 60,000 in 1793. In 1801, 77,653 inhabitants were enumerated, excluding suburbs and about 6000 seamen away on voyages. See Thomas Baines, *History of the Commerce and Town of Liverpool*, London and Liverpool (1852), p. 492 and John Langton and Paul Laxton, 'Parish Registers and Urban Structure: the

example of late eighteenth century Liverpool'. *Urban History Yearbook* (1978), pp. 74–84.

2. Paul Mantoux, *The Industrial Revolution in the Eighteenth Century*, London (revised edn. 1961), p. 108.

3. William Enfield, *An Essay towards the History of Liverpool*, London (1774), p. 90.

4. William Moss, *Liverpool Guide* (4th edn., 1801), p. 117.

5. Liverpool Record Office (henceforth Lpl.R.O.), Holt and Gregson MSS, vol. x, pp. 371–9.

6. C. N. Parkinson, *The Rise of the Port of Liverpool*, Liverpool (1952); and F. E. Hyde, *Liverpool and the Mersey*, David and Charles (1971).

7. The growth of overseas trade in the late eighteenth century is exaggerated by figures of tonnages entering and clearing the port because of the institution of a new method of measuring shipping tonnage in 1786, which could have the effect of increasing the weight attributed to particular vessels by an average of thirty per cent. See D. P. Lamb., 'Volume and tonnage of the Liverpool slave trade 1772–1807', in Roger Anstey and P. E. H. Hair, *Liverpool, the African Slave Trade, and Abolition*, Liverpool (1976), pp. 91–112.

8. Calculated from tables in John Corry, *The History of Liverpool* (often referred to as 'Troughton's History of Liverpool'), Liverpool (1810), pp. 261–2; and Lpl.R.O. Holt and Gregson MSS, vol. xix, p. 49.

9. Moss, op. cit., pp. 1–2.

10. Anstey and Hair, op. cit.

11. Hyde, op. cit., pp. 72–94.

12. T. S. Willan, *The Navigation of the River Weaver in the Eighteenth Century*, Manchester (1951); and T. C. Barker, 'Lancashire coal, Cheshire salt and the rise of Liverpool', *Trans. Hist. Soc. of Lancs. and Chesh.*, **103** (1952), 83–101.

13. J. R. Harris, 'Trends in the industrialization of Merseyside 1750–1800', *Colloque sur l'industrialisation en Europe au XIX*[e] *siecle*, Lyon (1970), p. 57.

14. Baines, op. cit., p. 489.

15. John Aikin, *A Description of the Country from Thirty to Forty Miles round Manchester*, London (1795), and Baines, op. cit., give thorough early accounts. The turnpikes are dealt with in G. H. Tupling, 'The turnpike trusts of Lancashire', *Mems. and Procs. of the Manchester Lit. and Phil. Soc.* **94** (1952–3), 39–62; and F. A. Bailey, 'The minutes of the trustees of the turnpike roads from Liverpool to Prescot, St. Helens, Warrington and Ashton-in-Makerfield', parts I and II, *Trans. Hist. Soc. of Lancs. and Chesh.* **88** (1936), 159–200 and **89** (1937), 31–80. All the waterways are treated in Charles Hadfield, and Gordon Biddle, *The Canals of North West England*, 2 vols., Newton Abbot (1970). Particular canals and navigations are examined in Willan, op. cit. and Barker, op. cit. and 'The beginnings of the canal age in the British Isles', in L. S. Pressnell, *Studies in the Industrial Revolution*, London (1960), pp. 1–22. Some of those proposed as well as built are treated in J. R. Harris, 'Liverpool canal controversies 1769–1772', *Jnl. of Transport Hist.* **2** (1955–6), 158–94. The coal trade of the Sankey, Douglas, and Leeds and Liverpool is described in John Langton, *Geographical Change and Industrial Revolution: Coalmining in South West Lancashire 1590–1799*, Cambridge (1979). Material in the text has been taken from these sources unless otherwise referenced.

16. The 'burthensome' tolls on most kinds of vehicle carrying earthenware, glass and iron were reduced in 1746 but those on wagons were increased. All tolls were raised to their pre-1746 levels in 1753. Bailey, op. cit., (1936), p. 194 and (1937), p. 31.

17. Bailey, op. cit. (1936), p. 57; and Aikin, op. cit., pp. 302–6.

18. In the late 1780s vessels made only 36 journeys a year from Liverpool to Manchester on the river because of the effect of the shallows at low tides, whereas each boat on the Bridgewater Canal made 84 trips a year. Lpl.R.O., Holt and Gregson MSS, vol. x, p. 241.

19. Baines, op. cit., p. 431.

20. Between 1775 and 1782, christenings increased by 18 per cent, whilst the tonnage of English shipping entering and leaving the port fell by 20 per cent (although there was an increase of 4 per cent in English plus foreign shipping).

21. The Bridgewater was linked to Wigan in 1820 and the Leeds and Liverpool was connected to the Lancaster at Wigan in 1816, which completed the northern trans-Pennine route. The northern and southern ends of the Lancaster were linked by a tramway at Preston in 1803. The Rochdale crossed the Pennines in 1804, and the Standedge tunnel on the Huddersfield and Ashton canals was completed in 1811. The Peak Forest and Macclesfield line from Manchester to the Midlands was opened in 1831. The Chester Canal link to the southern end of the Ellesmere, giving a further link from the Mersey to the Severn and access to North-East Wales and the Borderland, was finished in 1805.

22. The dependence of Liverpool on inland waterways and its dominance of the North-Western network is illustrated by the assessments made in the military levy of 1803. Liverpool was considered able to supply 11 wagons and the rest of Lancashire 521, but 384 canal and river boats compared with 266 for the whole of the rest of Lancashire.

23. Willan, op. cit., pp. 208–28.

24. Lpl.R.O., Holt and Gregson MSS, vol. x, pp. 233 and 238–9 and vol. xix, p. 98 and Lancashire County Record Office (henceforth L.R.O.), DDBd/48/8 and DP/175, p. 65.

25. Hadfield and Biddle, op. cit., vol. 1, pp. 36 and 96.

26. Principally in *Gore's Liverpool Directory*, 1766, 1767, 1769, 1772, 1774, 1777, 1781, 1790, 1796, and 1801. Details of boats are given for only these two waterways probably because it was only on these lines that the proprietors were the sole authorized carriers, so that a single source of information could provide Gore with material, whereas numerous firms of carriers would have had to be consulted to gather equivalent information for the other waterways.

27. Mainly Lpl.R.O., Holt and Gregson MSS, which comprise material about Liverpool assembled in the late eighteenth and early nineteenth centuries, and P.R.O., RAIL, 827, which contains documents concerning the Ellesmere Canal.

28. Comparisons are difficult because the overseas shipping statistics—whether in terms of burthen (as before 1786), or conversions of dimensions (as after 1786), or numbers of vessels—refer to carrying capacity, not actual tonnages hauled; the burthen of the vessels plying the inland waterways to and from Liverpool would be much higher than the tonnages they actually

carried. To make matters worse, overseas tonnage figures are not available between 1793 and 1801 but only numbers of vessels. Using numbers of vessels to overcome the problems caused by the change in method of tonnage measurement and the gap in tonnage figures, it appears that overseas shipping increased by 104 per cent between 1771 and 1799 and 7 per cent between 1791 and 1799, compared with 285 per cent and 31 per cent by canal tonnages over the same periods. Overseas shipping tonnages were 150,566 in 1777 (burthen) and 539,676 (about one-third greater than burthen) in 1791, less than the canal tonnages despite their upward biases.

29. Sankey tonnages, including coal carried from St Helens to Cheshire, which is excluded from table 1.1, increased from 74,289 to 98,356 in 1787 to 115,828 in 1788. Lpl.R.O., Holt and Gregson MSS, vol. x, pp. 238–9.

30. Trade on the Bridgewater between Liverpool and Manchester fell between 1791–3 and 1800–2. This must have been at least partially due to large increases in tolls made in 1794 and 1800; the rate on cotton, for example, went up from the 6*s*. per ton allowed under the Act to 10*s*. 6*d*. in 1794 and 16*s*. 8*d*. in 1800. Hadfield and Biddle, op. cit., vol. 1, pp. 92 and 96.

31. The Wigan to Liverpool traffic was even more voluminous than this, because in addition to the 89 vessels on the Leeds and Liverpool Canal 'between Liverpool and the River Douglas 36 boats are imployed' (Lpl.R.O., Holt and Gregson MSS, vol. x, pp. 238–9). It is not known whether these boats plied coastwise from the mouth of the river, or whether they sailed along the Leeds and Liverpool Canal from its intersection with the river at Newburgh, carrying goods from the length of the old river navigation which ran alongside the canal from Newburgh to Wigan. On the other hand, Preston has been omitted from the table because it is indistinguishable in the accounts. There was a regular service between Preston and Liverpool by 1791, and the traffic on this route will have been allocated to Wigan.

32. *Gore's Liverpool Directory*, 1805, p. 96.

33. Aikin, op. cit., p. 306.

34. *Gore's Liverpool Directory*, 1805, p. 96.

35. Aikin, op. cit., p. 302.

36. John Rylands Library, Manchester (henceforth J.R.L.), Haigh MSS, Canals Box/letters from Lord Balcarres to Mr Stanhope and to the Leeds and Liverpool Canal Co., 1788 and 1799.

37. Lpl.R.O., *Williamson's Liverpool Advertiser*, 28 Nov., 1766 (when the Sankey Canal was used by Wigan ironworks); *Liverpool General Advertiser*, 4 June, 1773 and 14 Oct., 1774; and Alan Birch, 'The Haigh Ironworks . . .', *Bulletin of the John Rylands Library,* **35** (1953), 326.

38. *Gore's Liverpool Directory*, 1805, p. 96. Wedgwood and his partner Bentley were leading promoters of the Trent and Mersey Canal. Bentley opened a warehouse in Liverpool, supplied wholesale by Wedgwood, in 1766, the year they began promoting the canal. Ann Finer, and George Savage, *The Selected Letters of Josiah Wedgwood*, London (1965), pp. 30–4 and 31.

39. The increases in tolls on cotton in 1794 and 1800 were matched by those on manufactured textiles. (See note 30). They illustrate the profitability of cotton carriage and inelasticity of cotton demand.

40. Willan, op. cit., pp. 208–28 and L.R.O., DDBd/48.

41. No accounts of traffic on this canal have survived. However, flats full of Lancashire coal bound for Chester were the first vessels to use it. Tolls on

coal were reduced to 1*d*. a ton mile just after the waterway opened, and to 9*d*. for the whole journey from the Mersey to Chester a year later. Because of the low price per ton and high demand elasticity of coal, reductions in tolls could greatly increase traffic; there was a continuous increase in total receipts through the late 1790s and a return of five per cent on capital, despite the reductions in coal tolls. P.R.O., RAIL, 827/5 and 7 and Joseph Hemmingway, *History of the City of Chester* (1831), vol. 2, p. 326.

42. Hadfield and Biddle, op. cit., vol. 1, p. 36. It should be remembered, too, that the Ellesmere and Chester line communicated with the saltfield at Nantwich (see fig. 1.2). The toll reductions on coal also applied to rock salt. P.R.O., RAIL, 827/5.

43. Of the rock salt produced, 45–50,000 tons a year were exported raw to Northern Europe, 5000 tons were refined at Nantwich and 8500 tons on the Mersey. Aikin, op. cit., p. 429.

44. These coal tonnages have been standardized to comprise tons of 120 lb. Liverpool exports were measured in chaldrons, which were Winchester rather than Newcastle measures. A Winchester chaldron was smaller in the ratio of 11:21 than a Newcastle chaldron, which contained 2.65 tons. *Customs Letter Book of the Port of Liverpool, 1711–1813*, Chetham Society Publ., Ser. 3, vol. vi (1954), letter 115; and British Museum, Additional MSS, 3874, fol. 32.

45. *Gore's Liverpool Directory*, 1805, pp. 96–7.

46. Ibid.

47. Langton, op. cit., p. 238.

48. Arthur Young, *A Six Months Tour through the North of England*, 3 vols., Dublin (1770), vol. 3, pp. 280–3.

49. Aikin, op. cit., pp. 205 and 237.

50. See note 43 and Barker (1952) op. cit. Salt refined from brine on the saltfield was also an important and increasing export (see table 1.5).

51. Aikin, op. cit., p. 429.

52. This list of industries was compiled from Lpl.R.O., HQ942.721ENF and Holt and Gregson MSS, vols. x and xix; *Gore's Liverpool Directories*; Moss, op. cit.; and J. R. Harris, op. cit.; and *The Copper King*, Liverpool (1964).

53. *Gore's Liverpool Directory*, 1794, p. 656.

54. Information on plant closures was taken from references cited in note 52.

55. M. A. Daunton, 'Towns and economic growth in eighteenth century England', in P. A. Abrams, and E. A. Wrigley, *Towns in Societies*, Cambridge (1978), pp. 245–79.

56. According to Young, weekly adult male earnings in the Liverpool porcelain, stocking, and glass manufactures were 8*s*. 11*d*., compared with 7*s*. 11*d*. in the Manchester fustian, check, hat, and smallware industries. Rates of wage increase in various Liverpool industries are given in Lpl.R.O., Holt and Gregson MSS, vol. x, pp. 277–99.

57. Harris, J. R., 'Skills, coal and British industry in the eighteeenth century', *History*, **61** (1976), 167–82.

58. According to Moss, op. cit., p. 153 'the number of Welch . . . is estimated at 6000, who occupy entire neighbourhoods, where scarce a word of English is spoken.' The influx of Irish increased considerably after the suppression of the rebellion of 1798.

59. Liverpool pottery craftsmen were attracted to Staffordshire by Wedgwood in the late eighteenth century. Finer and Savage, op. cit., p. 75.

60. Lpl.R.O., Holt and Gregson MSS, vol. xix, fol. 46.

61. Moss, op. cit., p. 75.

62. Langton, op. cit., pp. 176–81; and T. C. Barker; and J. R. Harris, *A Merseyside Town in the Industrial Revolution: St. Helens 1750–1900*, Liverpool (1954).

63. Aikin, op. cit., p. 363.

64. See note 41.

65. J. R. L., Haigh MSS, Alexander, 6th Earl of Balcarres, Management of mining estates, 1818–22, pp. 86–7.

66. Lpl.R.O., Holt and Gregson MSS, vol. xix, pp. 77–78.

67. L.R.O., DP/175, pp. 64–5.

2

Financial institutions and the capital market on Merseyside in the eighteenth and nineteenth centuries

B. L. ANDERSON

The development of a capital market and the emergence of financial institutions within it is of considerable intrinsic interest in a port-region such as Merseyside, where the links between finance, trade, and regional economic growth evolved over the classic period of the industrial revolution, and whose place in that wider process of change was of central importance to it. As a new metropolis of the west and the principal gateway to the northern manufacturing districts, the history of the financial sector of the Merseyside economy sheds considerable light on one of the key factors in economic growth generally. An examination of the organization and functions of the financial sector of a region's economy involves the whole system by which assets, both real and financial, change hands, and through which claims on resources accumulated by original savers are transmitted to those who ultimately use them for the creation of real capital or for other purposes.

In the early eighteenth century the relatively less developed economy of South-West Lancashire possessed no financial institutions of any significance and almost the only local body engaged in organized financial activity on any scale was the Liverpool Common Council. There is evidence that the Council raised some funds on a continuous basis through the issue of its own bonds from the beginning of the century to finance port and other local improvements.[1] At the same time local merchant and landed notables had been involved with a more or less regular collection of taxation and rental revenue, and its transmission to London, from at least the 1660s. With the extension of the Post road system during and after the 1690s regular remittance facilities must have permitted some interregional flow of funds, over and above those for taxation and personal maintenance purposes, though the size and direction of

Notes and references begin on page 51.

such flows has not so far been well documented. Thus by the eighteenth century the development of postal services, and the rise of individual intermediaries associated with them, meant that even a fairly remote and undeveloped region such as Merseyside was by no means isolated from the rest of the country, especially outside of the winter months.[2]

If the regional economy of the area was not completely isolated during the early eighteenth century its financial relations were still highly localized. For the most part these consisted of largely informal borrowing and lending between persons, much of which remains wholly without record. Considerable seasonality and a limited degree of specialization characterized this early interpersonal capital market. Not only agricultural activity but also trade were subject to seasonal fluctuations which, though they may have eased in the long-term with the growth of regional reserves held locally and in London, persisted until well into the nineteenth century. This seasonality in financial transactions also accounted in part for the emergence of specialist intermediaries, whose activities worked towards minimizing discrepancies in the availability of money and credit. These early eighteenth-century intermediaries often acted as nominees, testamentary executors, trustees, and assignees of 'powers of attorney'; but many more were key figures in the credit structure of the regional economy not because of any conscious specialization in finance but simply as a result of their pivotal positions in the organization of particular trades and manufactures. The former group of intermediaries stood between the original lender and the ultimate borrower, so that the actual identities of transactors, and their purposes, were often effectively hidden: for this reason alone information concerning these flows of funds can only rarely be related to a more general picture of total assets and liabilities.[3] In the case of the latter, and much larger, group of intermediaries information is more readily available, especially from the late seventeenth century on; though even here, much of the data relating to the credit relations of individual traders and small firms is barely discernible from the rather amorphous mass of financial activity taking place in what is now called the 'personal' or 'household' sector of the economy.

The general distinction drawn between these two groups of financial intermediaries can be extended further to include the two main financial markets in which they largely, though not exclusively, operated. For the country as a whole a broad dichotomy between a market in money and short-term credit instruments, and that in longer-term debt, is much older than the early eighteenth century even though both markets experienced an unprecedented expansion in the century after the Restoration. But in regions such as Merseyside the appearance of effectively delineated credit and capital markets seems to have occurred for the first time on any scale at this period. The mainstay of provincial capital markets for most of the eighteenth century was the private mortgage security; and this together with the purchase and sale of national debt securities became the chief preoccupations of the first group of intermediaries identified above. The bulk of mortgage transactions in South-West Lancashire in the eighteenth century appears to have been for a 'term of years' rather than 'in fee' and as such the real security remained in the hands of the borrower with only the title passing to the mortgagee for the time being. Real estate loans of this kind became extremely common as the land market became less active in the eighteenth century. As a corollary the demand for legal, administrative and trustee services grew considerably providing new opportunities for intermediation.[4] To a large extent these intermediaries were recruited from within the extended family circle, from friends and co-religionists, and from business partners or major creditors. At the lower levels of income and wealth little specialization was required on the part of the intermediary; indeed it was further up the social scale and in cases of unusually complex long-term indebtedness that specialist intermediaries came into their own. It was to this work that the provincial attorney, whose expertize and professional contacts linked land with trade, was increasingly drawn and who, before the rise of the country banks, was the archetypal financial intermediary in the South-West Lancashire capital market.

The local money market before the emergence of banking as a distinct institutional form was also largely inter-personal. Any coherence that it possessed owed much to the activities of a handful of wealthy and well-connected merchants in each of the region's principal trades. In this rudimentary money market three separate functions, frequently interrelated, can be identified: the provision, uses and adequacy of metallic currency (minted and token), of various financial instruments, and of book or trade credit. In the case of the first two considerable specialization is evident at the beginning of the century, whereas the third function was ubiquitous amongst individuals and firms. The English regions were far from being adequately monetized during the eighteenth century and more rapid economic advance brought acute pressure to bear on existing supplies of coined money. To some extent the effects of an unequal distribution of small denomination coinage and the gradual deterioration of its condition over time, were offset by the use of privately-issued tokens. In Liverpool the most reliable of these token circulations was issued by Thomas Clarke, a saddler, but there were several others issued during the course of the century.[5] Before the great token copper coinages of Thomas Williams' Parys Mine Company and those made by John Wilkinson and Matthew

Boulton after 1787, these tokens circulated alongside a variety of domestic silver and some foreign coins in differing degrees of deterioration with the result that areas such as Merseyside were frequently starved of low denomination coins.

The inadequacies of coinage as a medium of exchange lent some impetus to the growing practice of using certain kinds of financial instrument as a substitute. Chief among these was the bill of exchange, an instrument of great antiquity, whose use in foreign and internal trade grew by leaps and bounds during the eighteenth century. Because businessmen required a period of time during which to process and distribute raw materials or other stock in trade a gap existed, often a very long gap in the eighteenth century, between the time they were received, the time when payment for them was due, and the time of ultimate resale and reimbursement. The bill of exchange enabled these time periods between payments among buyers and sellers to be bridged to the satisfaction of all concerned. Although the bill mechanism developed most completely in the expanding Atlantic trades where long voyage times enabled its flexibility to be exploited to the full, its use in Lancashire's internal trade enabled it to replace conventional media over a far wider range of transactions than elsewhere in the country.[6] The extent to which bills were used for making quite small local payments appears to have induced some specialization in handling them from an early date. Prior to the emergence of private bankers in Merseyside in the 1770s, and long before the rise of the even more specialized bill-brokers in London in the early years of the nineteenth century, local bill-dealers arose to conduct elementary brokerage at the retail level and to arrange the sorting of bills by quality and usance for discounting locally or in London. As with bills, promissory notes were also negotiable but they rarely circulated beyond the confines of the locality in which they were issued and, during the course of the century, they appear to have given way to bills in the more rapidly growing regions of Merseyside and South Lancashire.

These early bill dealers operating in a small way were either important shopkeepers with numerous contacts in their neighbourhoods, or else merchants whose knowledge of the personnel and credit lines of specific trades enabled them to graft on bill-dealing to their trading function as a means of diversifying their interests and spreading their risks. Most remained intermediaries rather than principals in the bill system and to that extent their resemblance to the large broking firms who created the London discount market after 1815 is only superficial. The true successors of the bill-dealers were the private bankers, who extended specialization to the point where it became an independent business activity concerned with issuing their own notes and arranging for bills of exchange to be discounted locally or in London. These early provincial or country bankers did not operate a deposit and cheque system, unlike the Restoration goldsmith-bankers of the capital or the nineteenth-century joint-stock banks; nor did they give any statement of their financial position or offer anything more than their own personal character and worth in support of their dealings. They were also small in size and unitary in character. To some extent this was a consequence of the Bank of England's virtual monopoly of note-issuing which permitted only partnerships of up to six members to share their privilege. On the other hand the dominance of London and its region in the economic life of the country was greater from the late seventeenth to the late eighteenth century than at almost any other period, so that banking facilities there could have been expected to have been far in advance of elsewhere. Lack of banking specialization among merchants and manufacturers in the provinces probably reflected a lower level of banking requirements, especially note-issuing, as distinct from other financial services that could be met outside of banking for much of the eighteenth century.

On Merseyside, however, another factor making for the later emergence of the banking specialist was the financial organization of its main trades. These had always relied on the availability of discount facilities, rather than note-issues *per se*, to facilitate the smooth working of the bill system. With the rise of the cotton import trade in particular it was the demand for substantial bill-brokerage facilities and re-discounting in London which increased rather than bank notes for local circulation. Those who came to specialize in banking thus had to be merchants of considerable resources with established and dependable London connections. Indeed in the Merseyside financial system which depended crucially on mutual accommodation, trade credit given and received could obviate the need for extensive banking facilities locally for long periods, and did so long after the arrival of the banking fraternity. Before further discussion of the banking system, therefore, this important activity of informal borrowing and lending in the normal course of business and without any institutional assistance needs examination.

The extent to which eighteenth- and nineteenth-century economic activity was self-financed has often been allowed to disguise the ubiquity of interpersonal and interfirm accommodation. In part this arose from the relatively small size of most trading concerns. These tended to have a very low ratio of tangible fixed assets to total resources. Moreover, such firms typically held a high proportion of their assets in liquid form, and even if the proportion of stocks and work in progress was often not very different from that in the largest concerns of the period, the smaller the firm the more it was likely to be dependent on its debtors and creditors in trade. Such credit, given and received, enabled firms to economize on ready cash reserves by allowing interfirm settlements to become less frequent; this was particularly important for new enterprisers whose venture or equity capital might be barely adequate for commencing business. Trade credit possessed its own structure or hierarchy, with the largest merchants or manufacturers acting as lynchpins, which enabled the large firm to assist the smaller by, for example, sub-contracting or putting-out.

It is not surprising therefore that when banking first became a distinct enterprise activity on Merseyside, separate from the ordinary business of merchants, it was complementary to and in some degree competed with more traditional modes of credit creation. This occurred towards the close of more than a decade of sustained foreign trade expansion with only one major interruption, rising domestic consumption and accelerating population growth between the ending of the Seven Years War and the outbreak of the American Revolution.[7] The first banker mentioned in a Liverpool directory appeared in 1774 and it seems reasonable to infer that this foundation was one of a number of provincial responses to the London banking boom of 1769–73 which increased considerably the number of City banks with country and mercantile connections, and which culminated in the setting-up of the London Clearing House to handle the growing volume of inter-bank and country business. Not only was the notice of Liverpool's first banker unexceptional in national terms but the description 'William Clarke, banker and linen draper . . .' shows that even when a major shift in demand for credit and increased profit expectations took place the transition to independent banking was rarely complete. In fact from the early 1770s, when the English banking system became truly national in scope, and the mid-1830s, when the joint-stock banking boom at last brought bank development in most areas of the country, few Liverpool concerns conducted an exclusive banking business. Even at the beginning of the 1830s there were only seven private banks in the city, and two of these absorbed the bulk of its banking business.

The first known banker in Liverpool appears to have been John Wyke, a watchmaker and merchant middleman, who was active at mid-century; but the real watershed came in the years 1773–4. In addition to William Clarke & Sons, Arthur Heywood, and Charles Caldwell also established banks at this time, both having derived their capital from their involvement in the African and West Indian trades. Bill finance was crucial to the operation and expansion of these trades and, in this and subsequent periods of increased bill circulation, most of the important additions to the Liverpool banking fraternity were made. Leaving aside the frequent changes which took place in the partnership arrangements of banking firms, and the very brief lives of some of them, the next major increase in banking activity came in the last decade of the century. The crisis of 1772 had shown how dependent were ports like Liverpool on their traditional African and West India trades, and how crucial was the bill mechanism and London acceptances to their prosperity. Subsequently, the American War and its aftermath seriously disrupted these trades as well as the growing direct commerce with America. During the second half of the eighties all three main branches of Liverpool trade began to improve as the general economic outlook brightened. At this time, probably in 1786, William Gregson, West Indian trader and insurance broker, formed the banking partnership Gregson, Sons, Parke, and Morland. The fact that the principal partners in this bank had both pursued their earlier careers in the Islands trade may be significant.[8] During the eighties complex changes were being felt in the structure of Liverpool's trade, with import trades of recent origin such as that in American cotton growing more rapidly than its traditional commerce. The transition to full banking may have been an attractive exit for those who had prospered in slaves and sugar previously, but now found the outlook for them less sanguine.

As economic conditions improved with rising prices and increased port traffic through into the early 1790s, further additions to the banking establishment were made, including the partnership of Staniforth, Ingram, Bold, and Daltera founded in 1791 but dissolved four years later, and that of Cromie, Pownall, and Hartman the only known note-issuing bank which enjoyed barely a decade of activity. In fact the nineties, a decade in which the last great resurgence of the West Indian trade gave way to war, crisis, and uncertainty, saw only one bank established in the city. The concern of John Aspinall & Sons, founded around 1796, managed to survive two bankruptcies, in 1816 and 1832, and was floated as the Central Bank of Liverpool in 1836. At the same time the Clarke's bank, which had managed to survive the crisis of 1793, came close to insolvency after William Clarke's death in 1797 and only continued in existence by recruiting fresh energy and capital with the entry of William Roscoe into the partnership in 1800, and Thomas Leyland in 1802. Thus by the end of the eighteenth century Liverpool possessed only two banks of stature. Gregson, Sons, Parke, and Morland tended to be patronized by those of the West India connection, who set up the Liverpool West India Association in 1799, and who took their business to Leyland and Bullins bank after the dissolution of Gregson & Co. in 1805.[9] The age of this interest group, whose economics was enshrined in the navigation laws and whose politics were Tory, was drawing to a close. Clarke, Roscoe, and Co. was favoured by those of the new American interest; these men were free traders and Whigs, and it was they who formed the American Chamber of Commerce in 1801.

The liquidity crises of 1793, 1795, and 1799 had revealed the fragility of Liverpool's bill system under pressure and how easily its banking facilities were overwhelmed when large accumulations of commercial paper required liquidation. Only the issue of municipal bills in 1793 and loans of Exchequer bills by the Bank of England in the two subsequent shocks saved the merchant community from widespread bankruptcy. While precise evidence is lacking there is little to suggest anything more than a temporary lag in the growth and deployment of local savings behind the financial needs of the port's trades and related industries. Liverpool's population is estimated to have grown more than four-fold in the first half of the eighteenth century, and to have trebled again by its close without much assistance from outside immigration before the 1790s. This in itself suggests that economic growth in the area could be autonomously financed from an early date.

Even at the beginning of the eighteenth century it is now clear that the port of Liverpool's development was stimulated not just by its coastal and overseas trading connections, but also by a remarkably wide array of industrial activities in its hinterland.[10] In a region that was relatively isolated from much of the rest of the country were to be found almost all the traditional industrial activities associated with the onset of industrialization. These included the primary extractive industries of coalmining in the South-West Lancashire field from Wigan to St Helens, extending to Prescot and Whiston, and the saltworkings of Cheshire around the lower Weaver. Both these industries experienced phases of rapid growth during the course of the eighteenth century, characterized by considerable interrelatedness of capital and ownership. Mining was, of course, essentially still a rural industry and before the 1730s its progress in response to changing demand seems to have been largely dictated by the ability of local landowners to divert some part of the rising incomes from improved agricultural productivity into extractive activities.[11]

But with each successive improvement in communications which the growth of demand for coal and salt required—the completion of the Weaver navigation and the Liverpool-Prescot turnpike road in the early 1730s, the Sankey Canal in the late 1750s, and the Leeds and Liverpool Canal by the mid-1770s—the involvement of purely landed enterprise and finance diminished.

From mid-century when other industries of longstanding, together with some new ones, began to be conducted on a larger scale and to require much greater capitalization, the dominance of mercantile sources of finance from within and without the region becomes increasingly apparent. From this time also it is possible to detect the basic pattern of investment activity and economic growth that came to dominate the development of the regional economy for the remainder of the eighteenth and throughout the nineteenth centuries. This was a broadly inverse relationship between phases of foreign and coastal trade expansion, particularly exports and re-exports including the slave trade, and periods of heavy fixed capital formation in dock and transport improvements and urban construction. In the period *c.*1750–90 these interrelations are not clearly distinguishable and frequently overlapped. They are further complicated by the continuing growth in other local industries requiring finance, particularly the wide variety of secondary metal trades between Liverpool, Wigan, and Warrington, including an array of skills associated with the tool and watchmaking trades. These were of great longevity by the middle of the century and intermingled with a domestic linen manufacture focused on the Warrington sailcloth industry.[12] Other industrial developments involving much larger infusions of new capital were the St Helens glass industry, the Warrington copper and brass manufacture, with smelting extended to Liverpool itself in the 1760s, and an expansion of the earthenware industry into delftware and porcelain. Finally there were a number of port industries embracing shipbuilding, soon to be in relative decline; and rope and anchor works, sugar refining, brewing and distilling, all experiencing considerable expansion.

The precocious growth of Merseyside's communications network during the thirty years or more before the outbreak of the Seven Years War when compared with other regions of the country is a characteristic that was to reappear at intervals during the following century and a half. When viewed in perspective, however, the eighteenth-century developments at least were a response to relative backwardness and isolation in terms not only of the port's links with its hinterland, but of the region's links with the rest of the country. From the Seven Years War down to the early 1770s the pace of transport improvement appears to have slowed down within the region, partly a reflection perhaps of a deflection of the merchant community's financial resources into the growing number of overseas trade opportunities at this time. It was in these years that the positions gained by the Liverpool merchants from the 1720s if not earlier, in the sugar, tobacco, and above all the slave trades, came to fruition. Moreover, any redeployment of capital was facilitated by the fact that Liverpool's merchants had always been a more cohesive and purposeful oligarchy than their counterparts in Bristol, and even London, and had gained earlier and more complete political leverage over the town's Common Council. At the same time, before the American War at least, wartime conditions helped to expand rather than hinder Liverpool shipping, in contrast with most other ports, and were much less disruptive of the coal and salt trades.[13] These latter were also largely controlled by the same groups of merchants, the Cases and Gildarts, the Cunliffes and the Blackburnes, the Bolds and the Staniforths, who directly or indirectly developed the more distant trades. Further transport improvements were made during the American War and by the end of the century Liverpool's water communications with all the important industrial regions were largely complete. In the decade following the American War, however, there was a very marked resumption in the growth of the port's shipping capacity; in fact it was a key period in this respect, as in others, and must have involved a considerable net inflow of funds into the foreign trade sector of the regional economy. One estimate suggests that 349 vessels were owned in the port in 1783, and 606 ten years later, at which date Liverpool was the second ship-owning port in the Empire.[14] Out of a total of 879 different vessels registered at Liverpool between mid-1786 and the end of 1793, owned by 1207 individual investors, 76 per cent or 917 lived within the limits of the port, and another 17 had lived in Liverpool at some time during the period. These 917 owned 83·7 per cent or 3048 of 3643 part-ownerships of Liverpool-registered vessels in the period. Of the 1207 individual investors, 61 per cent or 736 were described simply as merchants in the registers, and another 5·6 per cent or 67 were sometimes so described. Together these 803 merchants owned 80 per cent or 2914 of total part-ownerships.

The picture of ship-owning in late eighteenth-century Liverpool, perhaps the most important single object of merchants' fixed capital formation, which these figures provide give some indication of the important part played by Liverpool in that great expansion of trade and manufactures after 1783 which was so crucial to industrialization. It is said that the number of vessels owned in the port increased by approximately 75 per cent in the decade following the American War, a reflection of the very large capital resources which the merchant community was able to dispose of when opportunities arose. For, as the figures make clear, the ownership of this enlarged fleet was overwhelmingly in the hands of local merchants who made up two-thirds of all shipping investors. The remainder were people with other business interests outside trade, or people who were exclusively ship-owners. These last, however, were almost certainly very few in number at this stage since ship-owning as a distinct business function does not appear to have been very important much before the 1830s. The purchasers of these ship-owning partnerships appear to have employed their vessels in their own trades, many of them in the profitable carriage of West India goods and slaves. Vessels at this period were largely trade-specific, partly for technical and partly for management reasons, and while most of them carried freights for merchants other than their owners at some time, very few appear to have been chartered for long periods. Large numbers of master mariners took shares in the vessels of which they were masters, and some even became sole owners though usually of small vessels, less than fifty tons, employed in the canal and coastal trades.[15] A ship-owning master ensured the better conduct of a venture and had an incentive to maximize profits. One such was Samuel McDowall who began as a part-owning master, graduated to become an independent merchant, and accumulated sufficient capital to quit seafaring altogether and become a ship-broker by the early 1790s.

Thus towards the close of the eighteenth century the shipping and trade of Liverpool was largely under the control and direction of around eight hundred merchants normally resident in the town. The growth of Liverpool's trades and the regular influx of new recruits to the merchant community had enormously increased and diversified its ranks in comparison with the small oligarchy of perhaps two dozen substantial merchants who had guided the fortunes of the port in the 1720s. There were, of course, always some investors in Liverpool's shipping and trade who retained their interests long after they had ceased to reside in the town or who had retired from active business. More important were the outside interests who were attracted by the great expansion of the cotton trade during the 1780s. Usually these were the London agents and correspondents of prominent Liverpool merchants who provided the discount and remittance facilities on which an expanding trade relied. These financial links with the capital, already extensive, were to become more rather than less important after the turn of the century as the continued growth of the cotton industry and trade produced overwhelming pressures towards greater inter-regional specialization within Lancashire.

The rise of the factory system and larger scale industrial units in the east of the county, and its failure to take permanent root in the south-western districts was already becoming evident before the end of the eighteenth century, and by the 1830s the eastward movement of industries such as chemicals, copper, pottery, and glass, in addition to the cotton manufacture and general engineering, was largely complete. These developments accelerated the trends towards commercial specialization in Liverpool, emphasizing the trading and financial functions of the port, including its continued importance as a centre for transport extension and finance.[16] Following the reforms of 1811 dock extension expanded rapidly, with a quadrupling of facilities between 1825 and 1861. During the 1830s the 'Liverpool Party' took the lead in promoting and financing railway expansion far beyond their own region. As with canals earlier, these initiatives helped to underpin the growth of the port's trades in the nineteenth century, especially the American trade, which produced a four-fold increase in its shipping tonnage between 1820 and 1850. By the end of the 1850s Liverpool possessed more than 200 acres of docks, more registered tonnage than the port of London, and was shipping virtually half of Britain's exports.[17]

This remarkable progress as a commercial centre that had now long since outgrown its purely regional functions had required a considerable expansion in Liverpool's financial institutions. After 1815 the merchant community was served by only two banking partnerships of high credit standing and ample resources, Leyland, Bullins & Co. and A. Heywood, Sons & Co. These two establishments shared the Corporation's account between them and conducted the bulk of the banking business of the town. In addition there were a half-dozen other firms who conducted banking as part of a larger business as merchants, brokers, and bullion dealers, but the frequency of dissolution and partnership changes among them suggests that their purely banking business was never very large. Two of these banking concerns failed in the financial crisis of 1825/6 underlining the fact that the demand for discounting facilities which had grown rapidly during the Napoleonic Wars could no longer be met by the existing local banks and their established London connections. An important step towards remedying this deficiency was the opening of a branch of the Bank of England in July 1827 in order to provide greater stability in the local money-market and to dampen the sharp fluctuations in liquidity requirements to which Liverpool's trades were extremely prone.

This new Bank branch enabled local bankers to place much larger sums in the hands of their London agents and discount houses with ease and safety, thereby ensuring that Lancashire trade-bills, the majority of which were now drawn on London, could be honoured without difficulty.[18] In addition to easier remittance facilities and more regular supplies of media of exchange the Liverpool branch could offer deposit facilities to the local banks, acting as a cash reserve; it also gave preferential rates of discount to non-issuing banks not, as elsewhere in the country, to discourage local note-issuing which had never been popular in Liverpool, but to replace the local bill circulation with its own Bank of England notes. It was not the activities of the Bank branch which led to the decline of the Lancashire bill system after 1815, however, but a variety of other factors such as the fall in interest rates, increased stamp duty on bills of exchange, and in the longer-term the rise of the joint-stock banks and the use of cheques.[19] A large proportion of Liverpool bills originated in the cotton trade during the first half of the nineteenth century, where the normal discount for cash payment was 5 per cent; thus when the market discount rate fell below this figure, as it frequently did in this period, there was an incentive for merchants to discount bills for cash with the bankers and to buy cotton for cash at the normal discount.

The main impact of the Bank of England branch, certainly before the Bank Charter Act of 1844, was in expanding the discount facilities available to the Liverpool money-market and by increasing competition among the local banks it helped to keep down market-rates of interest for much of the period.[20] At the same time when financial pressure arose from time to time, as on several occasions in the late 1830s and in 1847, the branch acted as a lender of last resort thereby maintaining the stability of the system. Liverpool interests played an important role in the promotion and investment booms of the 1830s and 1840s. The investment funds of the region were heavily engaged in the key growth sectors of the British economy, railway expansion and the booming Anglo-American trade. There was also considerable local investment in the new bank and insurance company promotions which were another feature of these joint-stock company booms.

In 1826 it had become legal for banks with more than six partners to be established outside London, and to issue their own notes beyond a radius of sixty-five miles from the capital. This, together with the establishment of the Bank of England branch the following year, opened the way for a renewed growth of banking facilities in the port to match its increasing commercial prosperity. The first joint-stock bank appeared in the town in 1829.[21] It was a branch office of the Manchester and Liverpool District Banking Company and was quickly followed by the full establishment of the Bank of Liverpool which, although it was actually the first joint-stock bank to be registered in the country in April 1826, did not commence business until 1831 under the management of the former sub-agent of the Bank of England, Joseph Langton. This bank, together with the Commercial Bank of Liverpool set up in 1833, set its face against the active branching policy of the District Bank preferring to emulate the unitary status of the private banks. The Commercial Bank was ultimately absorbed by the Bank of Liverpool in 1889. The easy credit conditions of the early thirties encouraged bank promotions, many of them under-capitalized and poorly managed like the Northern and Central Bank of England and the Commercial Bank of England both of which established branches in Liverpool in 1834.

Even before the foundation of the Liverpool Stock Exchange in 1836 there appear to have been some dealings in the shares of joint-stock companies, including banks. The regular advertisement of share auctions' dates from 1827 with local brokers and accountants like Thomas Coglan, Thomas Winstanley, and Harmood Banner were among the earliest to engage exclusively in share dealing. By 1833, for example, the shares of the Bank of Manchester and the Bank of Liverpool are quoted in the weekly share lists of the *Liverpool Mercury* among a range of railway, canal, water, and gas companies. Joint-stock banks were an important feature of the promotions boom of 1835–6. At its height the local stock exchange quoted 38 railway companies, 15 banks and other miscellaneous concerns. In fact, as with railways, banks with no branches in Liverpool attracted the interest of Merseyside investors at this time.[22] Virtually all of the eight Liverpool-based banks quoted on the exchange had very large proprietaries, with the North and South Wales Bank having over 700. Among other banks quoted in Liverpool, the Bank of Manchester had 600 proprietors and the District Bank had over 1000.

The absence of any legal regulation undoubtedly added impetus to these promotions of the 1830s and although a few suffered from inexperienced and even fraudulent management most of the new banks helped to expand the market in rediscounting bills of exchange and thereby to cater for customers' increased demand for loans and discounts by supplying them with Bank of England notes. The joint-stock banks were not necessarily more given to speculation than the older private banks for their liability was also unlimited, but in general they were more vigorous in extending the banking habit and often less rigorous in their standards when making loans and discounts. The American trades, particularly in cotton, were the backbone of Liverpool's commercial economy at this period and ample credit facilities were required by those who engaged in it.[23] Moreover, although bills of exchange had become the usual instrument of credit in almost all trades, buoyant conditions for the Anglo-American houses invariably meant that large quantities of American bills circulated on Merseyside, some proportion of them drawn for the purpose of accommodation rather than originating in the sale of goods.

At times of financial stringency and crisis this system, which was well suited to the conduct of Liverpool's trades, could become a major source of instability, as in 1836–7, 1839, 1847–8, and 1866. At such times the Merseyside banking fraternity became inordinately vulnerable in the face of a scramble for discounts and runs on their deposits. In the commercial crisis of 1847–8, for example, of the seven bank failures which occurred three were in Liverpool and the town witnessed a higher level of commercial failure than any other centre outside London. Although the larger private banks such as Leyland & Bullins had always been well capitalized and maintained large cash resources sufficient to discount extensively for other local banks, they were exceptional; and while the coming of joint-stock banking increased the volume of bill discounting the growth of deposits tended to lag behind other areas of the country. The working of the Lancashire bill system encouraged local banks to rely on the cash resources of banks in rural areas, where investment outlets were few, being invested with London agents in bills that had been endorsed by Lancashire banks. The quality of bills was thus crucial to the smooth working of the system, more so after the rise of joint-stock banks in the provinces where their resources never approached those of their London counterparts. Even as late as the 1880s

Liverpool's seven banks had little more than half the level of deposits of Manchester's nine banks.[24] Among other factors it was the disastrous failure of the Borough Bank of Liverpool in the crisis of 1857, brought on by another convulsion in Anglo-American trade and finance, that led to legislation extending limited liability to the banking sector.

The joint-stock bank promotions of 1832–6 gave way to a lull during the 1840s and 1850s when only one new bank was launched in the town, the Exchange Office Bank, and three ceased operations, the Albion, the Phoenix, and a branch of the Commercial Bank of England. These initiatives had done little to extend the basis of bank capital beyond the region so that share-ownership was largely in the hands of Liverpool investors; moreover it was characteristic of these banks to have large reserves of uncalled capital which tended to encourage speculation in their shares.[25] During the next bank promotion boom of 1862–5 rather more investment interest came from outside the region, reflecting the even stronger links between Liverpool banks and their London agents in what was now a national money-market; even more apparent is the much wider investing public which had developed by the third quarter of the nineteenth century within the region itself.

Although it was not until the last quarter of the century that deposit banking in the regions, and especially Merseyside, began to grow appreciably, in respect of one financial institution it had begun much earlier. The thrift movement had a particular, and early, connection with Liverpool because its founder Henry Duncan served his apprenticeship to the banking business in the town at Heywood's bank. The precursor of the savings bank was the Liverpool Society for Bettering the Condition of the Poor, a friendly society formed in 1809 for the provision of basic relief. It represented an attempt to divert the petty savings of people of small means away from the lotteries, tontines, etc. which had flourished in the town in the eighteenth century, and to create a safe haven for the surpluses of the thrifty alongside the many outlets which existed for the gambling instinct. In 1811 a sub-committee of the Society was appointed to draw up rules for a 'Mechanics, Servants and Labourers Fund' which by 1815 had become a recognized savings bank. The Liverpool Savings Bank was unique in the movement, for under the guiding influence of the prominent Anglican churchman, Archdeacon Jonathan Brooks, it alone maintained a long and close connexion with the charity which gave it birth until his death in 1855.[26] It soon had a 'Minor Bank' in association with it for encouraging thrift among children, and as early as 1818 had set up agencies in Huyton and Winwick. Although by 1829 the Manchester Savings Bank, though founded later, had also grown rapidly and actually had more depositors than Liverpool and funds of £200,000, Liverpool's funds were greater at £265,000.

By the 1850s the Liverpool Savings Bank was the fifth largest in the country in terms of number of depositors, after the three London banks and Manchester, with approaching £¾m in funds. The crisis of 1857, which brought down the Borough Bank of Liverpool and rocked the local banking community, appears to have had small effect on the thrift movement in the town and in the next two decades numbers of 'penny banks' and then 'school banks' extended their activities in the area, receiving active encouragement from the Established Church and legislation in the form of Forster's Act of 1870. Down to 1863 the Liverpool bank held the funds of other small savings institutions in the region. Though under independent management they were called branches and made annual returns to the Liverpool bank: these branch banks were at Huyton opened in 1817, Neston and Wirral 1825, West Derby 1838, Stanley 1845, and Crewe 1847. During the sixties and seventies the Liverpool bank was third in the national league table of savings deposits behind Glasgow and Manchester. In the period 1875–88 it purchased Corporation mortgages on behalf of its depositors, an anticipation of the rise of the special investment department later, but also reviving an older practice of Local Authority lending. The Liverpool bank was one of those which earned special approbation for its management in the debates preceding the Savings Bank Act of 1891; with 85,000 depositors its success was partly attributed to competition from the Post Office Savings banks established in Liverpool following the Act of 1861.

The early emergence of a formal securities market in Liverpool, within little more than a generation of its establishment in London in 1802, requires further comment especially in view of the common belief that such markets are difficult to establish and maintain in economies in the early stages of economic growth and that their functions are of little benefit to the growth process and are easily dispensed with. Yet judging from Britain's experience, particularly that of provincial centres such as Liverpool, any obstacles to the development of securities markets appear to have been relatively easily surmountable. The fact that stock market facilities made their appearance at the same time, or soon after, the rise of other than purely local private banking arrangements not only in London but in a number of major provincial towns is an important feature of financial development in England.[27] That securities markets, dealing in titles to capital combinations, were being given institutional form during the 1830s when joint-stock banking development was leading to an improved articulation of the country's money markets is very significant. It is indicative of the way in which a securely founded market system, in which financial innovation was now largely unregulated, was capable of expanding the financial sector under the stimulus of economic growth.

The processes of change in the money and capital markets were highly interrelated in Lancashire as the Industrial Revolution came to maturity in the 1830s. The growth of incomes and wealth during the previous half-century was promoting additional requirements of currency and credit instruments, discounting and remittance facilities; and at the same time a wider range of securities for investment. Thus as well as an expanded banking sector for short-term borrowing and lending, a securities market was also needed not, as in banking, to make any overall assessments of the competing claims for finance in the region, but rather to distribute investment funds in accordance with the perceived profits prospects of firms and other institutions competing for share capital. The contribution of the stock exchange to the development of the capital market, within and beyond the region, was that it provided a truly 'speculative' market in a major centre of new wealth creation. Such a market, in which people buy not for immediate use so much as in the hope of selling again later at a profit, at prices reflecting constantly changing balances of investors' expectations over time, was an important vehicle for promoting further specialization and the reduction of costs in financial activities.

For much of the eighteenth century the demand for easily transferable securities remained modest and most savers, even among the higher income groups, had little experience and were frequently mistrustful of more advanced forms of wealth-holding. Only those of considerable wealth, abroad as well as at home, found it advantageous to spread their risks by diversifying their portfolios and only they could afford to pay the relatively high transactions costs of doing so. The institutional demand for securities was very limited and the considerable price uncertainty associated with securities of fluctuating value reinforced traditional preferences for liquid resources, especially outside London where the scarcity and costs of obtaining accurate information were always likely to inhibit investors. Before the 1820s only the government and a small number of select private institutions benefited from the growth of regular share-dealing in London at the end of the seventeenth century. In fact during the eighteenth century only government could provide sufficient securities on a regular basis to warrant the existence of such a market. From the passage of the Bubble Act in 1720 to its repeal in 1825 company formation was narrowly confined in law, and the low ratio of equity to debt which characterized the financial structure of the majority of business firms before the late nineteenth century left little scope for the issue of business securities and ensured that stockbroking was mainly concerned with trading in the public funds. Even in the London market which evolved a centralized and relatively low-cost organization very early, and which required little more than a recognized meeting place and access to postal, advertising, and clerical services that were already developed by the early eighteenth century, the entire trade in company shares was handled by a handful of brokers and jobbers as late as the 1840s.

During the 1820s a major element in the growth of the London Stock Exchange, and subsequently of the provincial exchanges as well, was the issue and trading of a wide range of transport and public utility securities. Allowing for the fact that the Usury Laws had been contravened to some extent in the eighteenth century, and that government borrowing was anyway exempt from them, it is difficult to judge the effectiveness of interest-rate ceilings before 1825, but there is some significance in the fact that the great expansion in the range of securities and the numbers of shareholders over the next quarter-century took place against a background of stable to falling prices and liberalized interest rates. Moreover, the latter did not entail in this period, as so often, the budgetary consequence of higher service costs on government debt. Provincial holdings of the public funds during the eighteenth century, nor the speculative activity in canal shares in 1791–3 or in company promotions in 1807–8 and again in 1824–5, mainly in waterworks and gas companies, were never sufficient to sustain a continuous investment market in shares in the regions.[28] Only the rapid growth of railway capital after 1830 was capable of producing a supply of securities sufficient to create the possibility of a national market centred on exchanges in London and Lancashire. Established in Liverpool and Manchester in 1836, and even more extensively throughout Britain in the mid-forties, these exchanges were partly the product of, and in part created, an environment that was highly conducive to fostering the entrepreneurial skills of risk assessment and investment appraisal. The result was a remarkable expansion in the size of the investing public and an unprecedented influx of new men into the ranks of the traditional broking and underwriting fraternity of towns like Liverpool. The inter-connections between the principal investment channels in the Merseyside capital market extend well back into the eighteenth century, and appear to have derived from the central role of the merchant among the region's investing classes. It was a characteristic that became even more marked during the great expansion of the capital market in the nineteenth century and underlies the alternating emphasis between the growth of Liverpool's trade and regional capital formation noticed above, and for which recent nineteenth-century estimates show a clear pattern. Thus in the aftermath of the lengthy boom in dock construction which had peaked in 1819 investment was freed for other uses during the twenties. John Moss of the banking firm, Moss, Dales & Rogers, for example, took a lead in promoting the Liverpool and Manchester Railway. He became its first deputy

Table 2.1. *Merseyside: Foreign trade expansions and declines in capital formation compared.*

Period of trade expansion	*Periods of declining capital formation*
1848–57	1846–51
1862–73	1864–9
1879–89	1883–9
1898–	1901–

Source. A. G. Kenwood, loc. cit.

chairman in 1826 and chairman of the Liverpool and Birmingham Railway in 1831.[29] In addition to his large sugar plantations in Demerara he was a substantial subscriber for shares in the Liverpool and Manchester, together with another banker, James Macgregor, and Joseph Hornby and Robert Gladstone. These merchants were members of a larger group of early reformers and opponents of the slave trade which also included Adam Hodgson and George Holt, proprietors of the Bank of Liverpool, and its first chairman William Brown, who was also the first trustee of the Liverpool Fire Insurance Company, the first insurance company to appear in Liverpool share lists in 1833. This was later to become the Liverpool and London and Globe, the largest provincial insurance company whose first chairman was George Holt. Just as the town's largest Friendly Society, the Royal Liver, had close connections with and kept its account at the Liverpool Savings Bank until 1887, so from their foundation close links were maintained between the Bank of Liverpool and the Liverpool and London and Globe Insurance Company. Similarly Adam Hodgson was an important figure in marine insurance and cotton broking as well as being the managing director of the Bank of Liverpool for over twenty years. Insurance was another major investment outlet in the region, especially after the coming of limited liability from the mid-fifties, and produced its largest financial institutions.

Minimizing risk without at the same time incurring high costs so as to discourage, or suppress altogether, risk-spreading facilities, has proved a difficult combination to achieve historically. To suggest that the calculation of risk was an unusually early and continuing preoccupation of the Liverpool business community during the centuries of industrialization seems justified for two reasons. The dependence of the regional economy on long-distance trades on the one hand, and extensive road, water, and ultimately rail communications on the other—both requiring substantial increases in fixed investment over the long-term—meant that local business interests were peculiarly concerned with and very susceptible to the high variability of the expected outcomes of their activities in trade and finance. For such men the need to avoid risk if the cost of doing so appeared less than the gain from avoiding the risk, loomed large in their calculations. Accordingly, in addition to being active participants in commodity and other speculative markets wherein information on future trading conditions were disseminated, and to giving close attention to the possibilities for risk aversion when making investments, Liverpool businessmen showed some precocity in the development of those institutional arrangements by which the burden of risk is able to be dispersed to other individuals i.e. insurance.

It is important to differentiate actuarial risk calculation from other forms. In attempting to make intricate estimates of a calculable risk, such as the expectation of life of a specific population for which relevant information is available, the actuary is able to remove an important element of uncertainty from his lack of knowledge of the future. Risk implies ignorance, and since the calculation of risk represents an attempt to know something of what is inherently unknowable—the future—its calculation is only possible in a limited sense. An insurance company actuary, drawing up frequency tables on the basis of policy-holders' past performance in respect of a given type of risk, can set premium payments so as to cover anticipated losses which all policy-holders share equally. Thus actuarial risk calculation, the probability of a particular type of event occurring, is only calculation to the extent that it offers a method of mitigating the consequences of a particular eventuality. In this it is quite different from the efforts of an ordinary business entrepreneur to assess the risks arising from his ignorance of the future. The risks of entrepreneurial action are so potentially manifold in number and quality, yet so specific to the entrepreneur in question and the enterprise he contemplates, as to defy all efforts to apply a calculus of probability to them.

In his search for profit the nineteenth-century Liverpool merchant was exposed, more than most, to rapid changes in the structure of prices and costs that confronted him. Swift judgement and good timing were vital to success in the port's trades, and for much of the century the inadequacies of the merchant's own accounting informa-ion and the snatches of market intelligence coming to him offered a very insecure footing from which to operate in the markets. Shipping and warehousing costs and their attendant risks clouded expectations even more in the commodity trades. In such a situation, where no amount of foresight could possibly envisage all the risks which might befall a venture or the stocks which he held as a result of its successful outcome, the merchant became much concerned with safeguarding his position from the consequences of those risks which foresight revealed to him even as he embraced those which remained hidden. In such a community the taking of high risks went hand in hand with the arrangement of insurance.

William Blundell of Little Crosby nr. Liverpool in 1642 wrote that 'The greatest gamblers are those who in public gaming-houses, called the Offices of Insurance, do for a sum of money secure buildings upon the land from fire, and ships upon the sea from water, etc.' But it seems unlikely that he was referring to local insurance offices. More than a century later, Liverpool's first directory for 1766 lists five brokers and one agent. Of these only two, James Cotter and Matthew Forde & Co. appear as exclusively insurance brokers; the others, namely Samual Shaw, Slater & Caldwell, and William Williamson were described as 'merchant and insurance broker', with William Pole the 'agent for the Sun Fire and Stamp Officer'. Not until 1776 was the first Liverpool Fire Office established with the following proprietors: Gill Slater; Benj., Rich. & B. A. Heywood; Thos. & John Tarleton; Thos. Case and Thos. Peake. During 1778 the proprietorship was extended to include Richard Hughes, John Blackburne jnr., Thos. Staniforth, Thos. Earle, Samuel Shaw, James Clegg, Joseph Brooks jnr., and T. Trotter. The Heywood family appear to have been the prime movers in this establishment which by 1780 was calling itself the 'Liverpool Assurance Office from Fire and on Lives'.

This firm ceased to write business in 1795 and was taken over by the Phoenix, established in London in 1782 and represented in Liverpool since 1789. William Kemp, secretary of the Liverpool Fire Office became the new manager of the Phoenix business in Liverpool. The Royal Exchange Co. (1720) and the Norwich Union (1797) also had agencies in Liverpool from 1790 and 1799 respectively. The next local initiative in fire insurance came in 1802 when the Liverpool St George's Fire Office was set up with a capital of £300,000 by a large group of prominent merchants headed by Moses Benson, P. W. Brancker, George Case, John Gregson, A. Heywood, and Thos. Leyland. Its launch in June was very unfortunately timed, however, and the company was badly hit almost immediately by the huge conflagration at the Goree Piazzas in September when seventeen warehouses were destroyed. Fires continued to burn for three months and total damage amounted to upwards of £⅓m despite the fact that all local fire offices now kept their own fire engines. Fire extinguishing engines were supplied by the firm Merryweathers from the 1790s to the mid-nineteenth century. From 1825 there was a local fire engine manufacturer, William Tyror. The companies with most engines and firemen in their employ included St George's, the Phoenix, the Sun, the Royal Exchange, and the British Fire Office, as well as the Norwich Union, the Imperial, and the West of England and these appear to have written most of the city's fire business in the first quarter of the nineteenth century.[30]

As fire insurance spread to the provinces during the second half of the eighteenth century the major metropolitan companies became increasingly involved in firefighting, supporting brigades in such centres as Manchester, Liverpool, and Bristol. This was partly a result of the establishment of provincial agencies—the Royal Exchange had four in Dublin, Liverpool, Norwich, and Portsmouth by the 1830s—but it also reflected the much slower growth of independent fire offices outside London. It was only during the second quarter of the nineteenth century with the rise of such powerful provincial offices as the Norwich Union, the West of England, the Royal, and the Liverpool and London, that insurance enterprises outside London accounted for a substantial share of British fire business. There is little detailed information concerning the main concentrations of insurance activity outside London but it does seem clear that Liverpool, Manchester, and Dublin were already important in 1815. For Liverpool it has been estimated that sums assured on mercantile risks by the Royal Exchange alone exceeded £1m by the 1820s and during the following decade marine premiums averaged around £9000 p.a. Nevertheless losses were heavy on Liverpool risks in the decade after 1815, partly because of intense competition between the major offices and partly because the town and its rapidly growing port made risk estimation and premium rating very difficult. There was a marked tendency to seek co-operation among the offices on risk classification and rate quotation in the wake of heavy losses and one such effort, during 1825–6, produced the Liverpool mercantile tariff following unsuccessful attempts to write to increase rates.

The principal authors of the Liverpool tariff were those London offices, the Sun, the Royal Exchange, the Phoenix, and the Imperial, which had borne the largest losses of previous years. They agreed to write on a drastic lowering of standard premiums and to substantially increase the tariff for Liverpool risks. Eighteen other fire offices subsequently joined these four in agreeing a common tariff. Little progress was made in removing the root cause of the town's record and reputation as a centre of exceptional fire hazard, however; its numerous warehouses, built in haste and separated by narrow alleys, were filled with cotton, hemp, flax, spirits, and too many other inflammatory goods. It had no regular water supply before 1801, and no publicly organized fire prevention in spite of an enabling Act passed in 1826. The carefree character and natural turbulence of its population—'a grog-shop for every seven houses' it was said—was an additional factor in keeping fire-rates high. By 1833, when eleven warehouses and nine dwellings were consumed by fire in Lancelot's Hey, at the cost of £200,000 in damages, the Liverpool rates had risen to 8*s*. per cent for buildings and 12*s*. per cent for floating policies.

These penal rates, reflecting the exasperation of the London offices, had two consequences. The first was to stimulate local property owners and the civic authorities into more rigorous action in respect of fire protection and salvage. A Liverpool Police Fire Brigade was authorized in 1834 and established in 1836 and greater attention was given to the fireproofing of warehouses. The other effect of high rates was to induce local competition for fire business with the establishment of the Liverpool Fire and Life Insurance Company in 1836 by act of Parliament.[31] This company, subsequently named the Liverpool and London and the Liverpool and London and Globe, set the pattern for the future development of insurance business on Merseyside by advertising itself vigorously and by moving into the American market at an early stage. Significantly, even as it reduced its Liverpool rate to 10*s*. per cent it was accepting New York property insurance at 15*s*. per cent, an indication that the new company had even less confidence in the non-inflammability of New York than London had in that of Liverpool. Further fire disasters in 1842–3 led to the passage of the Liverpool Fire Prevention Act of 1842, providing for detailed requirements in the construction of warehouses, to the formation of the Liverpool Fire Salvage Association in 1846 and, after much delay, to a properly organized Salvage Brigade with two stations in 1867.

Insurance company shares became a major attraction for the joint-stock investors of Merseyside between 1844 and 1856 when the Joint-Stock Companies Registration and Regulation Act was operative, allowing the formation of numerous unlimited insurance companies. The Liverpool Stock Exchange's specialization in insurance shares dated from this time and it was soon to become the most active market in the country. In 1845 the Royal Insurance Company was formed, becoming in due course the largest fire insurer in the world; it was followed in 1858 by the establishment of the Queen Insurance Company, acquired by the Royal in 1891. Insurance company flotations remained at a high level, into the sixties, partly because of the intrinsic security which most of them offered investors after the main interest in railways and banks had subsided, but also because the outbreak of the American Civil War brought a large increase in the market for British offices, especially in the field of marine insurance. Indeed after the foundation of the London and Lancashire Fire Insurance Company in 1862, which had a large Liverpool interest headed by Francis Braun of Beasiq, Braun & Co. and which moved its headquarters from London to Liverpool in 1867, all the subsequent local company flotations were for the conduct of marine business.

The marine insurance market in Liverpool had taken permanent institutional form as early as 1802 when an Underwriters' Association was formed at the instigation of John Gladstone. Thirty-two founder members including William Neilson, the first chairman, met at a coffee-house in Exchange Alley. Few if any of the underwriters of the early nineteenth century were exclusively engaged, most being merchants and shipowners. They were risk-bearers, paying and receiving the balances due from time to time on their accounts, but leaving the active management of risks to the brokers. The brokers were specialists, each acting on behalf of their own list of underwriters, whose names they were authorized to subscribe to marine policies for amounts ranging from £100–500 each. The local marine market thus resembled Lloyds in its organization and by the end of the 1850s it seems to have been made up of about a dozen broking partnerships who were underwriting for about three hundred names, or perhaps two dozen names or more per broker. Writing in 1858, the local historian of underwriting John Towne Danson, himself a broker, was of the opinion that the '. . . individual system of underwriting, in a place like Liverpool, must, in the nature of things be, and is now felt and acknowledged to be, hazardous.[32] The safety of an underwriter is, directly, as the extent of his transactions, when compared with his liability on any given event . . . The danger arises from a want of combination; and the best safe-guard would be the adoption of the joint-stock principle. For this extends the basis of average; and thus imparts to Marine Insurance, the full certainty of the mathematical principle upon which all insurance mainly rests.'

There had been attempts at establishing marine insurance on a joint-stock basis during the thirties when the Liverpool Marine of 1831, the first Ocean Marine of 1834, and another Liverpool Marine of 1839 were set up; but none were strong enough to take a substantial share of local risks away from Lloyds. It was only after the coming of general limited liability that local marine companies became feasible, and most of these were essentially transforms of local syndicates and partnerships. When it came during the boom ending with the crisis of 1866, however, marine company formation was sustained into the following decade. In succession the Thames and Mersey (1860), which became the largest of the Liverpool concerns formed quite independently of the broking firms, the Albion (1862) which failed in 1866, the British and Foreign (1863), whose underwriter R. N. Dale was a partner in the brokers Dale & Ryrie: the Union (1863), which was an amalgamation of Charles Langton & Co. and Rawson, Aiken & Co., the Maritime (1864) formed on the basis of the Price & Case partnership, the Standard (1871) eventually acquired by the London and Lancashire in 1907, the Sea (1875) based on W. H. & S. Jones & Co. and the last remaining independent marine company in Liverpool, the International (1879) acquired by the Union in 1893, and the Reliance (1881) founded by C. B. Vallance former underwriter with the Maritime; all these companies transformed the old system of marine insurance in the period down to the First World War.[33] It was the vigour with which they established world-wide agency systems which accounted for much of the early and continuing success of the marine companies. Their growth reinforced the achievements of the great fire offices of late Victorian Liverpool; by the 1880s its stock exchange was the main trading centre in the shares of twenty or more large insurance companies which towards the close of the century received around one-third of British premium income.[34]

The growth of financial institutions in the evolving money and capital markets of Liverpool and Merseyside illustrates important features of the relationship between the market process and economic change in general over the longer term. The most obvious of these has been the close interrelations between the motor of expanding commodity trades and the development of groups of financial intermediaries. It was the regular and successful exploitation of new trade opportunities both overseas and in the home region—the African, West Indian, and domestic coal and salt trades in the eighteenth century, and those with the Americas, the Far East and in emigrants in the nineteenth—that produced the surpluses and the demand for financial machinery upon which the growth of specialist intermediaries could proceed. The growth of trade was by no means automatic; new commerce had to be created as much as competed for and this required major re-deployments of personnel and resources, after 1713, after 1807 and in the American Civil War, for example. Nor was the geographical location of the port of unmixed benefit. The fact that its position was further removed from the main privateering routes in the wars of the eighteenth century, which permitted its trade to grow in wartime by contrast with London and the other outports, needs to be set alongside the fact that its port facilities were not natural but periodically extended at relatively large capital cost.

The characteristics of its merchant community were a key factor in the growth of trade and financial institutions alike. Here the relative openness of its mercantile interests for long periods was crucial, producing more scope for entry and exit and ensuring that the presence of oligarchy failed to stem the influx of new blood for very long. Thus it is noticeable that at times of major changes in trade patterns, Liverpool's most pushful merchants as distinct from its most prosperous were frequently outsiders. Throughout the period new men came from the rest of Lancashire, Cheshire, and the West Riding, but also with important contingents from London, Scotland, and Ireland in the eighteenth century and from London, Germany, and Spain in the nineteenth. These features of the local merchant community contain an important clue to the reasons for their successful development of financial services over the period. For common to the growth of banking, insurance, and securities markets alike is the improvement in the quantity and quality of market information at lower costs. This was increasingly necessary for those engaged in high-risk trades. Thus in banking access to the London money-market and the importance of close links with London correspondents, in insurance the key role of world-wide agencies, and in the stock exchange the regular listing of a widening range of company shares all served to relate the regional economy ever more strongly to that of the nation and beyond.

NOTES AND REFERENCES

1. Corporate bond debt of Liverpool, 353 TRE kf 156, Lpl.R.O.

2. On the remittance of rental revenues at this period see, for example, Margaret Gay Davies, 'Country gentry and payments to London, 1650–1714', *Economic History Review,* **xxiv** (1971); and on tax revenues, L. S. Pressnell, 'Public monies and the development of English banking', *Economic History Review,* **v** (1953).

3. For South Lancashire generally see B. L. Anderson, 'Money and the Structure of Credit in the Eighteenth Century', *Business History,* **xii** (1970); and for London see R. Grassby, 'English merchant capitalism in the late seventeenth century: the composition of business fortunes', *Past and Present,* **46** (1970).

4. B. L. Anderson, 'Provincial aspects of the financial revolution of the eighteenth century', *Business History,* **xi** (1969); and 'The Attorney and the early capital market in Lancashire', in F. Crouzet (ed.), *Capital Formation in the Industrial Revolution* (1972), pp. 223–55.

5. P. Mathias, *The Transformation of England* (1979), ch. 10.

6. T. S. Ashton, 'The bill of exchange and private banks in Lancashire 1790–1830', *Economic History Review,* **xv** (1945); and B. L. Anderson, 'The Lancashire bill system and its Liverpool practitioners: the case of a slave merchant', in W. H. Chaloner and B. M. Ratcliffe (eds.), *Trade and Transport: Essay in Economic History in Honour of T. S. Willan*, Manchester (1977), pp. 59–97.

7. J. Hughes, *Liverpool Banks and Bankers 1760–1837*, Liverpool, (1906); D. M. Joslin, 'London Private Bankers, 1720–1785', *Economic History Review,* **vii** (1954); and B. L. Anderson and P. L. Cottrell, 'Another Victorian Capital Market: A study of Banking and Bank investors on Merseyside', *Economic History Review,* **xxciii** (1975).

8. S. G. Checkland, 'American versus West Indian traders in Liverpool 1793–1815', *Journal of Economic History,* **xviii** (1958); and 'Finance for the West Indies 1780–1815', *Economic History Review,* **x** (1958).

9. G. W. Daniels, 'American Cotton Trade under the Embargo and Non-Intercourse Acts', *American Historical Review,* **xxii** (1916); and F. E. Hyde *et. al.*, 'The Port of Liverpool and the Crisis of 1793', *Economica,* **xviii** (1951); and B. H. Tolley, 'The Liverpool Campaign against the Order in Council and the War of 1812', in J. R. Harris (ed.), *Liverpool & Merseyside . . .* (1969), pp. 98–146.

10. T. Baines, *History of the Commerce and Town of Liverpool* (1852), p. 492.

11. T. C. Barker, 'Lancashire Coal, Cheshire Salt and the Rise of Liverpool', *Trans. Hist. Soc. of Lanc. and Chesh.,* **103** (1952); T. S. Ashton, 'The

Domestic System in the Early Lancashire Tool Trades', *Economic Journal*, Ec. Hist. Suppl., I, (1926); G. H. Tupling, 'The Early Metal Trade and the Beginnings of Engineering in Lancashire', *Trans. Lancs. and Chesh. Antiq. Soc.*, **lxi** (1949); and J. Langton, 'Landowners and the development of coal mining in south-west Lancashire, 1590–1799', *Trans. Inst. of Brit. Geogs., Special Publication No. 10* (1979).

12. J. R. Harris, 'Trends in the industrialization of Merseyside 1750–1800', in *Collogne sur l'industrialisation en Europe en XIXe siecle'*, Lyon (1970), pp. 57–73.

13. T. C. Barker, 'The beginnings of the Canal age in the British Isle', in L. S. Pressnell (ed.) *Studies in the Industrial Revolution* (1960) pp. 1–22; J. R. Harris, 'Liverpool Canal Controversies 1769–1772', *Journal of Transport History*, **2** (1955–6); C. Hadfield and G. Biddle, *The Canals of North West England*, Newton Abbot (1970), 2 vols; and P. G. E. Clemens, 'The Rise of Liverpool, 1665–1750', *Economic History Review*, **xxix** (1976).

14. D. J. Pope, *Shipping and Trade in Liverpool in the late 18th Century*, University of Liverpool, Ph.D. thesis (1970), vol. 2, Ch. 5.

15. J. H. Andrews, 'English Merchant Shipping in 1701', *Mariner's Mirror*, **41** (1955); J. Wallace, *A General and Descriptive History of Liverpool*, Liverpool (1975), p. 254; and Pope, op. cit., pp. 312–28.

16. L. F. Vernon-Harcourt, *Harbours and Docks*, Oxford (1885); I. and A. G. Kenwood, 'Fixed Capital Formation on Merseyside 1800–1913', *Economic History Review*, **xxi** (1978); on housing see J. H. Trebble, 'Liverpool Working-Class Housing 1801–51', in S. D. Chapman (ed.) *The History of Working-Class Housing*, David and Charles (1971).

17. B.P.P., 1851, lii, pp. 213 ff; T. Baines, *Liverpool in 1859* (1859) pp. 62–3; and B. Poole, *The Commerce of Liverpool* (1854), p. 198.

18. M. Collins, *The Bank of England and the Liverpool Money Market 1825–50*, University of London Ph.D. thesis (1972), pp. 25–55.

19. S. G. Checkland, 'The Lancashire bill system and its Liverpool protagonists 1810–27', *Economica*, **xxi** (1954); and more generally S. Nishimura, *The Decline of Inland Bills of Exchange in the London Money Market, 1855–1913*, Cambridge (1971).

20. M. Collings, 'The Langton Papers: Banking and Bank of England Policy in the 1830s', *Economica* (1972); N. S. Buck, *The Development of the Organisation of Anglo-American Trade 1800–1850*, New Haven (1925); and B. C. Hunt, *The Development of the Business Corporation in England 1800–67*, Cambridge, Mass. (1936).

21. G. Chandler, *Four Centuries of Banking* (1964); and S. E. Thomas, *The Rise and Growth of Joint Stock Banking* (1934), vol. 1.

22. W. A. Thomas, *The Provincial Stock Exchanges* (1973), ch. 1; and B. L. Anderson and P. L. Cottrell, loc. cit.

23. M. Collins, thesis, op. cit., pp. 108–9.

24. Burdett's Official Intelligence (1884), pp. 1182–95.

25. J. R. Killick and W. A. Thomas, 'The Provincial Stock Exchanges 1830–70', *Economic History Review*, **xxiii** (1970).

26. H. O. Horne, *A History of Savings Banks*, Oxford (1947), p. 40; and A. L. Schuster, *Origin and Growth of the Liverpool Savings Bank*, Liverpool (1920).

27. See for example the discussion in E. S. Shaw, *Financial Deepening in Economic Development*, Oxford (1973), pp. 80–112.

28. W. A. Thomas, op. cit., ch. 4.

29. B. L. Anderson, 'The Financial Revolution in the Provinces', *Business History* (1969); B. C. Hunt, The Joint Stock Company in England 1800–1825', *Journal of Political Economy*, (1935); and M. C. Reed (ed.) *Railways in the Victorian Economy* (1969).

30. G. Chandler, op. cit., pp. 239 and 244–5; G. F. Ibbotson, *Banking on Merseyside*, Liverpool and District Bankers' Institute Address (1953); also see the Account Book of Hugh Hornby, 920 MD 380, Lpl.R.O.

31. B. Supple, the Royal Exchange Assurance. *A History of British Insurance 1720–1970*, Cambridge (1970), pp. 124, 127–8, 161–3; Royal Insurance Company Ltd., *Liverpool and Fire Insurance. A Retrospect*, Liverpool (1903); and H. Brotherton, 'History and Development of the Liverpool Mercantile Tariff', *Journal of the Chartered Insurance Institute*, **12** (1909).

32. P. C. Brown, 'Fire Insurance in Liverpool', *Trans. Hist. Soc. of Lancs. and Chesh.*, **78** (1926).

33. J. T. Danson, *Various Papers of...* (1878), 3 vols.

34. *History of Liverpool Underwriters' Association*, Liverpool (1902); and B. L. Anderson, 'Institutional Investment before the First World War. The Union Marine Insurance Company 1897–1915' in S. Marriner (ed.) *Business and Businessmen: Studies in Business, Economic and Accounting History*, Liverpool (1978).

APPENDIX 1

Chronology of banking in Liverpool

Bank	*Established*	*Failed/dissolved/ absorbed*
John Wyke	*c.*1765–6	1773
A. Heywood, Sons & Co.	1773	1883
William Clarke & Sons	*c.*1774	1820
Charles Caldwell & Co.	*c.*1774	1793
Lowry, Roscoe & Wardell	*c.*1774	1827, 1833
Thomas, Samuel, & Joseph Crane	1786	1788
William Clarke, Sons, Parke & Morland	1790	1807
Staniforth, Ingram, Bold & Daltera	1791	1795
R. Hobson & Co.	—	—
Sir Michael Cromie, Bart., Pownall & Hartman	*c.*1793	1801–2
J. Aspinall & Sons	*c.*1796	1816, 1832, 1893
Joseph Hadwen	*c.*1803	1826
R. Hanly	*c.*1803	1807
Leyland & Bullins	1807	1901
Moss, Dales & Rogers	1807	1864
J. Barned & Co.	1809	1865, 1866
Samuel Hope & Co.	*c.*1812	1823, 1836
Evans, Chegwin & Hall	*c.*1816	1825
John Threlfall	1818	1824
Robert Fairweather	1818	1825
Mersey Bank	1821	1822
Bank of England Branch	1827	
Manchester and Liverpool District Bank	1829	1969
Bank of Liverpool	1831	1918
Commercial Bank of Liverpool	1833	1888
Commercial Bank of England	1834	1840
Northern and Central Bank of England	1834	1836
Liverpool Union Bank	1835	1876
Accommodation Bank		1836
Borough Bank of Liverpool	1836	1857
Central Bank of Liverpool	1836	1839
Isle of Man & Liverpool Banking Company	1836	
Liverpool United Trades Bank	1836	1837
Manchester, Liverpool & Birmingham Banking Company		1836
North & South Wales Bank	1836	1908
Royal Bank of Liverpool	1836	1867
Tradesmen's Bank of Liverpool	1836	1837
United Banking Co. of Australia and Van Dieman's Land	1836	
Liverpool Banking Company (1)		1836

	Established	*Failed/dissolved/ absorbed*
Liverpool Banking Company (2)	1837	1847
Albion Bank	1837	1839
Phoenix Bank of Liverpool	1837	1839
Exchange Office Bank	1843	1867
Edward Bates & Sons	1848	
Adelphi Bank	1861/2	1899
Alliance Bank of London and Liverpool	1862	1871
National Bank of Liverpool	1863	1883
North Western Bank Limited	1864	1897
Barned's Banking Company Limited	1865	1866
Eastern Exchange Bank	1865	
E. W. Yates & Co.	1867	1904
Bibby Brothers & Co.	1874	
National Provincial Bank of England Ltd.	1880	1917
Union Bank of Manchester	1904	
United Counties Bank Limited	pre-1907	

Sources. J. Hughes, *Liverpool Banks and Bankers*, Liverpool (1905); 'Notes on some Unchronicled Liverpool Banks', *Lanc. and Ches. Hist. Soc. Trans.*, **21** (1905); 'Liverpool Banks', *Mersey*, **4** (1925); G. Chandler, *Four Centuries of Banking* (1964); J. Dun, *British Banking Statistics* (1876); S. E. Thomas, *The Rise and Growth of Joint Stock Banking* (1934); G. F. Ibbotson; *Banking on Merseyside*, Liverpool and District Bankers' Institute Address (Oct. 1953). In addition to the ordinary commercial banks listed above a number of other merchant and 'in-house' banking concerns operated in Liverpool for periods during the nineteenth century. These included the Banco Espanol en Londres; the Bank of British West Africa; Baring Brothers & Co.; The Chartered Bank of India, Australia & China; Kleinwort, Sons & Co.; Lewis's Bank Ltd.; F. Huth and Co.; Brown, Shipley & Co.

APPENDIX 2

Share list of the Liverpool Share-Brokers' Association, August 1836

RAILWAYS
Bolton and Leigh
Bolton and Preston
Birmingham and Gloucester
Birmingham and Derby
Birkenhead and Chester
Chester and Crewe Junction
Dublin and Drogheda
Dublin and Kilkenny
Eastern Counties
Edinburgh and Glasgow (old)
Edinburgh and Glasgow (new)
Edinburgh, Leith, and Newhaven
Glasgow, Paisley, and Greenock
Glasgow, Paisley, Kilmarnock and Ayr
Grand Junction
Great Western
Grand Connection (Worcester)
Kenyon and Leigh
Liverpool and Manchester
London and Birmingham
London and Southampton
London and Brighton (Stevensons)
London and Greenwich
Leeds and Manchester
Leicester and Swannington
Manchester, Bolton & Bury
Manchester & Cheshire Junction
Manchester, South Union
Midland Counties
Preston and Wyre
North Midland
South Midland
North Union
Newcastle and Carlisle
South Eastern
St Helens and Runcorn Gap
Warrington and Newton
Wigan Branch
Ulster

BANKS, etc
Liverpool
Commercial of Liverpool
Liverpool Union
Royal of Liverpool
Northern and Central
Tradesman's
United Trades'
North and South Wales
Bank of Manchester
Bank of Manchester and Liverpool District
Bank of South Lancashire
Borough Bank
Commercial Bank of England
Wilts. and Dorset
East of England
Exchange Buildings
Liverpool & Harrington Water Works
Bootle Water Works
Liverpool Coal Gas Company
Liverpool New Gas & Coke Company
Liverpool Marine Insurance Co.
Ocean Assurance Company
Liverpool Fire and Life Assurance
Manchester Assurance Company
Harrington Dock
Anderton Carrying Company
Woodside Ferry Company
Rock Ferry Company
Monk's Ferry Company
Steam Tug Company
Apothecaries Company
Liverpool Fish Company
Manchester and Liverpool Fish

Sources. List of Past and Present Members, and List of Prices of Liverpool Stock Exchange.

APPENDIX 3

Members of the Liverpool Share-Brokers' Association, 1836

APRIL
Thomas Barber, F, merchant
George Batley, F, broker
Thomas Coglan, F, auctioneer
Richard Crewe, F, attorney
John C. Da Costa, F, Port wine merchant
Richard Dawson, F, merchant, broker
Thomas Forsyth, F, merchant
Thomas Hampson, Snr, F, ship-broker
Thomas Harris, share-broker
Samuel R. Healey, F, accountant
George Highfield, F, ship-broker
Joseph King, Snr, share-broker
Arthur Rawson, merchant
Thomas Read, share-broker
William Reynolds, Jnr, agents and accountants
William Thompson, Jnr, accountant
George A. Tinley, ship-broker
Thomas Tinley, ship-broker
C. J. Townley, broker
Matthew Witherspoon, wine merchant
Jonathan Flounders, share-broker
William Okill, share-broker
Thomas Addison, gentleman
Harmood Banner, accountant
Harmood Walcot Banner, accountant
E. S. Boult, accountant
Daniel Neilson, merchant
John Richardson, merchant
William Sudlow, Corp. Treasurer's clerk
Samuel Woods, Jnr, merchant

MAY
A. J. Chuel, wine merchant
C. J. Tattersall, cotton-broker
Walter Clarke, insurance agent
William Reynolds, Snr, agents & accountants
Richard Scholes, cotton-broker

JUNE
C. G. Cowie, book-keeper

JULY
R. H. Poole, merchant

SEPTEMBER
T. M. Myers, customs & excise agent
Robert J. King, share-broker

OCTOBER
Thomas Cooke, druggist
J. Redish, accountant
W. Bird, accountant
W. Prince, draper
John Sudlow, Corp. Treasurer's chief clerk

F signifies founder-member

APPENDIX 4

Trades classification of depositors, Liverpool Savings Bank, 20 November 1850

	£	*s.*	*d.*	*No.*	*Av. dep. £*	*% of depositors*
Small farmers, farm servants, and gardeners, or their wives	22,388	15	9	448	49·98	1·92
Carters, porters, labourers, and firemen, or their wives	88,674	8	1	2,669	33·22	11·46
Retail dealers, shopkeepers, boarding-house keepers, or their wives	34,305	5	11	945	36·30	4·06
Blacksmiths, boilermakers, founders, moulders, pattern-makers, engineers, mill-wrights, machinemakers, plumbers, coppersmiths, tinsmiths, gunsmiths, watchmakers, opticians, or their wives	48,027	2	4	1,574	30·51	6·76
Sawyers, plasterers, joiners, wheelwrights, coach-builders, coopers, turners, cabinet-makers, upholsters, painters, carvers, gilders, or their wives	45,588	10	10	1,412	32·29	6·06
Masons, quarriers, brick-makers, stone-cutters, slaters, or their wives	12,517	2	1	370	33·83	1·59
Curriers, shoemakers, saddlers. bleachers, dyers, tailors, hatters, spinners, or their wives	14,922	11	6	544	27·56	2·34
Ship-carpenters, rope-, sail-, and block-makers, or their wives	35,335	17	8	896	39·44	3·85
Millers, bakers, butchers, brewers, cigar-makers, confectioners, sugar refiners, soap boilers, or their wives	14,993	12	5	456	32·88	1·96
Printers, bookbinders, stationers, or their wives	4,514	8	11	209	21·60	0·90

	£ s. d.			*No.*	*Av. dep. £*	*% of depositors*
Seamen, fishermen, or their wives	43,625	1	5	1,164	37·48	5·00
Soldiers, pensioners, customs, excise, and post officers, policemen, persons in employ of public authorities, or their wives	18,505	12	8	472	39·21	2·03
Dressmakers, milliners, plain sewers, and shop women	1,436	13	4	108	13·31	0·46
Female domestic servants	70,139	7	5	2,578	27·21	11·07
Widows and spinsters	126,285	18	8	4,162	30·34	17·88
Coachmen, grooms, ostlers, waiters, shipstewards, house and private servants, or their wives	20,201	12	3	570	35·44	2·45
Clerks, shopmen, professional persons of small incomes, or their wives	48,554	6	9	1,609	30·18	6·91
Miners	32,799	3	1	2,354	13·93	10·11
Other descriptions unspecified	1,316	6	9	380	3·46	1·63
Charitable societies	5,234	1	8	101	51·82	0·43
Friendly societies	50,018	13	9	261	191·64	1·12
Totals	739,454	13	3	23,282		

3

A staple consumer industry on Merseyside

Sugar refining in the nineteenth century and the emergence of Henry Tate and Company

A. MURRAY

The growth of Merseyside as an area of concentration of the staple consumer industries was the outcome of the interaction of many factors. The first, and perhaps most significant, was that of population growth. As can be seen from table 3.1 the number of inhabitants in Liverpool increased from 82,000 in 1801 to 753,000 in 1911. This nine-fold increase implied a similar expansion in the size of the market for staple consumer goods. If the towns of Birkenhead and Wallasey are included in the estimation of market size, then the potential sales area for the staple consumer good producer had increased by a factor of between eleven or twelve.

Table 3.1. *Population of Merseyside 1801–1911 ('000s)*

Year	*Liverpool and environs*	*Birkenhead*	*Wallasey*	*Lancashire*
1801	82	—	1	673
1811	104	—	1	828
1821	138	—	1	1053
1831	210	3	3	1337
1841	299	8	6	1667
1851	395	25	8	2031
1861	472	38	11	2429
1871	540	66	15	2819
1881	627	84	21	3454
1891	630	100	33	3927
1901	704	111	54	4373
1911	753	131	79	4762

Source. B. R. Mitchell and P. Deane, *Abstract of British Historical Statistics*, Cambridge (1962) p. 22 *passim*.

Notes and references begin on page 75.

Table 3.2. *Index of average wages in a normal week: Cottonworkers, 1891 = 100*

Period	*Index*	*Period*	*Index*
1806–10	82	1861–70	65
1811–20	70	1871–80	83
1821–30	51	1881–90	92
1831–40	47	1891–1900	102
1841–50	51	1901–06	109
1851–60	59		

Source: B. R. Mitchell and P. Deane, op. cit., pp. 348–50.

It would be unrealistic to assume that the market for such goods produced in and around Liverpool would be solely and exclusively marketed in this area alone. The advances in transport associated with the development of a major port also brought about the extension of the market sphere for the producers of necessity goods. The potential target for the sales of such goods as sugar, soap, and flour was, in the first instance, Lancashire as a whole.

The population of the county expanded from 673,000 in 1801 to 4,762,000 by 1911—a six-fold increase. This was the primary market for the production of the Merseyside industries, but as the transport infrastructure developed, the secondary markets of Yorkshire, the Midlands, and the North-East became accessible to the Merseyside producers. These areas became lucrative markets for exploitation because of the nature of the activities which were embraced within their boundaries. Hence the expansion of the consumer goods industries was dependent upon the purchasing power of the ordinary working man and his family.

The level of income enjoyed by the working classes was largely a function of the state of the industrial employment within the market area. During the period 1806–1906, the fortunes of Lancashire's main revenue earner, textiles, were on average, satisfactory. The movements of income over the period can be seen in table 3.2.

Wage levels rose markedly in the 1850s and 60s; and between the 1870s and 90s falling prices also worked to the advantage of the average working-class family. Taken in conjunction with a moderate rise in money wages, falling prices increased the value of wages of a skilled worker significantly in this period. Even in times of hardship generally, the effect of reduced incomes would not materially affect the demand for staple goods which, in many cases, provided the basis of survival for the population. It was against the general backdrop of increasing population and increasing prosperity created as a result of industrialization that the staple consumer goods industries developed.

Apart from the availability of large hinterland markets, other factors also favoured the growth of Liverpool and Merseyside as a centre for consumer goods production. The importance of the city as a major port and trading centre was the most significant of these. The links made with the producers of raw materials world-wide in the general course of trading were invaluable in providing a reliable source of basic ingredients for many products. This was particularly true for the sugar industry, whose early links with the slave trade and the West Indian sugar producers had been instrumental in establishing Liverpool as an entrepôt of the sugar trade in the eighteenth century. Similarly the soap industry relied upon the importation of oils and fats from Africa and America. By the nineteenth century Liverpool's relationships with such sources of raw material supply was already long established.

The proximity of other suppliers was also important to Liverpool's development as a centre of staple processing. The location of the city near to the Lancashire coalfields provided a valuable and relatively inexpensive source of power. The quality of water supplied to the town was also important in ensuring the maintenance of acceptable standards in its staple processing industries. Here too the location of a diverse chemical manufacture within the Merseyside area brought further advantages in terms of low costs and reliability of supply.

II

During the period 1830–1914 the sugar refining industry witnessed a radical change in structure. In the first half of the nineteenth century, there were in excess of 200 refiners in Britain, most of whom had weekly outputs of 50 tons or less. By 1900 there were only 16 refiners of which two, Henry Tate and Co. of Liverpool, and Abram Lyle and Co. of Greenock, with outputs of approximately 1800 tons per week each, controlled 62·5 per cent of the market.

During the period there were three main determinants of the progress of the industry; firstly the degree of intervention by government; secondly foreign competition in the form of bounty-fed sugar; and finally entrepreneurial performance. Government involvement manifested itself in different ways during the period. In the years prior to the abolition of the sugar duties in 1874, movements in the level of duties were the chief instrument of government intervention. These duties had a dual role, namely, that of providing protection for the West Indian planter and, to some extent, the British refiner as well as that of contributing to government revenue. With the abolition of slavery in 1833 and the failure of absentee landlords to innovate, the production of the British sugar colonies diminished. However, as the duty system was biased against the entry of foreign raw sugar into Britain, the supply of raw material to the refiner decreased as did home consumption.

By 1854, the campaign (which had begun in the 1830s) for the reform of the duty system had achieved some success by forcing through a Bill to equalize the duties between British and foreign sugars. But, by retaining the duty between raw and refined sugar, the refining industry was given the opportunity to exploit increased supplies of raw sugar while retaining protection to prevent the importation of refined sugar from abroad. Under these conditions the number of refiners increased from 51 in 1852 to 66 in 1864.

By 1874, when Free Trade in sugar was finally achieved, it was apparent that foreign competition, particularly from continental bounty-fed beet sugar, would play a decisive role in determining the structure of the British refining industry in its new trading environment. The period, 1874–1902, saw significant changes in the refining industry with the number of refiners falling to 16 by 1900. This decline in the number of refiners must be seen in the context of the emergence of the large-scale refinery which, by employing new technology and the use of various commercial techniques, could successfully compete against the inflow of foreign bounty-fed refined sugar. The epitome of these large concerns was the operations of Henry Tate and Abram Lyle who had only begun refining in the early 1860s. The inability of many refiners to compete was, according to the majority of refiners, caused by the bounty system[1] and, in particular, the failure of the British government to regulate these bounties by international agreement or by imposing countervailing duties. But this line of reasoning cannot be accepted without qualification. Tate's and Lyle's had competed under the same conditions as other British refiners, yet managed to remain profitable. Their enterprising approach to the threat of foreign dominance of the industry was the key to their success. By employing new technology and increasing investment by product differentiation, and by adopting cost control policies they ensured that they could compete sucessfully in the prevailing competitive climate.

The progress of the sugar refining industry of Liverpool between 1852 and 1900 relative to other refining centres is highlighted in table 3.3.

Although all refining centres experienced a reduction in the number of operational firms over the period, the extent of Liverpool's decline was less than that of her rivals. Among the reasons for this situation, Liverpool's location was important. Although London refiners were positioned at the centre of a large market area, they suffered certain disadvantages. Firstly, London was the nearest major refining centre to the Continent and consequently more

Table 3.3. *Number of refining firms in the UK.*

Year	*London*	*Greenock*	*Liverpool*	*Bristol*	*Others*	*Total*
1852	25	14	8	2	2	51
1864	30	17	13	3	2	66
1873	19	13	12	3	3	50
1880	12	10	12	2	3	39
1884	12	9	10	2	—	33
1900	3	6	6	1	—	16

Source: John M. Hutchinson, *Notes on the Sugar Industry in the U.K.*, Greenock (1901), *passim.*

susceptible to foreign competition. Secondly, the capital's safety regulations prevented the re-burning of charcoal (necessary for the purification of the sugar) inside a refinery. In other refining centres, the re-burning was carried out as a part of the normal refining process. As a result, it cost the London refiners an average of 22*s*. 6*d*. per ton to process the charcoal as opposed to 3*s*. 6*d*. which was normal in the other centres. It was also suggested that labour was more expensive in London for the refining trade. This was certainly true up to 1880, but the subsequent collapse of the loaf sugar industry (due to the pressure of foreign competition) meant that skilled labour became easier to obtain.

The Liverpool refiners enjoyed an especially favourable location for refining. As Henry Tate commented, 'The raw material is generally cheaper here than in Greenock, fuel is the same price; water, rent, and wages maybe a little higher, but there is an excellent market for the outcome and always at 6*d*. more than Greenock prices'.[2] Liverpool was ideally situated for coal from South-West Lancashire, and abundant supplies of soft water ensured a product of consistent quality, while Liverpool's position as the major British port meant low cost freight from the traditional sugar growing areas in the colonies. Liverpool was far enough away from the Continent to be able to survive more comfortably than London. Transportation advantages, especially preferential steamer/rail rates worked to consolidate Liverpool's position. The carriage of goods from Hamburg to Manchester via Goole was cheaper than the rate between Goole and Manchester.[3] The preferential rates did not apply to the Merseyside area. In the south of England, low price sugar entered from France through the Channel ports of Brighton and Newhaven at a cheaper rate than through London. The situation in the Midlands was similar, with French and German sugar entering through Hull and Goole as well as Cardiff and Bristol under the preferential rates system.

Liverpool's main threat arose in 1883 from imports by steamship from the US:

> the unusual lowness of freights must undoubtedly facilitate their export. The ordinary freight from the U.S. was formerly 30*s*. per ton; lately for wheat and such articles it has fallen to about 12*s*. a ton and there have been lower and even nominal rates.[4]

This situation lasted until 1885 when American manufacturers turned their attention to their internal market which was expanding rapidly with the growth in population stimulated by the Westward movement.

The progress of individual refiners on Merseyside during these years was mixed. Tracing the fortunes of two firms, Macfie and Sons, and Henry Tate and Co. will illustrate the differences in approach and success. Macfie and Sons was a family owned firm which began business in Greenock in 1788. By 1807, a second refinery had opened in Leith but production had to be discontinued temporarily at this plant in 1829 due to fire damage. Macfie's then bought a disused refinery in Edinburgh which took over production from Leith in the short-term. The transfer of business to Liverpool began in 1838 when the firm purchased Hutchinson's refinery in Temple Street. The next purchase was the Batchelor Street refinery of Wainwright and Company in 1841 which was followed by the acquisition of the William Street refinery in 1846. The transfer to Liverpool was to gain locational advantages; namely a steady supply of West Indian raw sugar, expanding local markets, and a good supply of water.

The Scottish plants were closed in 1852 consolidating Liverpool as the centre of the Company's operations. Macfie's was then a significant company in the refining trade; in 1864 they were the largest producer of soft sugar in Britain with an output of 500 tons per week which represented 6·3 per cent of total national output of this type of sugar. By 1880/1, they had been overtaken by two firms, Henry Tate and Co. and James Duncan. In 1839 at the age of 20, Henry Tate began his business career as a grocer in Liverpool. By 1858 he had six shops trading under the name of Henry Tate and Company. In 1859 he became a partner in the firm of John Wright and Co. sugar refiners. John Wright subsequently sold his interest in the business to Henry Tate who then started planning a new refinery at Love Lane, Liverpool. While building was in progress Tate bought the patent rights of the Boivin-Loiseau process for the purification of raw sugar liquor. This patent had been offered to many refiners before Tate was offered the rights. Although the work on the new refinery was well advanced, the new process was installed, a decision which was vindicated in the long run. By 1873 Love Lane was complete and it was apparent to Tate that his future was in refining and, as a result, he sold his remaining interest in the grocery business. The Thames refinery at Silvertown, London was built by 1878. This refinery housed the Langen process for the production of cube sugar, a new product which was pioneered principally by Tate and which proved to be a powerful weapon in the war against foreign competition.

The years for which comparable data on performance exist for these two firms are 1897 to 1903. The commercial background prior to and during these years was dominated by the influence of foreign competition upon the domestic market. Free trade in sugar existed in Britain between the years 1874 and 1902 and these years witnessed the most significant changes in the industry since its inception in the seventeenth century. With the removal of all duty barriers, the Continental states encouraged their best producers and refiners to use Britain as a market for cheap bounty-fed (i.e. subsidized) sugars. Assisted by favourable transport facilities mentioned previously, large amounts of beet sugar were systematically 'dumped' on the British market at prices which, to the British refiner, were below cost. In this way the foreign refiner could operate a discriminatory pricing policy in his own country and, by obtaining state bounties, export to Britain, make a profit, and ensure his domination in his home market. This was the background against which a comparison of Macfie and Tate has to be assessed. The imports of refined beet sugar reached an annual average of 19,048,000 cwts. in the years 1901–3, an increase of 29·4 per cent on the annual average for the period 1895–7. The performance of Macfie's reflected the impact of this foreign competition with an average annual net profit of £1523 for the years 1897–1903. Tate and Co. recorded an annual average net profit of £115,652 for the same period. Macfie's was a long established firm in the industry whereas Tate had been in business as a sugar refiner on his own account for less than thirty years. How can such differences in performance be explained?

In a study of the development of British industry and foreign competition it was observed that 'what makes a progressive entrepreneur is how he acts in a given set of conditions'.[5] Thomas Easton of Macfie's presented his view of the conditions under which his company operated in evidence to the 1886 Royal Commission on the Depression in Trade and Industry:

> The course of the refining trade is that a very large quantity is done in single refineries; for instance we do, we will say, 50,000 tons per year, if we are undersold one penny per cwt beyond what we can refine at, that means a loss to us of £4000 per annum.[6]

Each individual refiner approached the continental challenge in different ways, and with differing degrees of success. Henry Tate based his success on the extensive use of new technology which reduced unit costs. The basis of Tate's Love Lane refinery was the Boivin-Loiseau process which improved the purity and quality of sugar. The capital cost of this equipment was in excess of £10,000. Although a large sum, Tate raised the necessary finance to implement the process which would give a guaranteed quality of sugar. This was particularly necessary in a period when refiners had been prosecuted for the adulteration of sugar with glucose. Tate's insistence on quality was to become the foundation of the company's policy.

The second major innovation which Tate also adopted successfully was the Langen cube process. The firm had become joint licensees with Martineau and Sons, sugar refiners of London. Tate travelled to London to supervize the building of the Silvertown refinery especially to be used for cube production via the Langen process. The cost of installation of this new process was large and remains unknown but it involved a major financial crisis within the Tate family so much so that his daughter, Isolina, who was then at boarding school in Southport, had to be withdrawn for financial reasons. This product gave Tate's a buffer against increasing competition from abroad. Cube sugar was essentially the same product as loaf sugar but merely removed the necessity for the grocer to cut or crush the sugar for sale. This type of product differentiation gave Tate's a competitive advantage over the low-priced bounty-fed loaf sugar, since the firm was able to charge a premium price for cubes. By comparison the other licensee of the process, Martineau & Co., failed to take advantage of the process. This firm was the oldest sugar refining business still in existence in Britain. The reasons for the difference in success rates were, according to Mr Kearley MP:

> On the one hand you have a new man with new equipment, who, working according to modern ideas, kept himself to the front, feared no competition, faced the competition of Europe and was better for it, was not deflated and is now one of the greatest refiners. On the other hand you have this old firm, with the traditions of a hundred years of trade, working with obsolete machinery . . . (which) went under.

The Langen process was replaced in 1894 by the Adant process for cube production. Tate's commitment to new technology was unfaltering. By installing granulators in 1886, he successfully diversified his production again. Granulated sugar, known as 'Standard granulated', increased in importance over the period until, in the mid-1930s, it was Love Lane's major product.

From the limited records that have survived it is evident that Tate built his success on constant innovation. In addition to the major technological changes already mentioned, the largest vacuum pan ever built was delivered to Tate's Liverpool refinery in 1872. The pan was 12½ft. in diameter and 13ft. deep. It was capable of producing 'a skippen' of 27 tons of moist sugar every 2½ hours. The cost of the pan was £2800. There were many changes in technology over the years that followed: the Healey process for re-cycling waste heat, the installation of a Siemens generator in 1887, a Little evaporator in 1897 and a surface condenser in 1898. Research also played a part in the firm's success; it was constantly acquiring patent specifications to test the validity of the patentees' claims.

Tate, unlike many other refiners, was fully prepared to use the lower-priced bounty-fed raw beet sugar from the Continent. As competition with the foreign refiner increased, Tate used more raw beet sugar: in 1877, 60·5 per cent of raw sugar used was in the form of raw cane sugar, the rest was raw beet; by 1889 all the raw sugar used by Tate was beet sugar. Some refiners insisted on using solely raw cane. They believed, incorrectly, that beet was less sweet than cane. On the basis of this claim they charged a premium price for refined cane sugar believing it could compete with the lower-priced refined beet sugar. Crosfields, of Liverpool, was one such firm:

> When my firm decided 16 years ago that we would confine ourselves exclusively to cane sugar we believed it would recommend itself to the consumer and we should make it a special trade . . . the prejudice had gradually died out.[7]

Such beliefs were a result of the supply system which had prevailed earlier in the century: these refiners clung to the trade which had predominated in the 1830s based on the supply of raw cane from the British colonies.

By combining careful attention to new technology with a flexible policy for purchasing the cheapest supplies of raw sugar and the use of the best personnel available (both general managers were from Greenock; the chief sugar boiler was Ernest Wedekind, a German), the firm was able to claim in 1903 that:

> The factories, both in Liverpool and London, include refineries with the most modern and efficient sugar refining machinery and also include electric light producing plant . . . The plant has been kept up in a state of the highest efficiency.[8]

The situation at Macfie's was in marked contrast to Tate's. Total gross investment in this firm for the period 1852–71 was £30,200. The largest single investment in any one year came in 1873 when £35,000 was authorized for a new refinery. The Boivin-Loiseau process was available to the firm but they, unlike Tate's, failed to recognize the potential of the new technique. The decision to invest in a new refinery at this time was explained by Thomas Easton, general manager of Macfie's:

> We built a sugar house in 1874 for making moist sugar with the expectations that our old sugar house (Batchelor St.) would be occupied entirely in the making of loaf sugar. That was at the time when the National Assembly in France had voted refining in bond, and we thought everything was going to be made straight.[9]

In fact, the anticipated change in French law never materialized but James Duncan, the London sugar refiner, had also miscalculated and built a new refinery on the basis of the same expectation: 'I saw that the French were not getting the same advantage that they did formerly, and I thought that there was an opportunity of starting'.[10]

Duncan's new house had a capacity of 400–800 tons of loaf sugar per week. His decision to continue expanding loaf production showed an inordinate faith in the French desire to modify their laws. They had failed consistently since 1864 to make any significant change in their legal framework which would have benefited the British refiner. Duncan's myopia with regard to French law was surprising, considering that in other respects he was very far-sighted. He was, for example, one of the first refiners to cultivate beet sugar to supply his refinery. Even if the optimism of Duncan and Macfie's had been warranted, Macfie's would still have been in difficulties. Their new refinery had a capacity of 100–150 tons per week, 'keeping in mind it might be desirable to increase to 600 tons per week'.[11] In comparison to the undertaking by Tate, the commitment of the company to large-scale production is distinctly questionable. Tates produced an average of 413 tons per week at Love Lane in 1875; by 1881 this had risen to 1146 tons per week.[12]

Macfie's decision to purchase the Rawcliffe beet refinery in Goole in 1893 appears at first sight to have been sound enough. But in fact the firm failed to investigate the market situation around the refinery at that time. Goole was the centre of the 'dumping' area for continental bounty-fed refined sugar brought in under the preferential steamer and rail agreement. Secondly, Macfie's ability to refine beet sugar (after specializing in refining cane sugar) was in doubt. In 1866, Macfie's had made a loss because beet sugar 'did not harmonize with our way of working'.[13] The firm recorded in 1899 that the high cost of cane sugar prices had forced them to use beet sugar exclusively in the Liverpool refineries; the result was predictable: 'the staff and plant are not accustomed to refining beet only'.[14] It is not surprising that the firm had a disastrous experience of beet technology at Rawcliffe:

> the result had been disastrous both as regards the expenses and

> the margin on refining to pay them. A great many difficulties have arisen in the working of the Langen process and with regard to the plant required.[15]

Macfie's did not even recruit any new skilled personnel for Rawcliffe; Thomas Easton was made manager of the refinery and he had no experience of beet refining. As Macfie's discovered, the expertize required for beet refining was substantially different from cane refining.

In addition to refining sugar themselves Macfie's had invested in three other sugar refiners; firstly ten shares valued at £90 each in the Electric Sugar Refining Company; secondly fifty preference shares in David Martineau and Company at £11 per share, and lastly £1010 in Continental Sugar Factories Limited. These investments show a distinct lack of confidence in their own firm's ability to produce a comparable rate of return. This £2460 could have been used to re-train personnel to handle beet sugar. In this particular respect, the management of Macfie's was distinctly unimaginative.

The lack of a fully coherent investment policy can only be attributed to top management. Thomas Easton, when asked in 1866 whether human ingenuity could improve the industry, replied that 'there is not room for much'.[16] In the case of Rawcliffe the firm, arguably, should have realized that if James Duncan, a pioneer in the beet industry, was unable to make the refinery into a going concern then, given its limited experience with beet, Macfie's efforts stood little chance of success.

Macfie's ability to remain in business while so many refiners were closing was based, indeed, on the limited application of new technology. It began using the Langen cube process twenty years after Tate's had begun the construction of Silvertown especially for cube production. By this time Tate's had found a new method of producing cube sugar, and Macfie's was again ill-equipped in relation to Tate's.

Top management at Macfie's was in the hands of the family and some salaried personnel. These personnel were given a bonus if production was favourable, but partnership demands were delayed until the last possible moment. A chemist was employed but his impact was minimal. J. W. Macfie and Robert Marquis visited New York and Germany to investigate refining processes, but no action followed. The influence of the younger members of the family was significant in gaining the acceptance of the older members for the proposal to build the new refinery in the 1870s, but the younger directors themselves failed to recommend the type of process to be used in this refinery even though on some occasions they showed foresight in technical matters. For example, there was the recommendation that one of the family be sent to study engineering with the firm of Mirlees, Tait, and Watson, a major sugar machinery producer. Unfortunately, as in many firms of the period, the second or third generation of entrepreneurs also wished to follow non-business pursuits. J. W. Macfie returned from a trip around the world in 1882 but this 'adventure' does not appear to have included a search for new refining techniques. Thus in general Macfie's business attitudes reveal a growing apathy in comparison with those of Henry Tate, and it would appear that a serious technological lag resulted.

A comparison of Tate & Co. with Macfie and Sons raises the question of why Macfie's failed to respond to the commercial climate in which they found themselves, and why Tate and Co. recognized the solutions to the situation which prevailed. Was the gulf between these two firms due to financial or technological barriers to entry, to differing entrepreneurial performance, or to a combination of all of these factors? The cost of technology similar to that employed by Henry Tate was prohibitive to the average refiner. The value of Tate's 'fixed machinery, loose machinery, plant, houses, utensils, furniture and fittings' amounted to £314,300. 12*s*. 7*d*.[17] in 1903. In addition to this, a large amount of working capital was necessary especially for a large output: the value of stocks of sugar, raw and refined, and materials and stores was estimated at £337,441. 3*s*. 1*d*.[18] The total cost of all Tate's plant and stock was £651,741. 15*s*. 10*d*. even without considering the cost of land. Assuming that an existing refiner had sufficient land on which to develop a new refinery with similar capital equipment, the cost would have been beyond the means of most firms. By the time the less progressive refiners realized that the only way to compete was to install a totally new technology, Tate's and Lyle's lead was unassailable.

It is relevant to recognize the significance of the early-start thesis in the case of the sugar refining industry. Tate was a relatively new refiner, and had benefited from the research and development built up before 1870. However, this technology was only suited to refineries with a capacity up to 600 tons per week. Tate was thinking in terms of at least twice this size and consequently he had to find new technology capable of producing a large output as quickly and efficiently as possible. The older refineries would have to scrap most of their plant if they were to install new technology capable of such a large output. Such refiners argued that if the old machinery continued to make profits then there was little reason, apart from the prospect of increased foreign competition, to change. Not the installation of costly new plant, but the establishment of fair trading conditions was the solution.

Even if cost considerations could have been ignored, the availability of a similar technology to that of Tate and Co. was still problematical. The Patent system operated very efficiently in a high technology industry such as sugar refining. The rate of royalties for processes varied, but it was common for a rate of royalty per unit of output to be charged. For example, Howard's vacuum pan, which was one of the most widely used innovations in the industry, cost the refiner 1*s*. per cwt. This meant that Macfie's paid £20,000 p.a. in the 1850s, and larger refineries £50,000. According to R. A. Macfie, the profitability of the firm was seriously affected in such a situation:

> Our trade is one of those that we conducted with a small margin compared with many others. At one per cent profit we are remunerated. If we pay 5 per cent to the patentee where is our one per cent profit?[19]

Refiners were not prepared to pay large amounts for the use of specialist processes which, in some cases, had no guarantee of success. Macfie's did not use the Langen process (of which Tate was a licensee) until the patent had been proven and had, in fact, expired. Consequently Macfie's belated attempt to profit from cubes encountered difficulties because Tate's cubes were already well-known after 20 years of selling. Although it is easy to condemn Macfie's for their failure to diversify into cube sugar, the cost of installing the process and the license charge must have been prohibitive. By the time Macfie's had installed the Langen process it was already obsolete, the technology of cube making had been improved by the Adant process which Tate immediately installed.

The patent system combined with a policy of secrecy consolidated Tate's position in technological terms. Coupled with the high cost of new technology there was little chance of the widespread application of techniques pioneered by Tate's. There appears to have been a certain amount of inertia within Macfie's when considering the application of new techniques. And uncertainty about future trading prospects was cited by Macfie's as preventing them 'entering upon the improvements and extension which we otherwise would'. Uncertainty can be accepted as a major factor in determining a weak investment policy but only in the years up to 1884. In the period after 1864, there was a possibility that the French government might have considered abolishing bounties, but with the consolidation of the French system in 1884 and the introduction of a new duty system, the degree of uncertainty was much reduced. Increased bounties had now become a certainty.

The reluctance of many sugar refiners to follow the trend set by Tate's and Lyle's was not so much a function of the foreign competition prevalent in the British market as of a rational response to uncertainty. The bounties acted as a catalyst in the alteration of the structure of the industry. If the bounties had not existed and the massive imports of beet sugar had never entered Britain, then the result would have been the same; the large low-cost per unit refiners would still have cut margins and eliminated the less efficient refiners from the market. The bounties had the same effect without leading to charges of monopoly or oligopoly against Tate's and Lyle's.

While accepting that the cost of new technology was, in many cases, beyond the resources of the older refiners, the availability and desire to implement new methods did pose a challenge to entrepreneurial ability in the sugar refining industry. This is borne out by the fact that two firms, Tate's and Lyle's, who were relatively unknown in the industry in 1870, had become market leaders by 1903 and, more importantly, had achieved their dominant position in a period of intense foreign competition.

Henry Tate capitalized on the bounties by using the low-cost raw beet sugar in his process thereby restricting the impact of foreign competition. By using a cheaper transport medium, the canal, he cut costs. Using a new technology and producing larger amounts of refined sugar he gained economies of scale. By the use of product differentiation he obtained a premium price for his product in relation to cheap loaf and moist sugar. Tate was in every sense of the word a progressive businessman. Other refiners attempted to follow Tate's example by applying his methods piecemeal. Martineau's, who were joint licensees of the Langen process ran into financial difficulties. Jacob Schwartz, one of the few London refiners to make the successful transition from loaf production to moist sugar, was bankrupt by 1887 with assets of £49,990 and liabilities of £80,739. The success of Henry Tate was the result of a combination of many factors which were part of an overall strategy to produce a sugar of the highest quality at the lowest cost.

Tate's background may provide an indication of why he achieved success. He was the son of a Unitarian Minister in Chorley and joined his brother, Caleb, in the grocery trade. By 1859 he was a successful grocer in his own right, owning six shops. At this time he became a partner in a firm of sugar refiners, John Wrights. He had had no previous experience of sugar refining and this very fact could have been an advantage to him. It meant that he was free to absorb the relative merits of each system without any significant bias in his decision-making process. His desire to produce new types of sugar, which were easier to handle than loaf sugar, was obviously motivated by his experience in the grocery trade. With loaf sugar it had been necessary for the grocer to cut pieces of sugar off the moulded form. This process was time consuming and wasteful, requiring the use of cutters, tongs, and scales to weigh the sugar. Tate's production of cubes and granulated sugar meant that these processes ceased to be part of the grocers' trade.

Greater scientific and business acumen than that of Tate had been applied to the business of sugar refining and failed. Sir Henry

Bessemer had invented a suspended centrifugal machine to produce loaf sugar which he had then installed in a new refinery at a cost of £100,000. The refinery had gone out of business within a few years. Thus scientific knowledge was not a sufficient criterion for success. *The Times* of June 1914 contained an article on Tate's success and came close to identifying his business ethos:

> The history of the firm illustrates the truth that success only attends on conscientious and deliberate ambition and effort. The late Sir Henry Tate, who founded the business in 1859, based the policy of his business on the belief of the British consumers' appreciation of quality. He aimed at the production of a sugar which could be as pure as scientific knowledge and practical skills could make it—the cost of refining was not to be allowed to interfere with this ideal. Tate's sugar had to be the purest and best. Such a policy meant the temporary sacrifice of profits . . . and the scrapping of machinery, the purchase of patent rights which had been declined by all sugar refiners of importance, and heavy capital expenditure on new plant. The sugars produced by the new process of refining were unrivalled for purity and brilliance and they took a lead which has never been wrestled from them.[20]

Tate's motivation in business could perhaps be construed as the desire to improve his social status. Economists and historians have observed that the limitless pursuit of wealth for its own sake is a rare phenomenon. In Tate's case, his gifts to many charities, libraries, and galleries could be interpreted as a means to gain social improvement. His contributions are certainly impressive: he provided the library at Liverpool University at a cost of £20,000—plus £5500 for books. He built the Hannemann Hospital, Liverpool at a cost of £20,000; his greatest gift was of £150–160,000 for the building of the Tate Gallery. Tate's motivation in supplying these gifts, amongst many others, to the community was his desire to provide the nation with better facilities.

In the case of Henry Tate and Abraham Lyle, the idea of a loss of impetus among second or third generation entrepreneurs may then be pertinent. Both men were eventually first generation entrepreneurs who were loath to employ managers in the early years of the development of their business: they were architects of their own success. The older refining firms, such as Macfie's, were operated by second or third generation entrepreneurs. Tate and Lyle understood the conditions of foreign competition and, unlike the older firms who had enjoyed protection in the pre-1804 period, their business outlook was unhampered by illusion. As a consequence the younger refiners were the most successful participants in the industry.

The business careers of Tate and Lyle substantiate the claim of many economic historians that the performance of some entrepreneurs in the last quarter of the nineteenth century was dynamic. Nor can the advocates of the entrepreneurial failure thesis claim with any justification that Henry Tate and Abraham Lyle were exceptions, since they ultimately dominated their industry. The performance of the refiners apart from Tate and Lyle was certainly low in many areas, and some entrepreneurial weakness coupled with the influence of the bounties helped reduce the number of operational refiners in Liverpool from 13 in 1864 to six by 1900. Nationally, the reduction was from 66 to 16 in the same period. Of these 16 firms, Henry Tate and Abraham Lyle controlled 62 per cent of the production for consumer and industrial use.[21]

The growing importation of low-price refined sugar meant that the beneficiaries of concentration had become very low-cost producers. Instrumental in this achievement was a positive commitment to investment in new technology. Tate's success was based upon the Boivin-Loiseau process and the Langen cube process; Lyle's success on syrups and granulated sugars. Each was determined to reduce the cost of production by all available methods, but without the sacrifice of quality. The older firms faltered in the face of foreign competition. The closure of so many refineries would have been inevitable even if the bounties had not existed since the lowest cost output would have determined selling prices. The difference between Tate and Lyle, and other refiners, was thus largely entrepreneurial in nature.

NOTES AND REFERENCES

1. The bounty system was a Continental system which encouraged foreign refiners to export refined sugars to Britain. The foreign refiner would restrict domestic supply (thus gaining a profit), the excess was exported to 'Free Trade' Britain. The refiner gained a payment (bounty) from the state for the export.
2. J. A. Watson, *A Hundred Years of Sugar Refining,* Liverpool (1973), p. 16.
3. Royal Commission on Canals and Waterways, C3184 BPP 1906, vol. xxxii, p. 317.
4. B.P.P. (1886), vol. xxiii, p. 163.
5. D. H. Aldcroft (ed.), *The Development of British Industry and Foreign Competition, 1875–1914,* London (1968), p. 276.
6. B.P.P. (1886), vol. xxiii, p. 248.
7. B.P.P. (1898), vol. l, p. 152.
8. *Times New Issues,* 4 March 1903, p. 39.
9. B.P.P. (1878/9), vol. lxxiii, p. 85.
10. Ibid.
11. *Macfie MSS*, 380 MAC 31/1 (1871).

12. J. A. Watson, op. cit., p. 25.
13. *Macfie MSS,* 380 MAC 3/1 (1866).
14. *Macfie MSS,* 380 MAC 3/2 (1899).
15. *Macfie MSS,* 380 MAC 3/2 (1895).
16. Ibid., 1866.
17. Ibid.
18. *Times New Issues,* 4 March 1903, p. 39.
19. B.P.P. (1864), vol. xxix, p. 467.
20. *Times Food Edition,* June 1914, quoted in J. A. Watson, op. cit., p. 14.
21. *Hansard,* 1902, **126,** 702.

4
The service occupations of nineteenth-century Liverpool

G. ANDERSON

Economists and historians vary over the explanations for the long-term shift towards the growth of services. Most explanations have emphasized some combination of an increase in final demand (the operation of Engel's law), the growth of intermediate demand (through the increasing division of labour) or the relatively slow increase in per capita output in services compared to manufacturing.[1] Whatever the reasons for the growth of services as a sector, there is virtual unanimity that the most dramatic effect of this shift has been in employment rather than in output. The labour force characteristics of service employment, whether measured in terms of the sexual compositions of the workforce, the kind of work done, and the types of organizations people work for plus the location of service work have all had a profound effect in setting the dominant tone in a society.

This observation has much more force in contemporary societies, where the shift towards service output and employment has been marked, than in historical ones. Nevertheless the shift towards services has not been characterized by any major identifiable discontinuity in economic growth but rather by a gradual process occurring over time. In England the origins of this structural shift towards services have been ascribed to the changes associated with the Industrial Revolution with the resultant employment effects registering in the nineteenth century. The macro aspects of this shift are now quite well-known in the English case, but the effect at the micro-level of the local community or town has been rarely discussed.[2]

Although semi-rural or small-town societies (such as England in 1801 and the United States in 1839) generated a surprisingly high ratio of service occupations most of whom lived and worked in the

Notes and references begin on page 93.

Table 4.1. *Occupational structure of selected towns, Males, 1871 (selected sectors as percentages).*

	Liverpool	*Manchester*	*Birmingham*
MANUFACTURING			
Engineering	3·2	5·0	5·6
Textiles	6·8	17·4	8·4
Metals/minerals	3·2	5·3	18·8
Other manufacturing	2·4	5·2	9·6
% total male labour force	15·6	32·9	42·4
SERVICES			
Learned professions	2·5	2·9	2·4
Domestic service	1·4	1·2	0·9
Transport	14·8	5·9	3·7
Commercial	7·5	8·0	4·6
% total male labour force	26·2	18·0	11·6

countryside, it is generally accepted that one of the main social developments accompanying the structural shift towards services has been an increasing rate of urbanization. However, within and between the Victorian cities great differences existed in terms of the levels of service employment, the ratio of non-service to service employment and indeed the general extent to which service output/employment provided the dominant tone in a city's economic and social life. In all Victorian cities there was, of course, a whole range of hand trades and personal services both inside (domestic servants) and outside the home (blacksmiths and barbers) in addition to a cluster of professional and public services. However in some towns the spread of occupations and especially the ratio of service to non-service occupations was considerably higher than in others. Cities like Birmingham and Manchester were characterized by a fairly diverse occupational structure. Both possessed substantial manufacturing bases, in Manchester's case in textiles and engineering, and in Birmingham in metals, engineering, and general manufacturing. In addition both cities had a fully-developed range of service industries, although these were substantially larger in Manchester than in Birmingham. Liverpool, the subject of this essay, was in contrast much less diversified in terms of its employment structure.[3]

As is clear from table 4.1 Liverpool's industrial development remained small in the nineteenth century, it was a commercial rather than an industrial centre.

In Liverpool, foreign trade, especially exports, was the main determinant of levels of local investment which in turn led to capital formation in docks, warehouses, and offices (as well as in residential building) and dictated the structure and rate of expansion of employment opportunities in the port.[4] Although the purpose of this essay is to explore some of the more well-known and traditional service occupations (e.g. white-collar workers, merchants, professions, and domestic servants) associated with the city, the service characteristics of Liverpool's industrial structure determined the nature of its manual workforce as well. Liverpool was not characterized by a large manufacturing working-class, engaged either in factory-based textiles or metals and engineering so typical of other Victorian cities. Male factory employment, on a fairly small scale, was restricted to activities ancillary to the port such as food processing and tobacco manufacture. Only dressmaking and textiles had a sizeable sector (though still below Manchester and Birmingham) but this was mainly a workshop-based finishing industry and registered its biggest impact on the female labour force. Liverpool's working class was in fact largely engaged in the provision of 'manual' services (in distribution and transport and identified especially with dock labour) which were in turn ancillary to and supportive of the commercial/white-collar groups which form the heart of this study.

Liverpool's social and occupational structure, as well as its local economy, was shaped by its transport, commercial, and port activities. At one level Liverpool, like other major Victorian towns, experienced the considerable employment effect of the railways. In 1841 while the railways accounted for only 26 men or 0·2 per cent of the city's male workforce they employed some 9698 men by 1911 or 2·7 per cent of the city's male workforce.[5] At another level Liverpool's working class was closely connected to ocean navigation (seamen) and to the docks and warehouses. However, the top of Liverpool's service economy was characterized by a relatively small but strategically important group of merchants and shipping companies which were, in turn, supported by a range of financial and information-providing intermediaries such as banks, insurance companies, and brokers. In their breakdown of occupational change in nineteenth-century Liverpool, Lawton and Pooley showed that commercial services expanded rapidly over the seventy year period from mid-century to the First World War, reflecting Liverpool's pre-eminence as a port, the commercial functions of which, in their view, were almost on a par with those of London. Therefore, 7327 men were employed in Liverpool's commerce in 1851 (4·0 per cent of the city's male labour force) and that figure had increased to 24,659 by 1911 (6·9 per cent of the city's male labour force). These figures are, however, somewhat misleading for the purpose of this essay. Lawton and Pooley included under the general heading of commerce not merely general urban services (such as shopkeepers, dealers, and pawnbrokers) but also clerks, who, although they had close links with their employers, were really a subordinate group of employees and need to be treated separately. When merchants, brokers, and ship-agents are separated out then the history of their development is rather different.

In the first half of the century Liverpool's mercantile sector consisted of a group of specialist and general merchants supported by an, as yet, small but growing class of specialist brokers dealing either in the port's main commodities or providing insurance services. The connections of the port's merchants with the commodities of the old colonial trade (cotton, timber, sugar, and tobacco) were well-established, both in terms of imports and re-exports, while the city dominated the trade in finished textiles as well as having important connections with the trades in coal, iron, and machinery. In this period, according to the evidence marshalled by Cottrell, a local market of merchant firms had evolved, of roughly equal size and resources, which was approaching perfect competition.[6] Entry costs into merchanting/broking were apparently low, with office, warehouse, and shipping space easily rented. However, the cultivation of strong personal and business contacts was an important prerequisite for business success. As voyages became longer (more risky) and markets more distant (less certain) Liverpool merchants and brokers increasingly traded on behalf of others for a commission rather than simply, or even mainly, on their own account. In this respect the strategic location of Liverpool's merchants between the manufacturing districts in Britain and the sources of raw material supply and demand were maintained via apprenticeship (in other merchant houses) or by the use of the correspondence system (regular contact by letter) with other firms scattered along the trade route.

Many Liverpool firms developed a multi-branch structure. A good example was Alfred Booth and Company who acted as commission agents in the Atlantic leather trade providing specialist information to American manufacturers, regarding prices and quality, and even providing credit to small firms on both sides of the Atlantic. Booths' basic economic function, as with all brokers, was to provide accurate information regarding the probable future course of prices. To this end the presence of a partner and clerks in New York was thought vital. Via the branches of the broking and merchanting firms channels of upward mobility were created both for merchants' sons and the well-connected clerks in the trades. Commercial ties were often reinforced by religious and family connections. The careers of Alfred Booth and his brother, Charles, are illustrative of this pattern. Both were brought up in the close world of Liverpool's dissenting merchant families in the 1820s and 30s and both successfully exploited their background to obtain job experience and credit, before establishing their own business.[7]

The heyday for the brokers and commission agents in Liverpool was in the period down to *c.*1870. In the last third of the century a number of technological and institutional changes occurred which transformed the nature of commercial transactions. The wider use of iron steamships increased the speed and reliability of supply. The Atlantic Cable, laid down in 1866, plus the establishment of futures markets in the United States and England resulted in a further reduction of risks and price fluctuations by speeding up the supply of information. The net effect of these changes was that transaction costs were lowered. Some manufacturers now by-passed intermediaries and dealt directly with the producers. The role of the broker was much diminished.[8] Well established firms, like Alfred Booth, were prompted to lower their commission charges to the point where they incurred the possibility of carrying bad debts. Chance shippers with the firm which had previously been obliged to pay a higher rate were now charged the same as established clients. John Rankin, reminiscing on Victorian Liverpool from the standpoint of the 1920s, summed up the effects of these changes as representing an end 'to the law of chances and eventualities on which the merchant had hitherto operated. . . . Views, however shrewd, no longer availed, the remotest parts were on an even plane as regards information'.[9] The impact of these changes registered most directly on the brokers engaged in the commodities of the older colonial trade. For example, the port's 320 cotton brokers of 1870 had declined to 190 by 1914. Likewise the commission merchants declined in number from *c*.300 in 1870 to just over 80 in 1914. This reflected what was happening to the city's merchant class as a whole which having peaked at 727 in 1871 had contracted to 205 by 1891.[10]

Broking also provided the main entry point into the shipping side of Liverpool's commerce. As with commodity broking there was a premium on access to information, management skills and, of course, a reputation for honest dealing in shipbroking. It was an area of Liverpool's commercial life which attracted people with relatively few capital resources; in the first two-thirds of the century clerks and ships-masters could contemplate embarking on independent careers as ship-brokers, earning their commissions from chartering, agency work and insurance. Some Liverpool ship-brokers, by purchasing cheap ships or raising capital through their business connections, could anticipate becoming ship-owners in their own right as suggested by the histories of John Bibby, William Hall, T. H. Ismay, and the Harrison Brothers. However, like their commodity counterparts, the 'golden age' of Liverpool's ship-brokers was in the first two-thirds of the century. After the decline of sail and the advent of steam in conjunction with a growth in the scale of business organization the entry costs into ship-owning rose considerably. In addition information costs were much reduced by the establishment of specialized freight markets (e.g. Baltic Exchange in London). The management/information functions of the ship-broker were characteristic of the period when the ship-owners' capital needs were small and information costs were high. In the period before 1914, even though they retained a place, they were gradually superseded by the highly capitalized shipping empires offering regular services which were themselves the consequence of amalgamation and a more widespread capitalization through the issue of public stock.[11]

Liverpool's merchants, brokers, and ship-owners dominated the city's economy and society. Business life was centred in Liverpool upon the Exchange where brokers, merchants, and aspiring clerks rubbed shoulders. The merchant community generated a network of ancillary service institutions ranging from the Chamber of Commerce which functioned as a general forum for commercial interests to more specialist organizations providing information services for merchants trading in particular commodities or with certain regions (e.g. American Chambers of Commerce, West India Association, and Cotton Brokers' Associations). The social impact of the merchant class was just as significant. In a city where there was a strong tradition of upward mobility successful merchants were the most representative figures. If few had actually risen from 'rags-to-riches' many were self-made. Their careers and personality traits, models for social evaluation by many aspiring young clerks, were consistently propagated through the local media. Writers like Benjamin Orchard built professional careers around their pen portraits of local businessmen whom they transformed into social heroes.[12] The life styles of Liverpool's elite ranged from the fairly frugal world of some of the early and mid-nineteenth century merchants and brokers (described by John Rankin) to the conspicuous consumption associated with the largest ship-owners of the later period. Typical of the latter was the estate of Thomas Ismay, founder of the White Star Line, at Dawpool overlooking the River Dee with its thirty-three servants and 390 acres. Later the huge house with its high costs of domestic service and maintenance came to be regarded as a 'fetter' on the family resources.[13]

The expansion of the professions was a vital aspect of the sectoral shift towards service employment which occurred in the Victorian economy. Carr-Saunders and Wilson were among the first historians to identify a professional revolution in British society, a consequence in turn of the Industrial Revolution. Going further Colin Clark has singled out the expansion of the professions, of all the services, as the one most strongly symptomatic of economic growth itself. Moving to the social consequences of professionalization Reader and Perkin, in their different ways, have identified the emergence in the nineteenth century of a distinctive and independent professional class.[14]

The professions were certainly a rapidly expanding occupational group. According to Reader, the numbers employed in the professional occupations increased from 125,006 in 1841 to 473,697 in 1911. The largest category, over half in any particular census, were the teachers. In Liverpool, as elsewhere, the professions constituted an important and expanding group. Between 1841 and 1911 the number of men in the city's learned professions increased from 1819 to 7426, expanding their share of the city's total occupied male population from 1·5 per cent to 2·1 per cent over the same period. The professions also provided women with one of their few entry points into the city's labour market. In Liverpool between 1841 and 1911 the number of women in the professions increased from 776 (0·8 per cent of the female labour-force) to 7432 (1·9 per cent of the female labour-force). Moreover, by 1911 there were nearly as many women in the professions as men. However, the figures conceal important differences between male and female professional employment in the city. Female employment was overwhelmingly concentrated in two of the lower professions: teaching (3594 in 1911) and nursing (1692 in 1911). There was virtually no penetration of the top professions, with only eight female physicians enumerated in 1911 and no barristers, solicitors, or surveyors.

The demand for these professional services came from three sources within the city's economy. Firstly, households consumed a greater variety and volume of professional skills in this period. Many households increased their demand for medical advice, despite their low incomes. For example, the poorest Liverpool clerks joined the local Clerks' Association in order to provide basic medical provision in the event of illness and unemployment. Much of the demand for medical, legal, or architectural services came from the city's middle-class households who also, through their leisure activities, increased the need for music and art teachers, photographers, journalists, and writers. A second source of demand for professional services came from Liverpool's firms, many of which were engaged in trade and shipping. Many of the city's lawyers, solicitors, and accountants provided such firms with much needed legal and financial services. Hartwell also includes brokers under the broad umbrella of the professions and this group, as we have seen, was both numerous and important in Liverpool's local economy. Brokers did sell information and acted as intermediaries between other firms but it might be misleading to regard them as professionals in the strictest sense since they did not require any formal education but were, in fact, marketing their experience rather than their educational skills. Finally, government itself was an increasing employer of professional services whether in the form of engineers, to tackle the city's physical needs, or in the form of doctors and nurses to tackle the population's welfare needs. Certainly the enormous increase in teachers, both in Liverpool and elsewhere by 1911, is only explicable against a background of increasing government intervention in education.

Several characteristics marked the professions off, both from the other service occupations and the rest of society. Firstly the professional class, as Perkin has noted, occupied a more independent position within the class structure than either the working class or the entrepreneurial middle class. To some extent the professions were insulated from the market pressures which affected the businessmen and the workers in their respective struggles for profits and wages. Part of professional ideology may even have been distrustful or critical of the 'acquisitive aspects of industrialism and thought more of duty than of profit'.[15] Of course, the conflict between service and profit motives should not be taken too far. After all the professions invested their savings in capitalist enterprises and they held directorships in companies.

In Liverpool the inter-play between the professions and the commercial middle class is well-illustrated by the activities of the local Literary and Philosophical Society. Established in 1812 the Society acted as the city's most important meeting place for the professions and the commercial community. Within the Society, the professions fulfilled two functions. Firstly, they acted as a support group for the merchants and brokers providing expert information on a range of useful topics from compass guidance in ships to the adaptability of colonial regions for cotton or sugar-beet production. Secondly, they acted as moral teachers to the merchant class. In mid-century the Society was warning Liverpool's merchants, and through them the entire commercial middle-class, that despite their wealth and power they 'should acquire a higher knowledge above the merely utilitarian' and that if they 'pursue a wiser course then possibly as much zeal for the acquisition of knowledge would be found among traders as among doctors and clergymen'.[16]

This sense of intellectual superiority is the second major distinguishing characteristic of the professions. The underlying difference between the professions and other occupations was, in economic terms, a human capital one. Quite simply most professions were characterized by their unique educational requirements. However, these requirements were by no means clear-cut for all or even most professions in the nineteenth century and indeed one aspect of the process of professionalization was the insistence upon a clearly-defined and exacting professional training. Some important professions had produced their own organizations fairly early in the nineteenth century. The architects had realized themselves as a profession by 1834–5 when the Institute of British Architects was founded. The Institution of Civil Engineers was founded earlier in 1818 though not incorporated until 1828. However, the Institution of Mechanical Engineers was not formed until 1847 and that of the

Electrical Engineers not until 1871. The doctors, although one of the oldest groups, did not really achieve full control of their profession until the formation of the British Medical Association in 1855 and the Medical Act of 1858.

Thomas Bickerton, in his classic *Medical History of Liverpool*, argued that prior to the Medical Act there was no medical profession, because there was no distinction between qualified and unqualified men.[17] Certainly in Liverpool in the first half of the century a doctor's training was as much on a par with a trade apprenticeship as with a formal academic education. Robert Banning, recalling his medical training in Liverpool in 1848 when he was apprenticed to a local doctor after the payment by his father of a large premium, observed that: 'Not very much time was wasted in those days over preliminary instruction and a very few months after my apprenticeship commenced I was sent to my first midwifery case'.[18]

Demarcations between the professions were also a feature of the early moves towards professionalization. In Liverpool, for example, the long-standing enmity between pharmacists and doctors over responsibility for dispensing drugs led to the formation of the Liverpool Apothecaries Company in 1836, which sought to control the retail and wholesale trade in drugs. This organization was founded upon the assumption that 'medical practitioners could not depend upon the accuracy of chemists, or the purity of drugs, and that the formation of the Company was necessary for the safety of the public'.[19] In retaliation the local chemists founded the Liverpool Chemists' Association in 1849 which tried to appeal to industrial as well as pharmaceutical chemists. This organization failed and it was not until the Pharmacy Act (1868) which clarified the training and responsibilities of pharmacists that the group developed as a separate profession.

What of professional life itself in Liverpool? The local Literary and Philosophical Society acted as an important meeting place for both the old (doctors and clergy) and new (engineers and architects) professions in the first half of the nineteenth century. Doubtless such societies had a similar function for the provincial professional class elsewhere in England. Topics both of a local, pragmatic nature, and those dealing with more abstract, intellectual questions were endlessly debated. However, later in the century scientific papers which might formerly have been read to the Society were being given to the Royal Society or to the specialist professional associations in London. From the 1880s the establishment of the University College acted as a new filip to Liverpool's intellectual and professional life. By the end of the century a fairly distinctive intellectual and professional circle had established itself in Sandon Terrace, an area occupied mainly by learned societies, such as the Deutscher Club, or professional bodies attached to the University. Some of the academics had rooms in Sandon Terrace and the area was the centre of a vaguely Bohemian but materially comfortable professional middle-class elite.[20]

Clerical employment was one of the most important occupational categories in nineteenth-century Liverpool. While employment in large-scale manufacturing industry and in the smaller craft-trades either declined or stagnated in Liverpool after 1841, the opportunities for clerks proliferated. Some clerks were, of course, employed in Liverpool's local industries, having as it were an intermediate function, reflecting the growing division of labour within firms and helping to smooth the process of production. Given the relatively small size of Liverpool's industrial base these clerks were in a minority. In contrast to other industrially-based towns most of Liverpool's clerks worked in the commercial service sector—in shipping, broking, merchanting, banking, and insurance. Still others were employed as support services to the professional class while the growing demands of local government (especially after 1900) gave rise to a virtually new category of local government clerks and officials.

According to Lawton and Pooley commercial service employment rose from 4·7 per cent to 6·9 per cent of all male employment between 1841 and 1911. These figures are slightly misleading for our purposes for they include not merely the clerks themselves but also the merchants, brokers, shippers, agents, and insurance companies who employed them. More precisely the number of male commercial clerks in Liverpool increased from 3008 in 1851 to 9278 by 1881 and 13,668 by 1911. For the most part these figures exclude the large numbers of clerks employed in the railways, government services, and specific areas such as banking and the law. Between 1861 and 1911 the number of male railway officials and clerks in Liverpool increased from 876 to 2253. For most of the nineteenth century Liverpool's government sector remained fairly small. In 1871, for example, there were 1126 civil servants, many in the Customs Department, and 481 local government officers. After 1900, however, the first signs of the inexorable growth of a government sector became evident. Between 1901 and 1911 the number of local and national government officers and clerks increased from 4682 to 6285.

Women's involvement in clerical work remained limited until the turn of the century. Until then employment opportunities for women in Liverpool had been largely restricted either to domestic service or to textile and dress manufacture. Clerical work was thus an important factor in the diversification of women's employment in Liverpool as elsewhere. Down to 1871 no females were recorded as commercial clerks in Liverpool. Only 29 were listed in that year and although by 1891 the figure had increased to 489, it was after 1900 that the expansion really occurred. Between 1901 and 1911 the number of female commercial clerks increased from 1699 to 3267. In the same period the number of female clerks employed in local and national government in Liverpool rose from 547 to 1306.

What of the clerks themselves? We are fortunate in possessing a good deal of information about their incomes, relations with employers, chances of mobility, and social attitudes.[21] Liverpool's clerks were not a homogeneous group. There were distinctions based on income, self-esteem, and chances of mobility which marked some clerks off from others both within and between industries. Clerks engaged in banking and insurance were often virtually guaranteed upwardly mobile careers ending in management. Still others, in brokers and merchant houses, might set up in business for themselves although it seems that such opportunities were more likely in the Liverpool before 1870 than after. The question of timing is important. In the early and middle parts of the century Liverpool's relatively small clerk stratum was a secure and fairly aloof group closely attached to the merchant elite.

Henry Lucas, writing in the 1820s on behalf of his fellow clerks, was quite confident about their position in local society. 'There is one institution wanting in a great commercial town like Liverpool', he wrote, 'and that is a Commercial Institution, for while the Royal Institution is adopted to the recreation of the scientific and that of the Mechanics may serve to instruct artisans, neither of them is very appropriate to the information of a very numerous class of individuals in the town—the commercial clerks. From this class most of the merchants have risen to their present stations of respectability'.[22] Benjamin Orchard reinforced the point in 1871 when he dedicated his classic piece of investigative journalism *The Clerks of Liverpool* to that group 'from whose ranks not a few, after serving with capacity, zeal and faithfulness, rise to the position of employers'.[23]

Later in the century, during the Great Depression years, more is heard of the economic problems confronting clerks. Complaints (appearing regularly in the press from the 1870s) indicate the difficulties of equating a small income with a certain accepted level of expenditure. Those clerks in the £70–£80-a-year range were unable to afford the basic requirements of a middle-class lifestyle. In Liverpool as elsewhere, £150 a year was regarded as a minimum income for expenditure on the 'paraphernalia of gentility' especially the employment of servants.[24] The expenditure of the £70–£80-a-year clerk was restricted to the absolute necessities of food, fuel, rent, clothing, and travelling expenses. Of course, many of these low-paid clerks would not anticipate remaining at such a level. A time or career element typified much clerical work, especially in the banks, insurance companies, and larger shipping offices.

However, the activities of the Liverpool Clerks' Association indicates that numbers of the city's clerks did not enjoy work of a permanent and dynamic quality. Those clerks who joined the Association sought the reassurance of its employment register, medical and unemployment benefits. In the last third of the century, during the so-called Great Depression years, increasing numbers of clerks made use of the Association's facilities. Many suffered as their employers sought to reduce their labour costs in the face of falling prices and profits. Half the clerks who found work through the Association were placed in temporary jobs while the overwhelming majority of all jobs found were valued at less than £100-a-year.[25]

The size and structure of Liverpool's clerical workforce by the turn of the century reflects the increasing move towards clerical work of a routine and less skilled nature. Changes in workplace organization especially the introduction of the large, departmentally-based offices, typified by the Cunard, Liver, and Mersey Docks buildings on the water-front, were allied with changes in technology (typewriters and telephones) and new basic skills (shorthand). By the end of the century the pursuit of commercial education was the obsession of many young clerks, male and female, in their determination to improve their job chances. In Liverpool the Mechanic's Institutes led the way in providing commercial education courses from mid-century, supplemented by the YMCA and later by the School Boards as well. The benefits from commercial education flowed most strongly to the female rather than the male clerks. With shorthand and typewriting, women entered Liverpool's offices for the first time but before 1914 it is likely that the girl typist was the only woman employed. Although women were initially feared by men for their competition they did not, in fact, occupy the same band of the labour market. They were employed as, and remained, shorthand-typists whereas many male clerks could anticipate careers ending in management.

The clerks of Liverpool provided the city with much of its character and tone. They were the most numerous section of the central business area's working population and the most representative of the new suburbanites. In a sense they might be usefully contrasted with the other distinctive group servicing Liverpool's burgeoning commerce: the dock workers. Occupying the bottom end of the manual labour market the dock workers increasingly gave Liverpool its reputation for toughness, working-class militancy, and rigorous trade-unionism. In sharp contrast the expanding, if heterogeneous, class of commercial clerks provided much of the snobbishness, social striving and respectability which was the other face of Liverpool.

At the bottom of the service economy were the domestic servants. A number of characteristics marked this group off from the other service occupations which we have so far examined. Firstly the servants were far and away the largest of all the service occupations in the nineteenth century. They were also one of the most rapidly expanding at least down to the 1890s. In 1831 the English servant population was 665,709 or 12·6 per cent of the labour force and by 1891 the number had increased to 1,549,502 (15·8 per cent of the labour force) though by 1911 the servant sector had contracted to 1,314,024 (13·9 per cent of the labour force).[26] To some extent the increase in total service employment between 1841 and 1901 meant 'predominantly increasing numbers of female domestic servants'. Domestic service was the 'classic' female occupation of the period. In the years from 1861 to 1881 nearly 12 per cent of the total female population was in domestic service. In 1851 there were 784,000 female domestic servants and in 1881, 1,269,000 and the numbers are much larger if allied occupations (such as charwomen and washerwomen) are included. In the same period male domestic servants fell from 74,000 in 1851 to 56,000 in 1881 though large numbers continued to be employed as grooms and coachmen. Indoor domestic service then was predominantly a female occupation.

These characteristics of domestic service were repeated in microcosm in Victorian Liverpool. Lawton and Pooley have shown that domestic service was the single most important female occupation in the city although as a proportion of Liverpool's total female labour force, domestic servants were decreasing over the whole period. In 1871, therefore, domestic servants represented 14·46 per cent of Liverpool's total female domestic labour force but by 1911 they had declined to 8·4 per cent. The figures for domestic servants show them peaking in 1881 and then declining slightly down to the First World War.

Domestic servants in Liverpool 1851–1911

Year	*1851*	*1881*	*1911*
Male	917	245	189
Female	21,940	22,870	20,562

How is the increase in domestic service to be explained? One thing is clear, although servants have a long history dating back to pre-industrial times, the enormous expansion in their numbers in the nineteenth century was, in any long-term view, a temporary phenomenon. By the middle of the twentieth century domestic service had virtually disappeared. The growth of domestic service in the nineteenth century was closely related to the emergence of a particular pattern of household consumption. The determinants behind the increase in the demand for this particular type of household service can be explained at two levels.

In a purely economic sense the determinants of demand for domestic service were principally variables measuring income, the allocation of time to work and leisure and the price of the available services. The growth of domestic service closely paralleled the expansion of middle class income groups, especially in the mid-Victorian period. Between 1851 and 1871 the number of people in the middle income bracket (£200–£500 per annum) doubled.[27] Moreover, much of the increase in the number of middle-class households can be explained by the growth of middle class service occupation in commerce, government, and the professions. This was certainly the case in Liverpool which had no large industrial entrepreneurial class but was characterized, as we have already seen, by an expanding middle class service sector. This was particularly so in the middle of the century. The commercial service sector increased its share of the city's male labour force in Liverpool from 4·0 per cent in 1851 to 7·48 per cent in 1871. More specifically the number of merchants and brokers increased from 1175 in 1851 to 1954 in 1871. Likewise, the learned professions over the same period increased their share of the male labour force from 1·5 per cent in 1851 to 2·53 per cent in 1871.

The expansion of middle class purchasing power only goes part of the way towards explaining the increasing demand for domestic service in Liverpool, as elsewhere, in the mid-Victorian years. Much of the explanation must be sought in the psychic benefits derived by the middle class from the employment of servants. Theresa McBride has acknowledged that while not every family which, in objective terms, could be defined as middle class necessarily employed a servant, nevertheless their employment 'helped to define the distinctiveness of the entire middle class despite the tremendous disparity in income levels and social status.'[28] Domestic assistance provided a visible division between the middle and lower classes. It was an essential status symbol. J. A. Banks placed servants top of his list of the 'paraphernalia of gentility' while J. F. C. Harrison thought domestic assistance represented 'the essence of middle classness'.[29]

It could be, as Hartwell has suggested, that the conspicuous consumption aspects of domestic service outweighed any more measurable economic gains flowing from it and that in the end it represented an opportunity cost (the forfeiture of money income in order to obtain additional utility). The marginal utility gains from domestic assistance were probably greatest at the bottom end of the servant employing stratum. For the low-income clerk or small tradesman who employed one housemaid the psychic benefits (in the form of a subjective sense of middle classness) were substantial. Banks, the historian of the Victorian middle class, could not see how many clerks, given their incomes, could possibly afford the essential middle class comforts, including servants. He was correct but many poor clerks tried to do so.[30]

In Liverpool the struggle of status-conscious but low-level clerks to enter the servant-employing class was the source of fierce debate. When, in the 1870s one Liverpool clerk suggested that he could still live comfortably on £80-a-year and employ a servant, he was treated with incredulity by others in the same position.[31] Certainly according to B. G. Orchard, in his well-known survey of Liverpool's clerks, £150 was the barest minimum for the maintenance of a domestically-assisted middle class lifestyle and even then an extra source of income (e.g. from a lodger) might be a necessary supplement to the family wage.[32]

We are fortunate in having an account of this marginal servant-employing group in Liverpool in the 1860s. *Porcupine*, a popular satirical magazine, described, in rather sneering terms, the clerks, foremen, and 'respectable mechanics' who lived on the 'outskirts of town' in small villas with 'fittings supplied by the landlord' and with 'a girl to do the housework'.[33] In *Porcupine's* view the employment of this cheap untrained domestic assistance was unnecessary because the houses were small and the wives could, with proper management, have run them adequately. There were two reasons why they did not do so. On the one hand, many wives were untrained in housework and anyway regarded such activity with disdain and, on the other, 'the worship of appearance' (or put another way the pursuit of psychic benefits) led thousands of young married couples to keep young girls when they possessed neither 'the proper means nor cultured judgement to be entrusted with the keeping of anything so sacred'.

The condition of the servants in some of these lower middle class houses was the source of disquiet in mid-Victorian Liverpool. Usually it was young girls, often from Ireland or the country and seeking their first employment, who entered such homes for ninepence/one shilling per week (a wage-rate which, if correct, compared unfavourably with the £10–£25 usually quoted for housemaids in this period). Once there they might be 'driven without mercy and abused without stint and eventually got rid of in a hurry'. Moreover, according to *Porcupine*, the non-monetary component of the servant's wage was open to abuse and quoted as evidence a servant's narrative in a Liverpool house in which she was eventually forced to leave.

The unemployed domestic servant in mid-Victorian Liverpool faced a number of difficulties. Firstly, there were few reliable agencies which could provide much needed 'job search' information about the local labour market.[34] Girls, many of whom were recent arrivals in the city, often had to resort to unscrupulous Register offices in some of which they might lodge until they were 'suited'. The object of the offices was to keep the girls unemployed for as long as possible until their savings were exhausted. Those girls without money were vulnerable to prostitution though it is not clear that these offices actually acted as fronts for such activity. Not all servants' registry offices in Liverpool had this tarnished reputation. Some had close links with employing families and acted as intermediaries between them and better quality servants seeking work. In any event most servants in Liverpool were recruited via the more traditional channels of the newspaper advertisement or personal contacts.

According to Hugh Shimmin, writing in the 1860s, domestic service was loathed by the poorer people of Liverpool who evinced a strong preference for the comparative freedom of jobs in trade.[35] In the middle decades of the century young women entering the city's labour market had little choice other than domestic service. Only dress-making provided alternative female employment (of comparable size) and from the 1870s this sector was declining in terms of the proportion of the city's female labour force it recruited. However, from the 1880s onwards (and especially after 1900) alternative employment in public services and commerce (as clerks and typists) and in retailing (as shop-assistants) offered competing employment opportunities. These employments probably appealed more to the better-educated girls who might previously have entered more skilled areas of domestic service (e.g. advancement to cook or housekeeper status) while the expanding urban services in restaurants and bars provided good outlets for less skilled female labour for whom general domestic service had been the previous attraction. Coupled with this, there was a fall on the demand side. Servants were the largest component in a middle class household's costs and as middle class budgets became more constrained from the Great Depression years onwards the number of domestic positions was declining.[36]

In the twentieth century the special qualities of Liverpool's service structure which developed over the course of the nineteenth century, have been irreversibly altered. Domestic service, which defined the social status of so many Victorians in Liverpool and elsewhere, and which in terms of its sheer size as an employment sector lay at the heart of any notion of a service revolution in the nineteenth century, has all but disappeared in the second half of the twentieth century.[37] The network of small brokers, merchants, and ship-owners which characterized Liverpool in the age of sail and which provided employment and even avenues of upward mobility for armies of commercial clerks was already changing in the period before 1914. In the twentieth century Liverpool's pre-eminence as a seaport has gone and with it the merchant community which gave Liverpool its distinctive and dominant tone in the nineteenth century. This commercial decline has in turn affected the nature of manual work in the city. In mid-Victorian Liverpool dock employment was the only occupation open to much of the male population; in recent years dockwork has declined to negligible proportions.

NOTES AND REFERENCES

1. See V. R. Fuchs, *The Service Economy* (1968) for an explanation of the growth of services which favours the relatively slow increase in per capita output in services compared to manufacturing. For an explanation which favours some combination of a variation of Parkinson's law and the high social status attached to white-collar work see S. Pollard, 'The Rise of the Service Industries and White-Collar Employment' in Bo Gustafsson (ed.) *Post Industrial Society* (1979).

2. See R. M. Hartwell, 'The Service Revolution' in C. M. Cipolla (ed.) *The Fontana Economic History of Europe*, vol. III (1973).

3. The material used in this section including the occupational figures in table 4.1 is derived in the main from R. Lawton and C. G. Pooley, *The Social Geography of Merseyside in the nineteenth century* (Final Report to the S.S.R.C. 1976). The author wishes to express his gratitude to Professor Lawton and Dr Pooley for making sections of the S.S.R.C. report available to him. These were invaluable in the preparation of the essay.

4. See A. G. Kenwood, 'Fixed Capital Formation on Merseyside 1800–1913', *Economic History Review* (1978).

5. Occupational figures, unless otherwise stated, are derived from Lawton and Pooley, op. cit.

6. See P. L. Cottrell, 'Commercial Enterprise', in R. Church (ed.) *The Dynamics of Victorian Business* (1980) for a good account of the structure of Liverpool's commercial community in the period down to *c*.1870.

7. See A. H. John, *A Liverpool Merchant House, A History of A. Booth and Company 1863–1958* (1958).

8. For a brief outline of the effect of these technological and institutional changes see G. Anderson, 'The Social Economy of Late-Victorian Clerks', in G. Crossick (ed.) *The Lower Middle Class* (1977).

9. John Rankin, *History of our Firm*, Liverpool (1921), p. 268.

10. Figures derived from Gore's *Directories of Liverpool*.

11. For a good account of the Liverpool ship-brokers see R. Davis, 'Maritime History; Progress and Problems', in S. Marriner (ed.) *Business and Businessmen*, Liverpool (1978).

12. Various sources emphasize the tradition of social mobility in Victorian Liverpool. See G. Anderson, *Victorian Clerks*, Manchester (1976) and Francis Hyde, *Liverpool and the Mersey* (1971).

13. W. J. Oldham, *Ismay Line*, Liverpool (1961), p. 68.

14. A. M. Carr. Saunders and P. A. Wilson, *The Professions* (1933); Colin Clark, *The Conditions of Economic Progress* (1940); W. J. Reader, *Profession Men* (1964); and H. J. Perkin, *The Origins of Modern English Society* (1969).

15. S. Rothblath, *The Revolution of the Dons* (1968), p. 91.

16. Proceedings of the *Liverpool Literary and Philosophical Society*, session 37(V), 1848.

17. T. Bickerton, *Medical History of Liverpool* (1936), p. 129.

18. Ibid., p. 131.

19. See B. R. Edwards, *Origins and Development of Pharmaceutical Education in Liverpool, The First Forty Years of the Chemists' Association* (1975).

20. See R. F. Bisson, *The Sandon Studio Society and the Arts* (1965), a study of professional/intellectual life in Liverpool at the end of the nineteenth century.

21. The fullest account of Liverpool's clerks are B. G. Orchard, *The Clerks of Liverpool* (1871), and G. Anderson, *Victorian Clerks*, Manchester (1976). In addition many of the city's excellent shipping histories contain information on clerk/employer relationships.

22. *The Liverpool Repository of Literature, Philosophy and Commerce*, November, 1876.

23. B. G. Orchard, op. cit., p. 41.

24. The notion of the 'paraphernalia of gentility' was developed by J. A. Banks, *Prosperity and Parenthood* (1954).

25. For a detailed assessment of the Liverpool Clerk's Association see G. Anderson, *Victorian Clerks*, ch. 5.

26. T. McBride, *The Domestic Revolution* (1976), p. 36.

27. See G. Best, *Mid-Victorian Britain* (1972), pp. 82–3.

28. T. McBride, op. cit., p. 18.

29. J. A. Banks, op. cit.; and J. F. C. Harrison, *The Early Victorians* (1971), p. 110.

30. See R. M. Hartwell, op. cit.

31. See Anderson, op. cit., p. 68.

32. Ibid., p. 69.

33. *The Porcupine*, 15 June 1861.

34. Ibid., 21 June 1862.

35. Hugh Shimmin, *Domestic Servants*, Liverpool (1862).

36. McBride, op. cit., points to the increasing difficulty of the English middle-class to be able to afford servants after *c.*1880. (p. 67) plus their desire to privatize their lives and their consequent disinclination to employ live-in servants.

37. The idea that the increase in service employment in the nineteenth century meant predominantly increasing numbers of female domestic servants is made by J. Gershuny, *After Industrial Society* (1978), p. 62.

5

The Port of Liverpool: Employers and industrial relations, 1919–39*

R. BEAN

Prior to the Second World War Liverpool remained pre-eminently a great maritime and distribution centre—the principal export port of the country, a world market in the cotton trade, and the largest grain marketing centre outside the United States. The port was the primary focus of the Merseyside economy and in 1931 it was estimated that more than half of all insured workers there were located in industries associated with shipping, transport, and distribution as compared with less than a quarter of workers so engaged for the country as a whole.[1] The Liverpool, Bootle, and Birkenhead docks constituted the greater part of the Port of Liverpool and for port transport in general it has been said that, with the exception of coal-mining, no British industry in the twentieth century presented more intractable labour problems than those associated with the docks.[2] As in other industries it was the inter-war years which saw the consolidated development of a centralized, uniform system of minimum wages standards, and terms of employment for shipping and port transport, thereby enlarging the scope of the bargaining unit to encompass *national* (industry-wide) agreements in place of individual, and widely varying, port rates set by local negotiations. It was also a period in which the British system of industrial relations itself, founded upon voluntaristic, self-regulatory principles, has been said to have 'matured'.[3]

The object of this essay is to examine the major factors determining the character, dimensions, and evolution of industrial relations in the docks and shipping industries between the wars from the standpoint of a major port.[4] The attitudes and reactions of Liverpool port employers towards the emergence and conduct of national collective bargaining during the 1920s will comprise a particularly important

Notes and references begin on page 115.

aspect. The study also has wider implications beyond the immediate Merseyside context. It will investigate aspects of the new institutional machinery set up for collective bargaining, the National Joint Industrial Council for Dock Labour and the reconstituted National Maritime Board for seamen, especially the uncharted territory concerning internal relations between the Employers' Association of the Port of Liverpool (EAPL) and other constituent employer groupings on these national bodies.

I

Liverpool had been the first port before 1914 to establish its own autonomous disputes and conciliation mechanism, initially for dock labour and later for sea-farers, to underwrite peace-keeping and for the negotiation of order and stability in a fragmented industry susceptible to a succession of minor disputes and sporadic stoppages. Upon the initiative of Alfred Booth, recently appointed chairman of Cunard, the employers had been persuaded to adopt a new and more positive approach towards port labour relations so as to make them less overtly conflict-prone.[5] The White Book agreement of 1911 had granted union recognition on a general basis, part of the primary procedural norm[6] of acceptance by employers of the union's right to represent and negotiate on behalf of legitimate interests, after years of unsuccessful endeavours to secure more than partial recognition by the dockers' union. In return, the union was to assist in labour regulation and control by requiring its members to process their disputes in an orderly manner without job disruption through a joint committee composed of an equal number of employer and union representatives. There was the added proviso that the union's aspirations towards more comprehensive, unilateral control of work practices would be confined within appropriate limits, in that no interference was to take place with the existing methods of working cargo on ship or quay. A later amendment to the agreement specified that the union undertook to use all measures permitted by its constitution to maintain discipline among its members, either on an individual or sectional basis, to prevent breaches of the agreement and that the employers would not engage non-union labour at the hiring stands when union labour was available.[7]

Employers claimed that between 1912 and the outbreak of war the Dock Labour Joint Committee had kept the port free from a large strike which could easily have occurred during a period of commercial prosperity with practically no 'free', substitute labour available.[8] The continuing success of these arrangements was attributed to the fact that the parties themselves at local level, 'at the essential point of contact with the actual labour employed', were responsible for their creation—instead of having them imposed by the State or by law as a cut-and-dried scheme from above. Employers maintained that it was vital 'not to make any agreement with the union that they say there is the least doubt about being able to carry out, because it will only lead to trouble'.[9] The emphasis was thus one of mutual responsibility for, and moral commitment towards, upholding the terms of negotiated agreements which self-generated initiatives at the local level were felt to be more likely to promote.

In industrial relations matters Liverpool port employers carefully avoided taking provocative action—they remained firm in principle but flexible on matters of detail, in the interests of a sound, continuing bargaining relationship. In particular, they were anxious not to do anything to undermine the authority of union leaders by granting concessions, in the face of pressure from unconstitutional action, which would be a direct encouragement to the rank and file in opposition to union officials. In fact, there was personal contact and reciprocal support between themselves and union leaders against those who sought to breach the terms of negotiated agreements. During an unofficial strike by coal-heavers at the end of the war Sexton, the local dockers' leader, warned the employers not to give way to the rebel elements otherwise it would be impossible for him to control the men thereafter, 'there would be an end of constitutional methods and his efforts to keep the peace in the future would be unavailing'.[10] He also 'castigated' one of his own officials and repudiated his action in threatening a work stoppage in support of a campaign (which was to recur) to get permanent foremen, time-keepers, and clerks on the docks to join the union, since the agreement expressly stated that they need not do so. When the dockers had struck unofficially in 1919, against an amendment to the local agreement specifying new hours of work and overtime arrangements which the union supported, Booth thought of a solution which involved altering slightly the hours of work but with a proportionate reduction in pay. He would put the idea privately to Sexton who then agreed, after securing the consent of his executive, formally to make a similar proposal to the employers. The purpose of this manoeuvre was to avoid any 'appearance of weakening on the part of employers', because if they were seen to be too ready to give way on the overtime question the men would consider immediately what other concessions they could secure.[11]

As a further aid to regulation of the port labour situation, to secure co-operation and support between employers themselves in carrying out agreements entered into with union representatives, the Employers' Association of the Port of Liverpool had been formed at the end of 1913. It was a comprehensive organization representing the interests of employers of all classes of port labour, both workers on shore and crews on ship. Although the main sections of labour directly employed by shipping firms and independent master porters and stevedores were dockers, seamen, and ship-repairers the Association also included tug and barge owners, the Mersey Docks and Harbour Board, and master carters,[12] since it was difficult to adjust wages and conditions for one class of labour in isolation without corresponding adjustments for the others. The rules stressed the need for employers in the port to hold together and for loyalty to collective decisions, under penalty of fines and possible expulsion. The Association also gained a wider significance as a representative of major shipping interests in labour matters at national level because it included the majority of the country's liner passenger and cargo tonnage, notably the Atlantic liners, not organized in the Shipping Federation which embraced mainly tramp shipping.

During wartime conditions of rapid and extensive economic changes, especially price increases to which wage standards and conditions of employment had to be adjusted, the government had been anxious to have war wage advances in the ports dealt with on a national and co-ordinated, rather than piecemeal, basis in order to prevent incessant work stoppages and continual disruption.[13] In 1917 a uniform cost-of-living increase was secured for dock workers in response to a national wage demand on their behalf. Ernest Bevin claimed that the formation of the Transport and General Workers' Union (TGWU) itself in 1921, which brought together the majority of previously competing unions so as to link almost the whole of British port labour into one organization, was primarily the outcome of wartime government intervention in the form of a national policy for dealing with wages and conditions of labour to which the transport workers responded. His dockers' union had strongly supported national wage settlements as 'the only sane method of dealing with any industry of national importance' and because in its view during the pre-war period the various unions had been used against each other by ship-owners and port employers, sometimes to the extent that 'one port's gain was another port's disaster'.[15] Moreover, when higher wages' rates had been conceded at a major port the dock union representatives were often asked by employers to endeavour to ensure that other competing ports were brought up to the new level. This had 'frequently left them with a tail like the tail of a comet, more difficult to deal with than the head of a comet'.[16] Consequently, the unions now sought to bring all employers in the industry together at the same time in order to secure their assent to a national and uniform settlement in place of uncoordinated, and possibly dissimilar, bargains. In the case of Liverpool day rates for dockers were lower than those paid elsewhere in the immediate post-war period because it had been the only port to adhere strictly to a minimum half day engagement.[17]

In 1919 the National Transport Workers' Federation (NTWF)[18] was pressing for the standardization of day and overtime rates in all ports and had submitted a claim for a national, minimum wage rate of 16*s*. a day for dockers. As the claim affected fifty-three ports and 125 separate employers' associations or individual employers the Liverpool Association, probably the most comprehensive and forward-looking employer grouping in the industry,[19] now took the initiative in calling together representatives of employers of dock-labour throughout the country to a meeting in London with a view to setting up a national organization of port labour employers. Booth wrote: 'Now that the organization on the men's side is so complete, we must have a strong and effective organization to deal with the problems of dock labour'.[20] It was agreed to establish a National Council of Port Labour Employers (NCPLE) to secure co-operation at all ports and 'act collectively' in labour matters, with a negotiating committee which would deal with the current wage claim and prepare the lines of united employer action. However, in an industry in which the generic term 'port labour employers' encompassed not only ship-owners but port authorities, master porters and stevedores and, in certain ports, wharfingers and water-side manufacturers as well as merchants, master lightermen, and tug-owners—all with their own separate and disparate commercial interests—the employers' side of national negotiations was to prove not only a very scattered constituency but also a very difficult one to unify and hold together. These various classes of employer were a reflection of the extraordinary diversity of circumstances found in the various ports, of local trading conditions, organization structure and methods of handling ships and different types of cargoes, loading and unloading systems, all of which differentiated one port from another.

Because the Council was intended to be a consultative and deliberative body, since neither it nor the negotiating committee would have power to bind individual employers or associations, it was believed that the inherent difficulties of forming a 'federation' of employers at national level in the port transport industry would be avoided.[21] There would be a maximum of five individual representatives from each port with equal voting rights, the intention being that the small ports would not feel that their interests would be overriden. Equally, the absence of mandatory powers would obviate the possibility of the smaller ports being able to work together in the Council to enforce their decisions.[22] In fact, it will be shown that soon after its formation the major ports, such as London and Liverpool, began to object to their restricted influence upon the outcome of deliberations in the Council which was not commensurate with their size and importance. They were to demand a greater degree of representation, thereby forcing an amendment to the constitution of the national body.

The employers' negotiating committee of the Council met the

Transport Workers' Federation at the end of 1919 in a joint conference convened by the Minister of Labour but refused to accede to the wage demands in view of the concessions which had already been granted in April of that year for a shorter working week of forty-four hours without loss of pay. They were, however, very ready to accept the Minister's proposals under his extended powers from the 1919 Industrial Courts Act to set up a court of inquiry under Lord Shaw to consider the dispute and make recommendations for a settlement. Recognizing that industrial relations were clearly the crux of the social problem in the immediate postwar period[23] the government wished to encourage collective bargaining, assist it to work smoothly, and help settle disputes. Earlier in the year at the time of a threatened dock strike in Liverpool as well as a national coal stoppage, a Liverpool port employer had been privately contacted by an official from the Ministry of Labour to press for a settlement of the local dispute and to convey official concern at the industrial situation, to an extent that 'it would appear . . . the government feared a revolution'.[24] The port employers welcomed the procedural device of a court of inquiry 'so that the public may be able to realize to what extent their interests are involved' through increased port charges for cargo handling and repercussions on wage claims in other industries should the national advance be conceded, in the belief that public opinion might then apply a moderating influence.[25] Furthermore, adopting a positive rate of time discount they felt that the actual (six month) delay in reaching a settlement, as well as staving off further demands in the interim, were also in the employers' interest by postponing an increase in wage costs.[26]

The outcome of the Shaw inquiry at which Bevin won a national reputation for his skilled advocacy of the dockers' case was acceptance of the standard minimum wage-rate, the setting up of a National Joint Council for Dock Labour as a deliberative, Whitley-type body and a recommendation that steps be taken by the industry to maintain dockers during periods of unemployment and under-employment i.e. for a minimum weekly wage whether employed or not. The reaction of port employers was one of reluctant acceptance coupled with dismay at the behaviour of one of their own nominees on the court who had 'gone over to the other side' and signed the majority report. There was also privately expressed resentment at the alleged lack of impartiality of the chairman, who kept employers 'dumb at the inquiry' and formed his views without giving employer representatives sufficient opportunity to expound theirs—'a more incompetent man for the job could not have been selected'.[27] So far as Liverpool was concerned the substantive terms of the White Book agreement, which would then be worked in conjunction with the national settlement, were duly amended but port employers soon came to appreciate that in the longer term they were to be constrained by national agreements which would have the inevitable effect of preventing their initiating local action, particularly for wage reductions, as and when they thought appropriate.[28]

In this respect a fundamental difficulty facing the employers' port labour organizations in negotiations both at local and national levels was the division of interest arising from the diversity of economic circumstances, organizational and trading characteristics as between their affiliated members. The less homogeneous the members of an alliance the greater the internal disagreement likely to emerge since, with divergent rather than common interests, it becomes difficult to find the common denominator on which all will agree.[29]

This problem was apparent even within the narrower confines of the internal port employers' grouping in Liverpool because of the importance and special interests of a leading shipping line, the Alfred Holt company which operated from the Birkenhead side of the Mersey. Birkenhead comprised the export section of the port and because of its particular requirements, such as the care needed in stowing cargo, had no piecework payments, higher time-rates than on the Liverpool side, different hours of work, and separate arrangements with the union on working conditions.[30] The Holt line had been reluctant to join the employers' Association at its inception and soon resigned from membership in 1917 since it wished to retain freedom to grant terms and conditions above the maximum scale which had been adopted. It regarded the advantages of such a collective grouping merely in terms of the mutual support which would be provided against 'whipsawing' union pay demands amongst individual firms.[31] In 1919 this firm broke the employers' united stand by giving way to an unofficial union ban on overtime against the new agreement on working hours. It agreed to pay enhanced overtime rates for the half-night in order to end delay in the turn-round of ships. Other lines operating from Birkenhead felt that they must follow Holt's lead and would resign forthwith from the employers' body unless this was permitted. In order to prevent the complete and imminent breakup of the Association, which Booth intimated would be 'madness' since the men 'would then do what they pleased with employers', it was agreed to accept defeat and take the 'very humiliating' step of officially sanctioning the deviant arrangements.[32] As a face-saving formula Sexton would be told that the Association had for some time been concerned at the continued postwar congestion in the port, resulting in a large number of ships having a lengthy wait for berths, and the Association whilst strongly maintaining its views on overtime payments felt that 'in the national interest it was necessary to yield its principles'.[33] The employers also decided to invite Holt back into EAPL membership, as evidently the actions of that company could not be ignored, in order to attempt to ensure a greater measure of employer unanimity in the future.

The difficulties of achieving employer unity and cohesion were even more manifest at national level. Here the NCPLE, the bargainer for the employer coalition in central negotiations with the union at the joint industrial council, had to reflect the different economic positions of constituent members within an industry typified by a heterogeneous structure, spatial divisions, multivariate interests, and commercial rivalries not only as between individual firms but also between ports. These basic divisions were further compounded during the inter-war years because the effects of the depression were by no means uniform in their impact upon the various ports.

The most significant international trading change which took place in this period was in the relationship between imports and exports; whilst exports fell sharply imports increased as a proportion of British trade from 37 per cent in 1913 to 57 per cent by 1937.[34] Liverpool, as the major export and liner port, with added costs as a result of the necessity of operating its liners even in the face of a severe drop in cargoes, suffered disproportionately from the effects of the depression. It was also losing trade to other UK ports between 1919 and 1939 at the rate of about one per cent of its own share in that trade each year.[35] Especially significant was the collapse in the export of cotton manufactures[36] (which had constituted 40 per cent of the value of exports out of Liverpool) and which meant that during the depths of the depression in 1931 the overall volume of Liverpool trade was only 41·8 per cent of the 1924 figure, much worse than the corresponding proportion for other ports such as London 72·9 per cent, Southampton 72 per cent, and even Manchester 48·1 per cent[37] i.e. in broad terms the northern ports were much more sensitive to the effects of depression than London or Southampton. In addition, the outward passenger trade to the USA and Canada declined by a quarter between 1924 and 1930 with a further loss of a large part of Liverpool's share of that traffic to Southampton because of its convenience for London and the continent. Finally, the port of Liverpool itself was expensive for shipping to use because it specialized in, and had appropriate handling facilities for, liners and high-value cargoes rather than for bulk commodities carried by tramp shipping. Thus, by the 1930s, with many of its facilities too dear and sophisticated for the world's depressed shipping and for the low value trades that the slump was making more important, Liverpool was less well placed to take advantage of the flood of cheap imports produced by the drastic fall in the price of commodities than competitive ports such as London.[38]

Such diversity of economic circumstances within the various ports was reflected in the deliberations of the NCPLE throughout the inter-war period. A number of ports led by Liverpool adopted a 'hard line' in urging resistance to wage advances which would increase charges and drive away trade to competitors, whereas other ports with a more favourable trading position were less resistant to union claims since they would face a heavier opportunity cost in the event of a strike.[39] It will be apparent that far from the employers' side at national level constituting a monolithic grouping designed to defend identical interests, internal dissension and cross-pressures were rife. They were a disunited and unstable coalition in which the alliances between ports on specific issues were often shifting rather than static.

Within a year of implementation of the Shaw award Liverpool employers had proposed giving notice to the unions for a £1 per week wage reduction in view of worsening trade and employment conditions and therefore a hardening market environment for the conduct of wage negotiations. In the employers' national Council the proposal met with general approval, especially from the smaller ports, and despite the reservations of London and the Bristol Channel notice was duly given. However, Bevin's counter proposal for a considerably smaller reduction instead of being summarily rejected by the employers' side was taken back to their constituents for further consideration. With many of the ports being 'in varying degrees in favour of a compromise', it was ultimately accepted. The reaction of Liverpool was to deplore 'the weakness shown . . . in negotiations' and to conclude that the port should now press for a greater measure of 'elasticity and freedom' to adjust substantive terms and conditions to meet local needs, even to the point of complete withdrawal from the national treatment of dock labour questions—fully recognizing that such a step might precipitate the break up of the national joint council.[40] In Liverpool's view there was no longer a useful role for the NCPLE to perform other than the exchange of information. It was vacillating and incoherent as a body, 'lacking unity of interests and capable leadership' and, as regards negotiations, 'each district should be left free to build up initiative and to put its own house in order'.[41] Indeed, between 1911 and 1914 Liverpool employers had been constructing very satisfactory relationships with their own employees through the port's Dock Labour Joint Committee which they felt would probably be gradually extinguished unless further developed on a local basis.

The possibility of Liverpool's impending secession from the NCPLE was averted temporarily only by a change in its leadership[42] and by agreement to some decentralization of authority in favour of a more appropriate measure of local autonomy, without which it is doubtful whether the Council could have survived on a long-term basis. Individual ports were now free to negotiate on working conditions, overtime hours and all other matters except the standard rate. The existing practice of referring local disputes to the adjudication of the national joint council would also be ended. Nevertheless, some months later in 1922 when the Council, at a 'very irresolute and conflicting' meeting, overturned a previous decision to press for a further, immediate pay reduction of 2*s.* a day and agreed to a longer, phased reduction—with only Liverpool, Middlesbrough, Southampton and, on this occasion, London dissenting—Liverpool formally terminated its membership of the national body. Despite a request from the Ministry of Labour to reconsider, since employers in a number of other dissentient ports were now also refusing to ratify the provisional settlement, the Liverpool employers' Association gave notice to Bevin to end the national agreement as far as the port was concerned and to Sexton to terminate the White Book agreement.[43]

Liverpool employers with predominantly ship-owning interests, unlike London where ship-owners were not the largest direct payers of dock labour, were concerned at this time not only with the level of dockers' wages as such but also with their repercussions on seafarers' pay, as well as the inter-relationship between wages paid to dock transport workers and those in kindred trades. Wishing to reduce the wage disparities within the 'unsheltered' industries, with a view to helping revive trade and improving the competitive export position of British goods, they maintained that dockers were overpaid in relation to craft and unskilled workers in ship-building and ship-repair (for which ship-owners paid the repair bills). They were also in favour of some wage reduction for the ship-repair trade itself since work was being sent away from Liverpool because of high labour costs in the port.[44] Indeed, they felt confirmed in their decision to secede from the NCPLE as a result of an application from the ship-building and engineering unions stating that a negotiated reduction in wages should now be withdrawn because a much more favourable settlement appeared to be maturing nationally for dockers.[45]

However, so far as dockers' wages were concerned the employers' Association in Liverpool soon discovered that it was unable to revert back to local bargaining on wage-rates and negotiate separately for the immediate 2*s.* reduction. Despite the union's concern in Liverpool at the employers' breakaway and the fear that there might be an immediate lockout in the port unless the new terms were accepted[46] the local officials, in accordance with TGWU instructions, refused to meet the employers. They insisted that the standard rate was now a national question which could not be settled on a local basis. Liverpool employers also came to recognize that any attempt to force the position would result in a certain strike in which local dockers would be supported financially by transport workers throughout the rest of the country. There was the added problem that even if a better settlement could be secured locally (which was far from certain) those Liverpool ship-owners who traded from other ports as well as from their home base would be unwilling to stand out and have ships held up at Liverpool for a lower wage-rate than they had to pay elsewhere. Moreover, the government would probably press them to act with other employers in the industry, and public sympathy would not be assured.[47] For all these reasons the Association had to modify its independent stance and follow the national reduction, which then applied unchanged to the port.

Similarly, because of the importance of the port itself Liverpool employers could not maintain their policy of complete isolation from the national employers' body either. When the union claimed an increase of 2*s.* in the daily, minimum wages on behalf of dock-workers at the end of 1923 to restore the previous cuts, the NCPLE wrote to the Liverpool Association requesting its views and inviting it to take part in formulating the employers' counter response. The Association was prepared to accede, after overtures from Glasgow port employers urging absolute employer solidarity in resisting the application, and believed that if the claim was conceded 'it would open the floodgates to further advances in other industries and check any improvement in trade'.[48] In the event, once again Liverpool found that most ports were prepared to compromize on the wage application rather than face a strike. The transport union, well aware from press reports that the employers' Council was disunited and that outside London some were prepared to give way to the full claim,[49] called a strike after negotiations had broken down. Pressure was put on Liverpool employers by Bevin who said that he could not recommend any settlement with which they were not agreed and by the Ministry of Labour after the government had set up another court of inquiry into the dispute. In these circumstances it appeared 'hopeless and invidious for Liverpool to hold out' and it was agreed to follow the national settlement of a one shilling immediate increase and a further shilling three months later.[50] One repercussion of the dockers' award was that in relation to an application for a wage advance in the ship-repairing trade Liverpool decided to depart from its practice as a non-federated district of following the Shipbuilding Employers' Federation, where negotiations were still pending, and to give a corresponding local advance 'quickly and gracefully'.[51]

It was felt in Liverpool that during this latest dockers' dispute the employers' side at national level, weakened by internal dissension, had once more woefully mismanaged its case and that at least some restructuring of sectional employer representation in the NCPLE was now essential. A basic perceived problem was that the interests of *ship-owners* were seriously jeopardized because of their insufficient representation on the Council, together with the difficulty of their formulating a coherent and unified policy in the absence of an employers' labour body which covered the interests of the shipping industry as a whole—as against the interests of other employers of dock labour. Therefore, at a meeting of leading ship-owners held in London a scheme was formulated to advance the special interests of ship-owners in national labour negotiations. They were to have improved representation on the NCPLE and a new organization would be established outside the Council, to be known as the Shipping Labour Committee, consisting of representatives of the Liverpool employers' Association, Shipping Federation, Glasgow Shipowners' Association, and the officials of the Chamber of Shipping. Its purpose was to 'act promptly and effectively as a united body in all labour questions' and to support and attempt to implement, 'actively and loyally', the Committee's policy within the NCPLE.[52] Liverpool also agreed to rejoin the NCPLE after it had been reconstituted in such a way that representation was based on the numbers of men employed at individual ports. The result was that Liverpool and London together then had virtual equality of membership with all other ports combined, as well as majority control of the policy-forming executive committee.[53]

In fact, the reorganization was not wholly successful over the longer-term in securing unanimity of collective attitude among the diverse interests represented by the ports for a firm stand against wage claims, particularly if resistance was likely to precipitate a work stoppage. In 1930 Liverpool had obtained general support within the national Council for a further wage reduction for dockers, except for London which claimed that such a move might prejudice its own negotiations with the union for a cut in locally determined piecework and overtime rates—which were of considerably less importance to Liverpool as the main timework port in the country. Although a reduction in the basic time rate was ultimately conceded after Liverpool had threatened that it might again have to consider its position on the Council, general support could not be secured in 1934 for resistance to the union's claim for a restoration of the wage cut during a period of reviving trade. Liverpool ship-owners were opposed to any increase in their working expenses at this time and once more exasperated with the Council considered withdrawal, since it was 'a useless body and served to make things easier for the leaders of the union'.[54] The pragmatic view prevailed, however, that secession would be justified only if it led to the breakup of that body, which seemed unlikely—otherwise Liverpool would still have to come into line with the council's decisions and therefore it would be preferable to remain and attempt to stiffen its resolve.

II

It has been shown that in negotiating arrangements for dock-workers although Liverpool employers favoured preservation of the related objectives of local autonomy and self-regulation these had to be considerably modified with the development of national negotiations and greater centralization of decision making in the changed environment of the interwar period. The employers were also at first unwilling to be linked in wider groupings outside the confines of the port transport industry and had soon resigned from the Confederation of Employers' Organizations since it was felt that ship-owners in a liner port had to be safeguarded from having their vessels detained owing to labour troubles or strikes at other centres. They were, however, persuaded by the Shipping Federation to rejoin in 1924 so as to ensure complete representation of ship-owners in the deliberations of that body.[55] In the same way, although the Liverpool Association usually followed national wage movements in the ship-repair trade, which involved some fifty firms on Merseyside, it had been reluctant to affiliate to the Shipbuilding Employers' Federation until 1926—after which agreement was reached between the Federation and non-federated districts for uniform, minimum wage rates in the trade to be applied on a national basis.[56] Prior to this the Association had eschewed formal links in order to maintain local autonomy when dealing with labour disputes and to avoid having to support any national lockout which might be called in that industry.[57]

A similar approach had been adopted also in relation to the wages of seamen. During the war Liverpool employers declined to serve on the new National Maritime Board set up by the government to deal with wages and the labour supply problem, that established for the first time national, standard rates of pay for the lower deck. The scheme had not arisen from within the industry, they disagreed with its terms of reference and if Liverpool employers voluntarily became parties to it then the actions of the Board would become 'morally binding' upon them.[58] When, however, the Board was reconstituted soon after the war as a joint industrial council for the shipping industry, without government representation, the Liverpool Association was then prepared to take part although it had believed it would be, '. . . a mistake to start with a national organization—such organization should be a natural growth from the local organizations; that port workers ought to be included as well as crews . . . and that any organization to be successful must by reason of its representative character be able to carry into effect its decisions'.[59]

The Shipping Federation and the Liverpool Association (Seafarers' Committee) would jointly constitute the employers' side of the

Maritime Board[60] and although the Federation would have majority representation consequent upon its greater tonnage, there would be little risk of Liverpool's being outvoted to its detriment because it was suggested that 'in practice moral weight would be the determining factor'.[61] This contention proved fairly accurate and the two bodies worked in close contact and (usually) harmonious accommodation with each other. There was less heterogeneity of employer interests—since all were ship-owners—and therefore less internal dissension than in the case of the NCPLE for dock-workers. Nevertheless, agreement on wage matters was not always immediately forthcoming on the employers' side of the Maritime Board as, in Liverpool's view, there was an 'extremist section' of Federation tramp-owners who would be quite prepared to press the union for very substantial wage reductions, even to the point not only of alienating public opinion but of breaking up the Board itself. These ship-owners felt that they could obtain crews at considerably less than the nationally negotiated rates, especially at some of the outports. Owners of passenger liners, however, were in a different position. They preferred greater certainty and stability since although a slight delay in securing a crew might be of no importance to a tramp-owner it was much more serious to a liner company with fixed sailing schedules.[62] The union claimed that in 1925 Liverpool owners had saved the day by insisting on only a £1 per month reduction in seamen's wages whereas tramp and cargo owners in the Bristol Channel and north-eastern ports favoured a reduction of at least £2. 10*s*., and possibly as high as £4.[63]

It is also a paradox that a further major constraint on the timing and extent of wage reductions in the shipping industry was a desire on the part of employers not to weaken the position of Havelock Wilson as president of the seamen's union (NSFU), or that union itself in relation to rival organizations such as the Amalgamated Marine Workers Union. The Liverpool Association was against employers pressing for a further national reduction in seafarers' wages in 1921 because the position of Wilson, who had been 'mainly instrumental in bringing about the previous reduction', was difficult *vis-à-vis* his own membership. Any precipitate action, by driving men into opposition unions, might make it a precarious one. Similarly, in 1932 it was felt that excessive downward wage pressure would be turned to advantage by competing unions, which would themselves be far less accommodating to employers. In contrast, seamen's union officials would go as far as they dared to meet the demands of ship-owners.[64]

The NSFU has been described as 'a company union working hand in glove with the employers'[65] and during the 1920s a priority for Wilson undoubtedly was that of maintaining harmony with the ship-owners in an industry which was difficult to organize, in order to preserve the closed shop. Crews on Shipping Federation vessels were obtained from a single source of supply jointly controlled by the Federation and the union, the practical effect of which was that a forecastle hand was not employed unless he was a member of the NSFU.[66] This arrangement enabled the union to keep up its numerical strength at a time when many unions experienced large membership losses because of the trade depression. Despite Wilson's complaint that certain ship-owners were not supporting his union as they claimed, the Liverpool employers' Association told Bevin that any proposed action by way of organizing a marine section of his union in competition with the NSFU would be regarded as 'unfriendly' and might lead employers not to ratify a new local agreement with the TGWU after the General Strike of 1926. When the union went ahead with recruitment after the expulsion of the seamen's union from the TUC in 1928 the Association retaliated by recommending local ship-owners not to retain the services of known members of the TGWU.[67]

There was, of course, also considerable rank and file opposition within the seamen's union to Wilson's close relations with the employers which in Liverpool culminated during the General Strike. The officials of the local branch had instructed their members not to sign articles, in defiance of the union executive—in Wilson's view the leaders of the strike were 'asses in lions' skins'. It was stated that the situation had been forced upon the branch because of the strong views of the local membership, in order to prevent the extinction of the union in Liverpool.[68]

III

Having delineated the growth of national negotiations for dockers and seamen, in terms of their effects on the port of Liverpool and especially within the context of employer reactions, it remains to consider the nature of purely local level bargaining—of specific rather than general applicability, on topics other than standard wage rates or hours of work—which took place during the inter-war period.

Although the most frequent business of the local Dock Labour Joint Committee was to resolve numerous, small disputes relating to the interpretation of agreements (appropriate payments for the discharge of particularly difficult or dirty cargoes, etc.) its major, and most difficult, negotiations during the early 1920s concerned the working arrangements and rules of the port. Because employers found that they were then unable to adjust labour costs via wage rate reductions to an extent sufficient to meet the competitive requirements of the port (constrained as they were by employer disunity and irresolution at national level), and faced with falling productivity on the docks,[69] they sought revisions in the secondary substantive norms relating to local working agreements. They wished to reduce what they regarded as exorbitant rates of pay for 'exceptional' working conditions and to amend the 'unduly burdensome' rules of shoregang work in docking and undocking ships, especially in relation to overtime and payment for weekend duties. The union's counter response to these overtures, however, was to put forward for employer approval a wider, consolidated set of 'port working rules' to standardize and codify across the port the methods of working cargo, numbers of men to a gang, as well as the weight and content of slings. All of these, the union claimed, were a formalization of existing custom based on union rules prevailing before the 1911 strike amongst those who worked under union conditions. Complaints had been made of employers' postwar 'driving' tactics on the Liverpool docks, overloading slings and increasing work effort by pruning the size of the gangs.[70]

The immediate reaction of employers was to reject the union rules which they estimated, if completely applied and literally interpreted, could increase cargo handling costs by up to fifty per cent. Also, the Mersey Docks and Harbour Board might refuse to sanction a further increase in master porterage rates to fall on the traders. Employers would stand by the White Book agreement which expressly stated that no union interference was to take place with the method of working cargo on ship or quay. The real questions concerned the authorship of the rules and employers' prerogative—they did not wish to be deprived of their discretionary power, in the interests of 'elasticity' of working arrangements, to regulate (and vary) the weight of slings and manning levels according to actual requirements at the various berths. Nevertheless, after a lengthy period of consideration together with detailed investigation of the cost implications of the rules, which were found to be less onerous than had been envisaged, it was decided to negotiate rather than attempt to enforce the White Book clause. The predominant considerations were the likelihood of recurrent sectional stoppages and the view that it would be preferable to establish jointly determined and administered rules by negotiation rather than have the union impose unilaterally, 'by pinpricks' and 'peaceful penetration', something less satisfactory.[71]

After two years of negotiations in which Bevin as well as the local union officials took part[72] the Port Working Rules for the Mersey were finally agreed at the end of 1925, despite the fact that the separate question of revised conditions for shoregang work which employers had raised was still pending—the union being accused of procrastinating. A settlement of this outstanding issue in favour of the employers was secured, however, in the following year as a result of the General Strike.

In fact, one significant consequence of the defeat of the unions during the 1926 General Strike was the opportunity presented to Liverpool port employers to partially rewrite existing, local agreements on their own terms after a prior warning to dockers that should they take part in the strike all agreements would lapse.[73] Liverpool had secured an earlier resumption of work than any other port but was alone in not having reached a definite understanding between employers and the union as to their future relations. Most employers felt that pre-strike agreements should, with certain modifications, be renewed although a minority saw it as a chance to revert to local autonomy and refuse to have anything further to do with national union officials.[74] But, above all, the unions' defeat had provided employers with a windfall gain such that they were then able to secure advantageous settlement of matters which had dragged on in negotiations for several years. The revised agreement stated that not only would the transport union refuse to countenance either sectoral or general stoppages without first exhausting the existing conciliation machinery, but also shoregang and port working rules were to be appropriately revised. Sunday work by the shoregang would now be remunerated on an hourly basis, the permissible weight of slings and number of cases for a 'fall' would be increased and latitude allowed to employers in interpreting the port working rules in specific cases.[75] The employers' actions in these respects were not so much vindictive—although certain of them such as the Mersey Docks and Harbour Board favoured more punitive retribution[76]—rather, with the unions in a weakened position a bargaining opportunity had presented itself which should not be passed over.

In the case of Liverpool cotton porters, however, the General Strike was instrumental in the formation of a sectional, breakaway union founded with employer support. The bulk of imported cotton passed through Liverpool on its way to the spinning mills, warehouse workers in the port being employed by cotton merchants and buying brokers organized for labour matters into the Cotton Porters Employers' Committee. Recognition had been secured by the Liverpool based National Warehouse and General Workers' Union (after amalgamation in 1921 the Distributive and Allied Workers' Union), whose largest section comprised cotton workers, towards the end of the war when the union met the employers in conference for the first time. Subsequently the union's working rules, consistent with prevailing customs in the trade, were tacitly accepted by the employers' committee to regularize standard and uniform conditions. A preference for employment of casual warehousemen taken on from the stands would also be given to union men as opposed to outsiders.[77] Nevertheless, 'permanent' (or regular) employees[78] had never favoured the union and others believed that their interests would be better served in a union devoted exclusively to cotton workers rather than by a general organization. Opposition to the General Strike by those porters who had remained 'loyal' throughout the nine days, together with employer dislike of the warehouse union's links with the wider labour movement, led to the formation of a separate Liverpool Cotton Workers' Union.

Although the first moves had come from the men themselves it was also, *de facto*, fostered unofficially by the employers[79] and was said to be the first, seceding union to be set up in response to disagreement with the calling of the General Strike.[80] Its intentions were to concentrate on benefit society provisions for members, to favour arbitration as against strikes in dispute settlement, and to 'create a closer feeling between men and their employers' by remaining unaffiliated to any other organizations. Officially the employers remained strictly neutral by negotiating with both unions, in view of the warehouse union's threats to involve dockers and carters in widespread blacking. Yet as the new organization grew by the late 1920s to represent a majority of cotton workers in the port and faced, as it then was, with financial difficulties consequent upon the severe depression affecting the trade employers agreed to contribute to its funds and to give first preference of employment to its members.[81]

A further question which had concerned the cotton trade was that of the irregularity and casual nature of much employment in an occupation subject to pronounced seasonal influences and widely regarded as a 'dumping ground for outsiders', especially during the winter months. In 1922 a registration scheme was devised by the employers' committee, with union approval, to confine employment to bona fide workers in the trade. Employers who wished to engage surplus men in addition to their regulars would apply to the warehousemen's union which would submit a list from which employers could choose.[82] In the event the scheme proved abortive as it was overwhelmingly rejected by a mass meeting of employers, whereupon all the existing committee resigned. Employers were not ready to accept the implications of the scheme, resolving to retain their freedom of action and employ whomever they pleased in the warehouses.

However, the major, national discussions on decasualization and regularization of employment for port workers during the inter-war years, in which Liverpool played a leading part, took place for dock labour. Liverpool had been the first port to attempt, in 1912, the organization of dock labour via a registration scheme and the introduction of tallies under joint employer/union control. The purpose was to enable the port to 'turn off the tap' of additional labour supplies in an overstocked labour market with fluctuating employer demands, thereby protecting the regular port workers from an influx of casuals pouring into the docks.[83] Yet during the next twenty years little overall improvement was forthcoming. The achieved reductions in the total number of Liverpool dockers were not proportionate to the decrease in demand for labour consequent not only upon depressed trade but also increased mechanization and technological improvements, thereby reducing the labour (and specialized skill) content in cargo handling at the quayside. These included pneumatic suckers in place of 'bucket' elevators for the discharge of grain, electric bogeys for transporting timber and meat, and electric piling machines for sugar cargoes.[84] The problem of the 'floating' labour surplus therefore remained.

In this respect one of the recommendations made by the earlier Shaw inquiry was for maintenance payments for unemployed dock labour, Liverpool employers being in principle in favour of such a scheme on the grounds that it would improve both the type of dock labour secured and the amount of work done. Also, if local employers did not take an independent initiative then it was felt that something unsatisfactory would be imposed on them.[85] A scheme devised by Alfred Booth was approved by the EAPL in 1921 whereby each employer would engage the maximum number of men who could be so employed on a weekly basis, any remaining balance to be provided each day from the casuals. Employers were then to contribute into a pool or fund out of which maintenance pay would be granted to registered casual men who applied unsuccessfully for work. The standard rate of pay would be reduced and the contribution to the pool would be higher in respect of casuals than for regular men. The intention was to make it more expensive for employers to take on men for a short, than for a longer, engagement and to avoid the inherent limitation of previously drafted schemes which would have worsened the position of the margin of casual men who could not be regularly employed. However, given that discussions were taking place at national level Liverpool employers were unable at that time to proceed with their own scheme without approval from the NCPLE.[86] Furthermore, with worsening trade conditions the employers' over-riding priority was to bring down wage rates. For several years even Bevin ceased to press the question of maintenance.

After the settlement of the 1924 dock strike, discussions on the extension of registration and maintenance schemes were again renewed and a number of government sponsored inquiries undertaken— but with little practical result. Only in 1937, at a time of trade revival and the rearmament boom, did employers at national level enter into serious negotiations by countering the union's claim for a substantial wage increase with an offer to make improved employment conditions and decasualization a first priority. In Liverpool, as elsewhere, local negotiations took place on the detailed viability of a scheme but met with opposition from certain employers. Some were against any proposals for a scheme run on a collective, port-wide basis which would take work away from efficient men (by reducing overtime, for example) and spread it among the less efficient so as to provide guaranteed employment for a large proportion of waterfront workers, in view of the resultant increased costs via reduced output. Others were not prepared to support any scheme unless *all* employers working in a cargo handling capacity at the docks were included in order to protect the competitive position of individual firms.[87] In fact, in view of the difficulties encountered it was not until 1941, at a time when a stable dock labour force was needed for the war effort, necessitating regular employment, that a (minimum) guaranteed weekly wage on a statutory basis was introduced by Bevin, by then Minister of Labour, at first for Merseyside and the Lancashire ports and later elsewhere.

IV

In this chapter we have surveyed the course of industrial relations over the inter-war years in the port transport industry as they affected Liverpool, with particular focus on employers' reactions at local level and their inter-action nationally. During the period a growth of national wage bargaining took place together with greater centralization of decision-making. To Liverpool employers this development led to an unwelcome compromise in the course of action to be pursued, and therefore less effective resistance to the union in dock wage negotiations—given that there was less homogeneity of interest among port employers at national level. Yet they found that it was by then no longer possible to revert to the *status quo ante* and again conclude purely local agreements on the primary substantive norms of wages and hours. The national employer grouping also proved to be a somewhat negative influence on local employer initiatives and innovations regarding secondary issues, such as decasualization. Thus, for the Liverpool employers' Association 'voluntarism', in the sense of being able to order its own labour relations affairs autonomously in the interests of spontaneity and flexibility with as little external interference as possible (not only from the state), was already being seriously eroded.

For the transport union the change to a 'national' policy for industry-wide wage determination also led to some difficulties with rank and file members on Merseyside especially in Birkenhead, typified by different work specialization and arrangements as well as a long-standing and separatist, independent labour tradition which persisted in the face of national unionism. In 1932, for instance, the Birkenhead men had been one of the few branches to vote against the national agreement for a wage reduction and new conditions of employment, culminating in unofficial strike action. The local communists were also actively agitating against the reduction which they referred to as 'Bevin's slave terms', but their leader who came to address the strikers was pulled off the platform by the dockers and rolled in the mud. Bevin complained of his Birkenhead members' lack of appreciation of constitutional procedures. He, himself, had to come up to Merseyside in order to secure their acceptance of agreements after employers had threatened to invoke the sanction of suspending the entire registration scheme in that section of the port and no longer confining employment to tally holders.[88]

In summary, we have detailed from the perspective of a major port aspects of the evolution and dynamic character of collective bargaining within an important formative period—adjusting, albeit uncertainly on the part of employers, to new conditions and changing circumstances, re-locating decision making, and thereby helping to determine the shape and direction of industrial relations in port transport for the next forty years.[89]

NOTES AND REFERENCES

* Acknowledgement is made to the Nuffield Foundation for the award of a research grant and to the Employers' Association of the Port of Liverpool, Transport and General Workers Union, Merseyside County Museums, and the Modern Records Centre at the University of Warwick for access to primary source material.

1. In contrast, only 37 per cent of Merseyside's insured workers were engaged in production, as against an average of 63 per cent for the whole country. See Board of Trade, *An Industrial Survey of Merseyside*, London (1932), pp. 13–14; and D. Caradog Jones (ed.), *The Social Survey of Merseyside*, vol. III, Liverpool (1934), p. 8.

2. A. Bullock, *The Life and Times of Ernest Bevin*, vol. I, London (1960), p. 248.

3. 'Foreword' in R. Charles, *The Development of Industrial Relations in Britain, 1911–1939*, London (1973), p. 16.

4. Charles' book—the major, national study for this period—deals with port transport only briefly as the author was not granted access to the official records of the industry. See also W. R. Garside, 'Management and Men: Aspects of British Industrial Relations in the Inter-War Period', in B. Supple (ed.), *Essays in British Business History*, Oxford (1977), pp. 244–67.

5. See R. Bean, 'Employers' Associations in the Port of Liverpool, 1890–1914', *International Review of Social History*, **xxi**, (1976), pp. 358–82. Booth admitted that he had not been involved in, and knew little of, port labour relations in Liverpool before 1911. A fresh approach was therefore made more feasible and Sexton in his autobiography, *Sir James Sexton, Agitator*, London (1936), p. 233, described Booth as 'a new type of employer'.

6. 'Procedural' norms in collective bargaining govern the attitudes of the

parties towards each other and the methods of establishment, application, and interpretation of agreements. 'Substantive' norms regulate the standards and adjustments of wages, hours, and conditions.

7. *Agreement Between Employers' Labour Association of the Port of Liverpool and the National Union of Dock Labourers and Riverside Workers* (22 April 1919). (Amendment to the White Book Agreement.)

8. Colonel H. Concannon of the White Star Line in Royden files, Cunard Papers (University of Liverpool library).

9. Evidence of Alfred Booth to *Court of Inquiry Concerning Transport Workers—Wages and Conditions of Dock Labour* (the Shaw Inquiry), Sessional Papers (1920), XXIV, p. 297; and *Journal of Commerce* (13 October 1917).

10. Employers' Association of the Port of Liverpool, 'Committee Minutes', (10 September 1918 and 24 April 1919). (Hereafter, EAPL Minutes).

11. Ibid. (25 April 1919).

12. Close contact was maintained with the Liverpool Cart and Motor Owners' Association since, although the EAPL did not negotiate wage-rates for carters or directly employ many of them, a carters' strike could dislocate the port. The practice was for the EAPL to put into effect wage adjustments as agreed between the master carters and the union locally.

13. Shaw Inquiry, p. 543.

14. TGWU, *Record*, **1** (August 1921). At that time the TGWU represented 95 per cent of the dock-workers in the country.

15. *Dockers Record* (February 1918) and TGWU, *Record*, **11** (March 1932). The Dock, Wharf, Riverside and General Labourers' Union (led by Tillett and Bevin) covered dockers in various ports in the south of the country, especially London and Bristol, whereas the National Union of Dock Labourers (led by Sexton) was predominant in Liverpool, Scotland, and Ireland. There were also a variety of other specialist unions and local clubs and societies to cater for the diffuse and splintered dock labour force.

16. 'Minutes of a Conference between a Sub-Committee of the National Council of Port Labour Employers and the National Transport Workers' Federation (27 November 1919). (Booth files, Cunard Papers).

17. EAPL Minutes (31 July 1919).

18. The NTWF had been founded in 1910 to bring together all unions with members in docks, road haulage and passenger transport to discuss mutual problems and co-ordinate action. In 1913 it included fifteen dockers' unions representing a total of about 100,000 dock workers. See R. Williams, *Report to the International Transport Workers' Federation Convention* (1913), British Library of Political and Economic Science, Webb Collection.

19. The Port of London had no comprehensive employers' labour organization similar to Liverpool at this time. EAPL Minutes (10 September 1918).

20. Booth files, Cunard Papers: A. Booth to Sir K. Anderson (1 June 1920).

21. Ibid., 'Memorandum' regarding the proposed National Council of Port Labour Employers', (10 October 1919). The Council was at first provisional but became a permanent body in the following year.

22. Ibid., A. Booth to Sir K. Anderson (1 June 1920).

23. G. D. H. Cole, *A Short History of the British Working-Class Movement, 1789–1947*, London (1948), p. 369.

24. EAPL Minutes (24 July 1919).

25. 'Resolution of a (national) Meeting of Port Employers' (2 December 1919) (Booth files, Cunard Papers).

26. Ibid., Sir J. Broodbank to C. Guthrie (11 April 1920). Off-setting the postponement of the incurring of higher wage costs there were, of course, the direct and indirect costs of time and resources devoted by the employers' side to preparing evidence for the hearing of the court, including legal fees of at least £10,000.

27. Ibid., Sir J. Broodbank to A. Booth (28 March 1920).

28. EAPL Minutes (9 February 1921).

29. Compare N. W. Chamberlain, 'Determinants of Collective Bargaining Structures' in A. R. Weber (ed.), *The Structure of Collective Bargaining*, New York (1961), p. 5.

30. See Shaw Inquiry, p. 345; and E. P. Cotter, *The Port of Liverpool*, US Department of Commerce, Washington (1929), p. 136.

31. A. Holt & Co. to Hill Dickinson (solicitors) (12 November 1913) (Royden files, Cunard Papers).

32. EAPL Minutes (26 August 1919).

33. Ibid.

34. H. J. Dyos, and D. H. Aldcroft, *British Transport*, Leicester (1971), p. 320.

35. G. C. Allen, F. E. Hyde, D. J. Morgan, and W. J Corlett, *The Import Trade of the Port of Liverpool*, Liverpool (1946), p. 22. The liner, as a regular means of communication between ports, was the recipient of consignments which were too small to justify the chartering of a special vessel, particularly goods of high value in relation to bulk.

36. Due to inability to sell British cotton goods abroad as a result of the fall in purchasing power of countries such as India: itself a consequence of the slump in the prices of their own primary products.

37. D. Caradog Jones, op. cit., p. 63.

38. W. Smith, *The Distribution of Population and the Location of Industry on Merseyside*, Liverpool (1942), p. 59.

39. In 1930, despite the general trade depression a record tonnage of shipping cleared the Port of London and, in consequence, employers there were not prepared to take any action which might even risk a stoppage at the docks. Sir Percy Bates to Walter Runciman (26 March 1931) (Bates files, Cunard Papers).

40. EAPL Minutes (18 April and 27, 30 June 1921).

41. Ibid. (24 February and 23 March 1922).

42. In effect Sir Joseph Broodbank was dismissed as chairman of the various employers' committees—no proposal being made for his re-election. Ibid. (23 March 1922).

43. Ibid. (13 July 1922).

44. Ibid. (2 April 1921) and *Journal of Commerce* (14 August 1922). By 1925 the percentage increase over pre-war rates of wages in the sheltered trades were generally above the average for industry as a whole. However, amongst the non-sheltered (exporting) type of industries dock labour had received increases substantially above the general average for industry as a whole, the disparity being most marked after 1920. See Committee on Industry and Trade, *Survey of Industrial Relations*, London (1926), pp. 85–6.

45. EAPL Minutes (11 September 1922).

46. *Journal of Commerce* (22 July 1922).

47. EAPL Minutes (30 June 1921).

48. Ibid. (29 January 1924).

49. See *Journal of Commerce* (14 February 1924); and TGWU, *Annual Report* (1925), p. 24.

50. EAPL Minutes (22 February 1924). The NCPLE felt that action behind the scenes via 'an eminent person . . . closely associated with shipowners and ship-builders' and the general manager of the Great Western Railway, both of whom had made proposals to the Prime Minister for a settlement, had cut the ground from under the feet of its negotiating committee.

51. Ibid. (24 April 1924). Although the Shipbuilding Employers' Federation deprecated the local settlement as being prejudicial to the national negotiations it was felt that any deferment would probably lead to an even higher wage advance.

52. Ibid. (12 June 1924). There was a London Shipowners' Dock Labour Committee and also a separate organization known as the 'London Ten' which was representative of *all* the employers of dock labour in London, including the Port of London Authority as the major employer.

53. Ibid. (14 November 1924 and 22 January 1925).

54. Ibid. (16 October 1935).

55. Ibid. (7 May 1924).

56. The Mersey Ship Repairers' Federation with whom the EAPL maintained close contact had become more convinced of the advantages of linking up in order to obtain the support of the Shipbuilding Employers' Federation.

57. During the 1922 national lockout in the engineering industry the private view of the chairman of Cunard was that the country was now suffering from a counter attack by 'Bolshie employers—all our trouble with Labour starts with the employers'. T. Royden to Captain P. Creed (15 March 1922), (Royden files, Cunard Papers).

58. EAPL Minutes (13 October 1917). For the reasons for Liverpool employers' objections to the Board see R. Bean, op. cit., p. 381.

59. EAPL Minutes (20 November 1918).

60. For the functions and organization of the National Maritime Board see Committee on Industry and Trade (1924–27), *Minutes of Evidence*, vol. II, pp. 1048–49. The Liverpool district negotiating 'panel' for sailors and firemen also had joint employer representation.

61. EAPL Minutes (18 November 1919).

62. Ibid. (19 January 1932).

63. Liverpool Trades Council, 'Minutes of Executive Committee' (2 October 1925). Statement by C. McVey, local official of the NSFU.

64. EAPL Minutes (14 October 1921 and 19 January 1932).

65. A. Bullock, op. cit., p. 411. In 1928 the seamen secured a favourable revision of overtime conditions on the basis of an undertaking from Wilson that his union would join with British shipowners at the forthcoming ILO conference in objecting to any international convention for the regulation of seamen's hours which went beyond the new British conditions. EAPL Minutes (16 March 1928).

66. In 1925 Liverpool shipowners agreed to give preference to Wilson's

union as against any rival organization when filling vacancies and to continue the existing joint supply system where applicable. Ibid. (4 December 1925).

67. Ibid. (22 June 1926 and 11 August 1929). The employers' recommendation was cancelled after the seamen's union later reaffiliated to the TUC and the TGWU had agreed not to enrol further seamen.

68. Statement by the Liverpool branch secretary, ibid. (5 May 1926), and J. H. Wilson to T. Royden (13 May 1926), (Royden files, Cunard Papers).

69. The Mersey Docks and Harbour Board estimated that the weight of goods passing through the docks had fallen from 248 tons per lineal yard of quays in 1914 to 192 tons by 1919. Explanations ranged from a slacking off of work effort on the part of dockers after the war to over-congestion on the quays reducing the speed of ship turn-round. See *Journal of Commerce* (18 July 1919).

70. TGWU *Record*, **2** (October 1922).

71. EAPL Minutes (8 November 1923 and 12 June 1924).

72. Bevin's view was that 'money, if lost, can be won back but it is not so easy to win back working conditions once they have been given up'. TGWU *Record,* **11** (March 1932). As well as being General Secretary of the TGWU he also acted as national secretary of its Dock Trade Group. See also Dock Labour Joint Committee, Minutes (28 August 1925).

73. For details of events in the port during the strike see D. E. Baines, and R. Bean, 'The General Strike on Merseyside, 1926' in J. R. Harris (ed.), *Liverpool and Merseyside*, London (1969), pp. 239–75.

74. EAPL Minutes (2 June 1926).

75. Ibid. (22 June 1926). 'Memorandum of Agreement Between Employers' Association of the Port of Liverpool and Transport and General Workers Union'.

76. For their own employees in the enclosed docks the MDHB proposed reducing the pay of men on their established list who had stuck to that of casuals, and employing them only from time to time as required.

77. 'Minutes of Cotton Porters Employers' Committee' (affiliated to the United Trades Association) (29 March 1919 and 18 November 1921), (Merseyside County Museums, Bryson collection).

78. 'Permanent' cotton porters were defined as those subject to one week's notice i.e. they had security of employment for at least a fortnight after engagement, for which they received a slightly lower rate of pay than the casuals.

79. 'Minutes of Cotton Porters Employers' Committee' (21 May 1926). Expenses for a hall in which to hold a meeting and the services of a clerk were financed by a leading employer.

80. *The Times* (15 June 1926).

81. 'Minutes of Cotton Porters Employers' Committee' (26 November 1928).

82. Ibid. (7 December 1922). The union would throw open its books for a six-week period to all those engaged in the cotton trade at a nominal entrance fee.

83. See R. Williams, *The First Year's Working of the Liverpool Docks Scheme*, London (1914).

84. F. G. Hanham, *Report of an Inquiry into Casual Labour in the*

Merseyside Area, Liverpool (1930) and EAPL Minutes (12 February 1934).

85. Ibid. (22 March and 21 December 1920). In 1926 Holts offered to transfer three-hundred Birkenhead dockers from the casual ranks to their permanent staff, but the union took exception on the grounds that decasualization was a matter for the entire port rather than for one employer.

86. Ibid. (4 November 1921). Nationally, certain of the employers strongly maintained the view that they had discharged their maintenance obligations under the Shaw recommendations by payments subsequently required when dockers were brought under the terms of the Unemployment Insurance Act in 1920.

87. Ibid. (26 May 1938). Further, the union was concerned about reductions in the size of the register and consequent withdrawal of tallies in order to make any scheme financially viable.

88. Ibid. (7 January 1932 and 11 September 1934); *Birkenhead News* (13 January 1932).

89. The Liverpool dockers' secession from national negotiations following the Scamp report in 1967 was said to be the start of the decline in importance of national negotiations on the docks. See R. Undy, 'The Devolution of Bargaining Levels and Responsibilities in the TGWU, 1965–75', *Industrial Relations Journal,* **9** (1978), p. 45.

6

The Port of Liverpool and the regional economy in the twentieth century[1]

P. J. M. STONEY

By 1900, the age of the sailing ship had been superseded by that of the steamship. Such a radical change in one of the most basic aspects of dock operations was to be by no means unique since the ensuing seventy years saw similar changes of a technological nature. It would have needed a clairvoyant in 1900 to foresee that by 1980 the entire system of docks to the south of the famous Liver Building would be lying fallow, virtually unused, and derelict. To the north of this famous landmark, the locus of one of the most impressive sky-lines in Western Europe, the twentieth century has seen a continuous run-down in the volume of bulk cargo-handling operations, both in terms of tonnage handled and number of dockers utilized to handle the goods. The Census of England and Wales of 1921 shows that in 1920 there were about 20,000 dockers in the employ of the Port Authority; in 1980, Mersey Docks and Harbour Company records show that there were no more than about 4000. Who could have foreseen in 1900 the technological revolution of containerized ships? At Seaforth, in the extreme north of the dock complex, there exists a modern multi-million pound terminal which is used exclusively for the handling of containers and the processing of their contents in the form of granaries and other modern facilities. The container revolution has affected Liverpool Port significantly. Other ports in Great Britain, like Felixstowe, have invested much money in modernization, in the form of container-handling facilities, including roll-on, roll-off (the so-called 'ro-ro') hardware. A developing outcome of this new technology has been a decline in the amount of non-fuel cargo handled by Liverpool compared with other ports (Kim Yee Chu, 1978),[2] see fig. 6.1.

Another very significant development during the present century has centred around the role of fuel oil. By the early 1960s, huge

Notes and references begin on page 145.

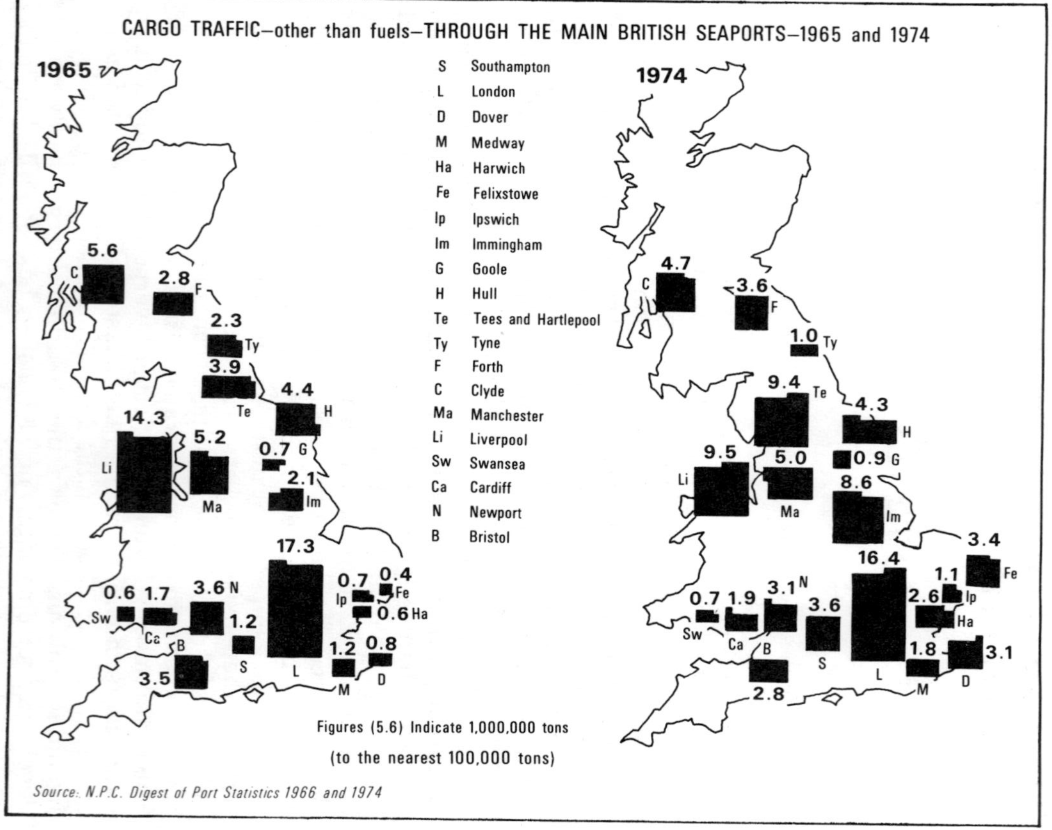
CARGO TRAFFIC—other than fuels—THROUGH THE MAIN BRITISH SEAPORTS—1965 and 1974
1965
5.6
C
2.8
F
2.3
Ty
3.9
Te
4.4
H
14.3
Li
5.2
Ma
0.7
G
2.1
Im
17.3
L
0.6
Sw
1.7
Ca
3.6
N
1.2
S
B
3.5
0.7
Ip
0.4
Fe
0.6
Ha
1.2
M
0.8
D
S Southampton
L London
D Dover
M Medway
Ha Harwich
Fe Felixstowe
Ip Ipswich
Im Immingham
G Goole
H Hull
Te Tees and Hartlepool
Ty Tyne
F Forth
C Clyde
Ma Manchester
Li Liverpool
Sw Swansea
Ca Cardiff
N Newport
B Bristol
1974
4.7
C
3.6
F
1.0
Ty
9.4
Te
4.3
H
9.5
Li
5.0
Ma
0.9
G
8.6
Im
3.4
Fe
16.4
L
1.1
Ip
2.6
Ha
0.7
Sw
1.9
Ca
3.1
N
3.6
S
B
2.8
1.8
M
3.1
D
Figures (5.6) Indicate 1,000,000 tons
(to the nearest 100,000 tons)
Source: N.P.C. Digest of Port Statistics 1966 and 1974

Fig. 6.1.

crude-oil and refined petroleum spirit discharging and loading facilities had been installed at Tranmere on the Birkenhead side of the river. Furthermore, it was less than twenty years after that refineries at Stanlow were given a source of supply overland via underground pipeline from an off-shore unloading terminal 90 miles away at a point off Anglesey Island.

Yet another change has been the almost total removal of passenger liners from the scene. As far as large liners in excess of 20,000 d.w.t. are concerned, the removal has been complete. Gone are the days of transatlantic journey by great liners into and out of the Mersey, although this did not happen until after the 1930s (Mountfield, 1965, p. 163).[3] Here are the days of the jumbo-jet and Concorde, which span the Atlantic, with just a few ferries crossing the river Mersey and the Irish Sea. Accompanying the permanent departure of the liners has been the re-location elsewhere in the United Kingdom of the headquarters of major shipping companies like the Cunard Line.

There has been a dramatic run-down in the amount of ship-building and ship-repairing along the river Mersey. Recent closures and/or shrinkage of companies in this business have decimated the number of active jobs and have left acres of docks with a ghost-like appearance. Added to this have been closures of commodity processing industries like sugar refining, which have left idle thousands of square feet of factory space.

I

An essential feature of the trade in passengers in the early 1900s was the uncertainty surrounding the amount of business to be undertaken. This was due in no small measure to the variability of the number of migrants, particularly those of Irish origin. Even in these years, long before the almost total extinction of passenger traffic, most of the dock space was occupied by cargo liners. Moreover, the exodus of passenger line companies was not unknown at the turn of the century. For example, in 1907 the White Star Line took its express passenger service to Southampton.

Both World Wars saw changes in passenger trade with consequences of decline. All shipping companies emerged from each war with smaller fleet sizes, and lost operational sea routes, because of intensified competition from Continental Europe, especially Germany, France, and Italy. But the final, killing blow to this trade was the arrival of the passenger airliner in ever-increasing numbers.

There have been many changes in the commodity throughput of Liverpool Port since 1900. Many authors have written on various aspects of this (for example Mountfield, op. cit.; Hyde, 1971).[3, 4] In the early 1900s, Liverpool was handling approximately 36 per cent of the export trade of Britain and about 25 per cent of her imports by volume (TNRUK, 1939).[5] In the early 1900s, the main imported commodities handled by the Port were very different from those handled fifty years previously and similar changes occurred during the twentieth century. In volume terms in 1913, cotton imports account for between 70 and 80 per cent of all cotton imported into the United Kingdom and this represented, in volume terms, 30 per cent of all imports into Liverpool. Both sugar and tobacco amounted to 2·4 per cent of total Liverpool imports by value. Newer imported goods included the grain products of wheat, barley, oats and maize which accounted for 8 per cent. Other newer imports were rubber, which accounted for 5·2 per cent, copper for 2·4 per cent, tin for 1·5 per cent, and hides and rice for 2·5 per cent. By 1913, timber had maintained its traditional percentage of 2·5 of all imports into Liverpool (TNRUK, 1913).[6]

The export trade was dominated by cotton yarn, piece-goods and other cotton textiles. In value terms, these amounted to about half of the total exports in 1901, and to about 40 per cent in 1913. This overall decline hides an increase in the volume of piece-goods which arose because of the increased demand in India. Over the same decade, there was an increase in handling of heavy engineering and railway equipment to India, South America, Mexico and South Africa from 16·7 per cent to 20·4 per cent of total exports. Another increase occurred in wool and woollen and worsted piece-goods which stood at about 6 per cent of total Liverpool exports by value in 1913 (TNRUK, 1913).[6] An additional feature of the early 1900s was the increased importance of re-export trade, mainly to Europe, which amounted to about ten per cent of total exports by 1913.

The years after 1913 to the present day were characterized with one overriding facet, namely decline in almost all aspects of port operations. The inter-war years to 1939 were characterized by a great deal of uncertainty throughout the trade routes to Brazil, India, the West Indies, Central America, the Persian Gulf, and the Far East. This uncertainty was caused largely by the years of the Great Depression throughout the world in the late 1920s and in the 1930s. As a consequence, there was a problem of keeping ships running to capacity and a concomitant, significant decline in the cargoes of traditional products such as cotton, sugar, wood, rubber, and tobacco in the import trade and of cotton piece-goods and certain classes of engineering equipment, heavy capital goods, and coal in the export trade. This, in turn, involved shipping companies in a search for new markets and new commodities, and, as a consequence, the creation of new voyage patterns. For example, one of the staple cargoes of the Booth Line prior to 1913 had been Brazilian rubber, whose export had accounted for 47 per cent of the entire world supply. In the late 1920s, there was competition from Malaya and

Table 6.1. *1939 Share (by value) of Liverpool in the trade of the United Kingdom, imports and exports.*

Commodity	*Percentage*
Imports	
Dairy products	5·9
Grain and flour	19·1
Meat	15·8
Fruit	23·4
Oilseeds	25·0
Timber	12·5
Wool	24·6
Woollens and worsted	1·2
Petroleum	6·2
Cotton and linters	67·5
Rubber	28·9
Tobacco	30·2
Sugar	35·0
Tin	89·1
Exports	
Cotton yarns and piece-goods	52·2
Woollens and worsted	33·0
Iron and steel manufactures	29·0
Non-ferrous metal and manufactures	40·5
Machinery	37·9
Vehicles (including ships, locomotives, and aircraft)	26·4

Source: Trade and Navigation Returns of the United Kingdom, 1919–39.

the Netherlands East Indies to such an extent that the share of Brazil fell to 5 per cent and, in the late 1930s, to about 2 per cent. Similarly, the general economic depression affected adversely the staple of cotton with the Harrison Line from the Gulf. Moreover, because of political unrest in India, of action by the Indian Congress in boycotting British goods and through the devaluation of the rupee, the export of cotton piece-goods to India, which was very important to Harrisons, fell to 20 per cent of the 1913 volume. Apart from rubber, the export trade of Brazil remained relatively prosperous until 1930, the main goods being cotton, sugar, and coffee and it was these three commodities virtually alone which showed increasing trade trends until 1939. There was also a significant trade in palm oil in bulk and fourteen ships were built for the United Africa Company for this trade in the 1930s. The overall tonnage of ships using the Port, however, fell away considerably up to 1939. (Hyde, op. cit., chapter 8).[4]

By 1939, the share (by value) of Liverpool in the total trade of the United Kingdom can be seen in table 6.1. The figures for imports conceal the fact that the share of total imports of Liverpool in the

United Kingdom fell from 36 per cent in 1913 to only a little over 20 per cent in 1939. Within particular commodity groups, there was a fairly high range of fluctuation. Raw cotton, on which much of the prosperity of Liverpool had been based, held a prime place until 1926. By 1931, however, her share had dropped to 67·7 per cent and never rose above 70 per cent during the 1930s. Indian and Egyptian cottons had gone increasingly to Manchester via the Manchester ship canal, whose history has been written about in other texts (for example in Redford, 1956).[7] By contrast, wool went against the general trend. Rubber maintained a constant share, mainly because Liverpool did not gain as much as other ports from the growth in rubber supply from the Far East. There was an increasing trend in the import of oilseeds and vegetable oils because of the prosperity of the crushing plants and soap-making factories at Port Sunlight, whose history has been documented well elsewhere, (for example, Wilson, 1954, Bibby & Bibby, 1978).[8, 9] In the oldest imported goods of tobacco and sugar, there was some fluctuation with an overall increase occurring in the latter. The importance of wheat fell, whereas that of tin remained constant at a very high level.

With regard to exports, by 1939 Liverpool remained the leading port in the country at about 30 per cent by value of exports, notwithstanding a sharp drop in the total amount exported by value. In addition, there were significant changes in market patterns during this period. With some particular commodity groups, a fall in export demand reverberated upon imports. For example, the very marked fall in the export of cotton piece-goods led to a fall in the demand for imported raw cotton. The wider implications of this marked fall can be illustrated from statistics of the composition of the total export trade. From 1922 to 1924, 55 per cent of the exports of Liverpool consisted of cotton yarn, piece-goods and other textiles; 24 per cent was metals, cutlery, road vehicles, machinery, and hardware and only 3 per cent chemicals. The main markets were the USA, Canada, the West Indies, West Africa, and the Far East. By 1934 to 1938, the composition had changed radically to 36 per cent cotton yarns, piece goods, and other textiles, 37 per cent metals, cutlery, machinery, and hardware, and 6 per cent chemicals. This trend of change proved to be long-term since, by 1950, cotton yarns, piece-goods and other textiles had fallen to 28 per cent, whereas metals *et al.* had risen to 45 per cent. Furthermore, by 1950, the main export markets from Liverpool, in decreasing order of importance, were the Far East with 22 per cent, South and Central America and the West Indies with 16·4 per cent, Australia, New Zealand and Fiji with 11·8 per cent, Europe with 10·5 per cent, West and South Africa with 6·9 per cent and the USA, Canada, and Newfoundland with 5·8 per cent (Hyde, op. cit., chapter 9).[4]

The Second World War saw a disruption of the above trends which manifested itself mainly in the transfer of much of the trade passing through London to Liverpool. Recovery of normal trade was slow after the War, due in no small measure to the physical devastation of dock systems. By 1950, the share of Liverpool in the total trade of the country was 28·5 per cent, compared with that of London of 31·5 per cent (TNRUK, 1950).[10] In export trade, Liverpool had regained first place from London, the respective shares being 32·9 and 30·8 per cent for London. During the 1950s there was a constantly changing pattern in the composition of trade and in the markets served. In 1950, Liverpool imported, by value, one-fifth of all grain and flour consumed in the country, one-fifth of imported meat supplies, nearly one-fifth of all fruit and vegetables, two-fifths of all oilseeds and vegetable oils, 15 per cent of timber, nearly two-fifths of raw wool and about three-fifths of raw cotton. The share of the major export goods was two-thirds of all cotton piece-goods, about two-fifths of woollens and worsteds, one-third of the exports of iron and steel, nearly 30 per cent of non-ferrous metals, 38 per cent of machinery, and 27 per cent of vehicles of all descriptions (TNRUK, 1960).[11]

By 1955, imports into Liverpool of raw cotton were down one-third on 1950, but the share of wool increased over the same period. Grain remained steady at about 40 per cent of total imports into the country during the 1950s. One of the main changes, however, was connected with the demand for fuel oil and petroleum which increased in importance following the construction of the oil port and refinery at Stanlow on the Wirral peninsula side of the Mersey.

With regard to Liverpool exports, by the mid-1950s, the share of all United Kingdom exports and re-exports fell to 27 per cent. The composition of exports in 1950, as a percentage of total exports out of Liverpool, by value, included cotton piece-goods down to 28, and metals, vehicles, and machinery up to 45. By 1960, still further changes had occurred: cotton yarns and piece-goods accounted for only 8 per cent of the total value, whilst machinery of all sorts, road vehicles, cutlery, hardware, and metal manufacturers had increased to 53 per cent. In addition, a large expansion to 15 per cent occurred in chemicals, salt, coal, soap, and vegetable oil. The geographical division for these products was about 50 per cent to Africa and the Americas, about 25 per cent to India and the Far East, 14 per cent to Australia and New Zealand, and 11 per cent to Europe, (Hyde, op. cit., chapter 10).[4]

By 1970, a main change in commodity flows was in fuel oil and petroleum. About one-sixth of all tonnage entering the dock system was oil-tanker tonnage, (MDHC, 1971).[12] Furthermore, the virtual closure of the Shotton Steelworks in 1979 led to a loss of iron-ore traffic.

The main change in the 1960s and 1970s, in the physical appear-

Table 6.2. *Trade through Liverpool, 1972–9 (000 tonnes).*

	1972	*1973*	*1974*	*1975*	*1976*	*1977*	*1978*	*1979*
Foreign imports								
Food, drink, tobacco	2,625	2,245	2,205	2,555	3,128	3,309	2,999	3,025
Raw materials	3,011	3,293	3,002	2,342	2,505	2,553	2,465	2,489
Manufactured articles	793	834	713	771	769	791	641	647
Petroleum in bulk	12,434	13,669	15,604	12,097	10,584	5,749	3,575	1,354
Foreign exports								
Food, drink, tobacco	224	136	153	280	253	193	317	278
Raw materials	114	74	48	40	31	37	268	236
Manufactured articles	2,669	2,634	2,531	2,640	2,443	2,335	1,850	1,627
Coastwise imports								
Petroleum in bulk	2,466	1,736	1,214	756	665	2,596	2,812	4,786
Livestock	94	77	97	98	42	65	63	24
Other	469	439	310	329	268	268	259	188
Coastwise exports								
Petroleum in bulk	115	145	42	63	10	—	1	9
Other	560	613	465	479	571	575	669	712
Total imports and exports	25,574	25,895	26,384	22,450	21,269	18,471	15,919	15,375

Source: Mersey Docks and Harbour Company, *Annual Reports and Accounts.*

Table 6.3. *Goods traffic: overseas trading areas of the Port of Liverpool in 1975 (000 tonnes).*

NEAR AND SHORT SEA TRADING AREAS

Near sea

	Irish Republic	*West Germany*	*Netherlands*	*Belgium Luxembourg*	*France*	*Total*
Imports	437	78	346	120	271	1251
Exports	294	5	22	9	2	331

Short sea

	Scandinavia Baltic	*Iberia Mediterranean*	*Total*	*Total*
Imports	456	687	1143	2394
Exports	53	349	402	734

DEEP SEA TRADING AREAS

	West Africa	*South Africa*	*East Africa*	*India/ Persian Gulf*	*Far East*
Imports	2869	265	398	8858	264
Exports	378	194	181	458	137

	Australasia	*North America*	*South America*	*Central America/ West Indies*	*Total*
Imports	260	1599	1581	297	16,392
Exports	282	225	311	216	2,381

Total of all trading areas = 21,902

Source: National Ports Council

ance of Liverpool Port was the obsolescence, which had started to show earlier, of the entire dock system to the south of the Liver Building. The 1980s are likely to see a continuation of the trend increases in those kinds of exports and imports which need more containerization (a new terminal costing in excess of £70 million over the last ten years was opened recently at Seaforth) and towards a decline in the utilization of traditional bulk cargo-handling techniques. The overall level of traffic, by both value and volume of both exports and imports, shows a constantly declining trend during the late 1960s and the 1970s. The obvious inference is that Liverpool has lost trade to other ports both in Britain and Europe, and particularly to the latter as a result of entry into the European Economic Community by the United Kingdom in the early 1970s. Trade has been affected severely and a decline in many trades can be seen in table 6.2.

Most of Liverpool's trade is with Africa, India, the Middle East, and the Americas, the EEC countries accounting for only 1·5 million tonnes out of a total of 21·9 million tonnes in 1975, as can be seen from table 6.3.

There is no doubt that Liverpool will continue to serve the country in particular bulk trades or that she will have a container role to fulfil (about 6 per cent of total traffic is containerized at Liverpool, a much smaller percentage than at some other ports such as Southampton), but it is a highly moot question as to whether or not the recent shrinkage in dock operations, including a decimation of the dock labour force, will continue.

II

From the types of commodities mentioned in the previous section, it is obvious that the port has served and will continue to serve as a transportation intermediary for many industries located in the Merseyside hinterland, which is defined as the Merseyside Metropolitan County in fig. 6.2; more than one such definition is possible (Gentleman, 1970).[13] For example, Pilkingtons had an established shipping office at Drury Buildings, Liverpool in the late nineteenth century (Barker, 1977, p. 168);[14] coal was shipped through Liverpool from the St Helens area (Hyde, 1953);[15] sugar refiners, seed crushers, and soap manufacturers have for long used the port; and more recent users have included the three motor vehicle assembly plants established in Merseyside in the early 1960s.

It is not obvious, however, as to the extent of the importance of the port, both for the hinterland economy and for the rest of Great Britain. There is a problem in defining what is meant by importance in this context and of deciding on an indicator of the importance. One indicator of quantitative importance is employment. This has been used in previous studies of the importance of industrial sectors of activity (for example by Port of Seattle Commission, 1971; Brownrigg, 1980).[16, 17]

The hypothesis to be tested is a variant of the classical statistical null hypothesis that if the Port of Liverpool were to cease operations, the consequence would be no effect on the employment level of Merseyside, with the exception of the dock labour employed directly in the port complex.

In order to assess the port's employment impact, firms related to the port in some way were examined. The analysis concentrates on the Mersey Docks and Harbour Company. Data were obtained from the Mersey Docks and Harbour Company, (MDHC), HM Customs and Excise, the Health and Safety Executive, and over 1600 firms both on Merseyside and throughout the UK. These firms can be classified into one or more major types of activity:

1. *The port and its related activities* wholly dependent upon it i.e. the MDHC, stevedoring, towing, rigging and pilotage firms. Figures on numbers of local seamen and employment in shipping companies, freight forwarders, and shipping agents were collected also.

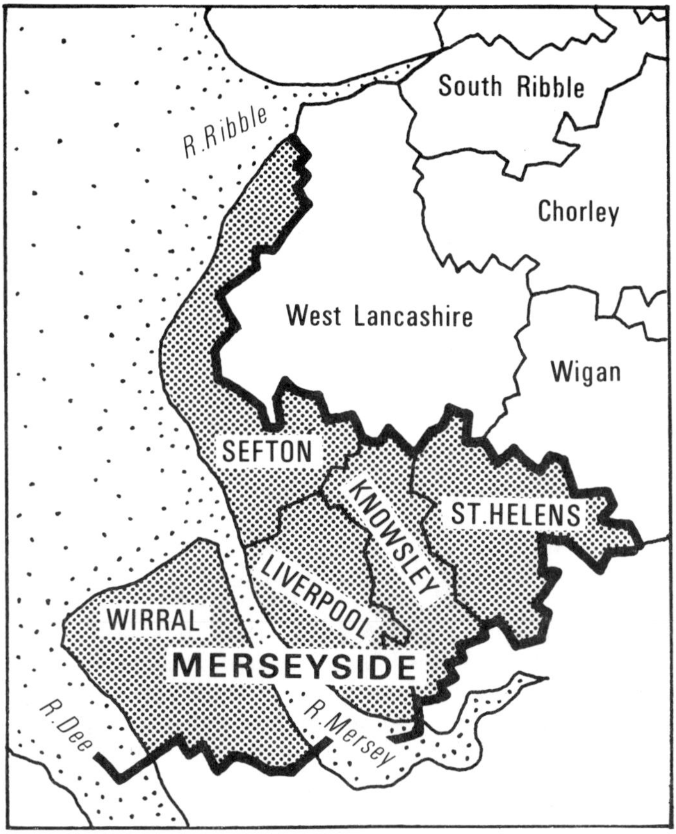

Fig. 6.2. Merseyside Metropolitan County.

2. *The port's suppliers.* Out of the MDHC's 2035 suppliers in 1976, it was found, by examining invoices of firms supplying the company with some goods or service, that the top 10 per cent accounted for 90 per cent of the total MDHC expenditure. Within this top 10 per cent it was decided to visit firms which were paid over £25,000 (since less than this figure was considered to represent less than one employee). This produced a list of 100 firms.

3. *The port's shippers.* From the MDHC's list of over 1000 major shippers, the Customs and Excise indicated the most important in terms of value. 105 firms were identified.

4. *The dockland zone firms.* This category includes 1400 firms in a narrow band adjacent to the docks defined by the Health and Safety Executive as 'Dockland' (fig. 6.4). Linkage with the port might or might not be present. The employment here is included very largely in categories 1, 2, and 3 above; but it is thought to be of sufficient intrinsic interest to be allotted a separate research category.

Table 6.4. *Registered dock labour in Liverpool (including Garston).*

Year (Jan–Jan)	*No. of registered dockers*		*Major events*
1966	13,551	1972	South Docks closed. MDHC became the largest stevedoring Co.
1967	12,845		
1968	12,186		
1969	11,885		
1970	11,197	1973	Seaforth officially opened. Jones-Aldington severance scheme.
1971	10,678		
1972	10,081		
1973	7,629		
1974	7,752	1977	Anglesey Oil Terminal opened.
1975	7,124		
1976	6,847		
1977	6,400		
1978	6,432		
1979	6,168		

Source: National Dock Labour Board.

Data were collected on (i) number of employees, (ii) the annual wage and salary bill, and (iii) turnover of each firm, together with (iv) the amount of business done with the MDHC, (v) the amount of trade shipped through the Port of Liverpool and (vi) the amount of trade shipped through all UK ports (in value terms). Once the percentage of a firm's turnover done with the port had been found, the corresponding percentage of employment and wage and salary bill could be calculated, in order to arrive at a measure of employment dependency. When considering the shippers using the MDHC, after the percentage of trade passing through Liverpool as a percentage of trade passing through all UK ports had been calculated, the corresponding percentage of employment, wage and salary bill turnover was calculated again. Upper and lower limits of this category of dependent employment are presented. Using these figures, the extent of linkages between the Port and other industries on Merseyside, the amount of dock-related activity in the area immediately adjacent to the docks and the actual number of jobs associated with the port could be estimated in terms of employment numbers.

The Mersey Docks and Harbour Company and related organizations wholly dependent upon the port were considered as providing direct employment. Firms in this category include the MDHC, the stevedoring, rigging, towage, and pilotage firms which had a workforce totalling about 10,800 in 1976 viz: 8529 engaged by the MDHC—dockers and white-collar staff (the number of dockers has fallen dramatically in recent years, as shown in table 6.4), 2000 working for private stevedoring firms, 200 employed in towing, the remainder in pilotage and rigging.

In addition there are an estimated 4500 employed in shipping and forwarding agents and shipping companies and an estimated 3000 seamen sailing in and out of the Mersey whose homes are on Merseyside. All these categories were estimated from Minimum List Heading, (MLH) data, (CSO, 1974).[18] The extent to which these two latter categories can be considered to be dependent upon the port, is indeterminate. However, assuming total dependency (i.e. 100 per cent redundancy without a port) the total number of people totally dependent upon the port in this section adds up to 18,300 (=10,800+4500+3000).

Whilst the MDHC had 2035 supplying firms, it was decided to concentrate on the top 10 per cent (which accounted for 90 per cent of the MDHC's expenditure to these 2035 firms) and to reduce the sample further by selecting and analysing firms within the top 10 per cent which received more than £25,000 (since less than this amount was assumed to represent less than one employee). 100 firms in the top 10 per cent fulfilled this criterion and it was found that their business with the MDHC represented on average less than 3 per cent of their individual total turnover in 1976. The total amount of business in all 100 firms accounted for by the MDHC amounted to £4·7m.

By relating the percentage of turnover accounted for by the Dock Co. to each firm's employment (on a plant basis) and annual wage and salary bill and totalling the results, a total number of 523 people in these firms can be said to be dependent upon the port and a total of £1·89m. can be said to have been generated in 1976 in wage and salary bills through the port. For example, if 2 per cent of a firm's total business is accounted for by the MDHC then 2 per cent of that firm's employment is considered to be dependent upon the port and 2 per cent of the annual wage and salary bill is considered to be generated by the port. Such calculations assume that average and marginal levels of turnover per employee are equal. This assumption is clearly oversimplified since marginal turnover gained by adding one employee (or lost by reducing the workforce by one employee) may be less or more than the average over a wide range of employment levels. Equally, the relationship would vary according to specific decisions or events. Thus the figure of 523 is likely to be an over-estimate, and it is more likely that small parts of several thousand jobs rather than 523 whole ones would be lost if the port were to (for example) close completely. On the other hand, the suppliers of other stevedoring firms and non-sampled suppliers are not taken into account. However, it seems unlikely that this would have much effect on the final number of dependent jobs.

The top 10 per cent of supplying firms receiving more than £25,000 was located mainly on Merseyside, see table 6.5. Originally an invoice address rather than the actual manufacturing address

Table 6.5. *Employment, wages and salaries, and turnover of the top 10 per cent of supplying firms receiving over £25,000 dependent upon the port in 1976.*

	Employment			*Wage and salary bill (£m.)*			*Turnover (£m.)*		
Sector of activity	*M'side*	*NW*	*UK*	*M'side*	*NW*	*UK*	*M'side*	*NW*	*UK*
Coal and petroleum	0	1	1	0·000	0·005	0·005	0·00	0·06	0·06
Metal manufacture	1	1	1	0·007	0·007	0·007	0·04	0·04	0·04
Mechanical engineering	1	6	21	0·000	0·017	0·076	0·00	0·11	0·45
Electrical engineering	1	1	4	0·005	0·005	0·045	0·03	0·03	0·17
S.B. & marine engineering	1	1	1	0·004	0·004	0·004	0·05	0·05	0·05
Other metal goods	0	0	0	0·000	0·000	0·000	0·00	0·00	0·03
Textiles	4	4	5	0·014	0·014	0·017	0·04	0·04	0·16
Other manufacturing	0	4	4	0·000	0·012	0·012	0·00	0·06	0·06
Construction	131	131	133	0·411	0·411	0·531	1·23	1·23	1·73
Transport & commun.	67	67	67	0·259	0·259	0·259	0·65	0·65	0·65
Distributive trades	0	0	1	0·000	0·003	0·007	0·07	0·17	0·20
Miscellaneous services	276	277	285	0·895	0·898	0·928	1·02	1·05	1·12
Total	481	493	523	1·595	1·635	1·891	3·13	3·49	4·72

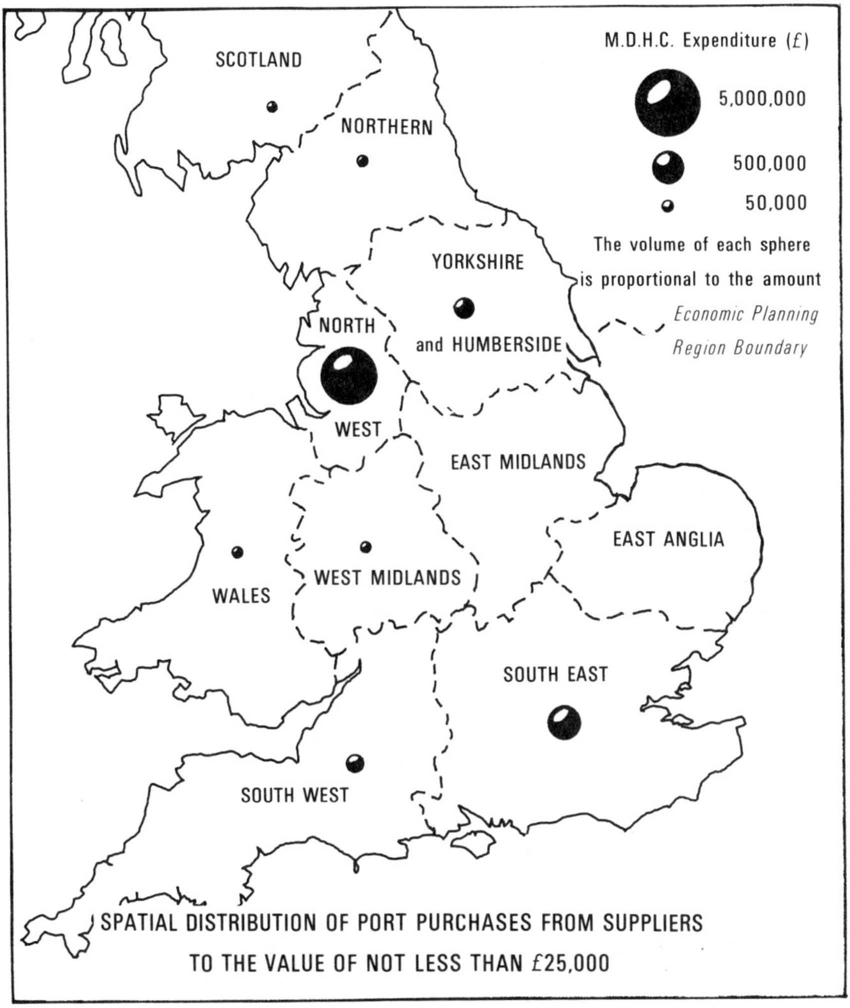

Fig. 6.3.

was often given. However, this was corrected so that figures which appear relate to the source of production/service rather than to an accounting office. Of the total £4·72m received by them, 74 per cent (or £3·5m) was accounted for by firms in the North-West, and 66 per cent of the £4·72m by firms in Merseyside alone. The next largest receiving region was the South-East with 16·9 per cent (or £0·8m), see fig. 6.3. The firms fall into four major sectors of activity. Construction ranks first (accounting for 36·7 per cent of the MDHC's for UK expenditure to these firms), followed by services (23·7 per cent), transport and communications (13·8 per cent) and mechanical engineering (9·5 per cent). In terms of dependent employment as defined above, services account for the most jobs (54 per cent) followed by construction (25 per cent) and transport and communications (12·8 per cent).

Thus in 1976 about 18,823 full-time equivalent jobs in UK and 18,781 full-time equivalent jobs on Merseyside were totally dependent upon the port.

18,823 is arrived at by adding 523—the percentage of jobs dependent upon the port in the supplying firms—to the 18,300 employed in the docks themselves. Similarly, 18,781 = the 481 dependent jobs in Merseyside + the 18,300 in the docks. No estimate has been made of the impact of suppliers to private stevedoring companies other than the MDHC. Although these firms employed 2000, the impact of their suppliers is likely to be extremely small since they are concerned solely with loading/unloading and storing cargoes. Unlike the MDHC they are not concerned with the maintenance of wharfs, locks, etc.

228,576 people were employed in the sample of 105 firms (the top 10 per cent by value) using the Port of Liverpool for their shipments. However, by relating shipments through Liverpool to total shipments and applying this percentage to employment, it can be said that 70,897 people (i.e. 31 per cent of the 228,576) are dependent upon the Port of Liverpool in this category. Since this employment estimate has been calculated from a sample of firms whose business accounted for only one quarter of total trade through Liverpool, it needs to be revised upwards in order to achieve formal logicality in the procedure. The precise amount of upward revision would be known only from a 100 per cent sample of these firms, but it is possible to gain an approximate upward revision by multiplying the estimate by four, a procedure which assumes linearity. Doing this gives a revised estimate of 283,588. Similarly all other figures given below and calculated on the basis of the sample of 105 firms, should be regarded as under-estimates. In view, however, of the nebulousness of this whole estimation procedure, for example with regard to the indeterminateness of the switchability of trade through other ports to the same markets, it seems a sufficiently refined course to leave most of the estimates as they stand on the basis of the sample of 105 firms, having made this caveat. In any event, the research team was advised by HM Customs and Excise that the 105 firms comprised the largest in terms of employers of people. In terms of wage and salary bill and turnover the figures for this sample after relating Liverpool shipments as a percentage of total shipments to them are £310·7m and £2091m respectively. The North-West is the most important region (accounting for 49 per cent of jobs) followed by the West Midlands (with 12 per cent) and Yorkshire-Humberside (with 10 per cent). Of the North-West's total, Merseyside accounts

Table 6.6. *Upper limit of employment, wages and salaries, and turnover of sampled shipping firms related to the port in 1976—calculated by relating Liverpool shipments as a percentage of total shipments to employment, wage and salary, and turnover figures.*

	Employment			*Wage & salary bill (£m.)*			*Turnover (£m.)*		
Sector of activity	*M'side*	*NW*	*UK*	*M'side*	*NW*	*UK*	*M'side*	*NW*	*UK*
Food, drink, tobacco	7,143	10,151	13,257	29·8	41·8	54·2	151·8	282·3	440·7
Chemical and allied	4,735	8,250	12,058	20·6	32·6	72·1	142·9	680·5	786·6
Metal manufacture	—	6	7,175	—	0·2	28·7	—	1·0	90·6
Mechanical engineering	9	2,134	9,292	0·1	6·3	33·0	20·0	45·8	200·4
Instrument engineering	—	—	275	—	—	1·1	—	—	2·5
Electrical engineering	3,241	6,920	14,811	13·1	28·4	59·2	44·4	109·1	219·8
S.B. & marine engineering	—	—	1,200	—	—	5·2	—	—	47·1
Vehicles	—	249	249	—	1·0	1·0	—	5·0	5·0
Other metal goods	—	—	2,192	—	—	8·8	—	—	24·6
Textiles	—	499	1,755	—	1·5	6·5	—	18·0	35·2
Bricks, pottery, glass	6,427	6,427	7,627	31·9	31·9	36·7	156·2	156·2	168·2
Timber, furniture	68	108	108	0·3	0·5	0·5	5·4	6·0	6·0
Other manufacturing	—	69	369	—	0·3	1·5	—	3·4	6·4
Transport and commun.	—	120	520	—	0·5	2·1	—	0·8	4·4
Distributive trades	9	9	9	0·1	0·1	0·1	53·5	53·5	53·5
Total	21,632	34,942	70,897	95·9	145·1	310·7	574·2	1,361·6	2,091·0

Table 6.7. *Lower limit of employment, wages and salaries, and turnover of sampled shipping firms related to the port in 1976—calculated by relating Liverpool shipments as a percentage of total turnover to employment, wage and salary, and turnover figures.*

	Employment			*Wage & Salary bill (£m.)*			*Turnover (£m.)*		
Sector of activity	*M'side*	*NW*	*UK*	*M'side*	*NW*	*UK*	*M'side*	*NW*	*UK*
Food, drink, tobacco	3,697	4,310	4,759	14·91	17·39	19·18	91·0	117·5	146·4
Chemical and allied	2,118	4,996	7,223	9·63	25·58	35·14	69·2	632·7	694·2
Metal manufacture	0	1	3,226	0	0	12·9	0	0·1	39·3
Mechanical engineering	6	1,012	4,521	0·02	3·36	13·8	12·0	24·95	97·3
Instrument engineering	0	0	220	0	0	0·88	0	0	2·0
Electrical engineering	1,324	1,833	4,011	9·8	11·88	20·42	44·0	52·3	80·2
S.B. & marine engineering	0	0	612	0	0	2·66	0	0	24·0
Vehicles	0	51	51	0	0·2	0·2	0	1·0	1·0
Other metal goods	0	0	708	0	0	2·83	0	0	7·3
Textiles	0	425	686	0	1·3	2·23	0	15·4	18·2
Bricks, pottery, glass	1,062	1,062	1,122	5·27	5·27	5·51	26·0	26·0	26·6
Timber, furniture	64	65	65	0·26	0·27	0·27	5·0	5·02	5·02
Other manufacturing	1	1	101	0	0	0·4	0·06	0·06	1·06
Transport and commun.	0	75	119	0	0·31	0·49	0·0	0·5	0·9
Distributive trades	8	8	8	0·03	0·03	0·03	53·0	53·0	53·0
Total	8,280	13,839	27,432	39·92	65·59	116·94	300·26	928·53	1,196·48

for 21,632 jobs (or 62 per cent of the North-West's total). This figure might have been much higher if the Merseyside County Council boundary to the south had not been used, since many of the firms were located just outside Merseyside in places like Warrington and Ellesmere Port. Most of the other firms not accounted for by Merseyside were in the Manchester region. Four sectors of activity predominate, viz: chemicals; food; drink and tobacco; mechanical engineering, and electrical engineering, see table 6.6.

The figures given in table 6.6 are certainly over-estimates since, for example, 30 per cent of a firm's trade through Liverpool might be only 10 per cent of its total trade (international + domestic) and therefore to take 10 per cent of the total employment figure in this instance could be more appropriate. This procedure ignores, for the time being, problems associated with the switchability of trade from Liverpool to other ports. In order to calculate a possible minimum level of employment, wage and salary bill, and turnover figures that can be related to the port, the percentages of turnover accounted for by Liverpool shipments in each firm were calculated. These were then applied to each firm's employment, wage and salary bill, and turnover figures. The results are shown in table 6.7. It would seem likely that the actual port-related employment, wages and salary bill, and turnover figures lie somewhere between these two limits (shown in tables 6.6 and 6.7). Thus the number of full-time equivalent jobs dependent upon the port in the shipper category in the UK in the 105 firms sampled, will be between 27,432 and 70,897 and in Merseyside between 8280 and 21,632. Similarly, the related wage and salary bill figure will be between £116·94m and £301·7m in the UK and between £39·92m and £95·9m in Merseyside, and the turnover figure between £1196·48m and £2091m in the UK and between £300·26m and £574·2m in Merseyside. According to the logical procedure, all these figures are under-estimates, as noted above, according to the extent that employment exists in those firms excluded from the sample of 105. In reality, the size of the under-estimate could be either less or more than a factor of 4. It is unlikely to be as much as 4.

Few firms were wholly dependent upon the port for their shipments in 1976. It was found that only nine of the original 105 firms in the sample put more than 80 per cent of their foreign and coastwise shipments through Liverpool. These nine accounted for a total of 5972 employees, a wage and salary bill of £24·2m and £93·8m in turnover, £62·7m in total shipments through all UK ports and £58·06m in Liverpool shipments. Seven of the nine firms were located in the North-West.

In the 'Dockland Zone', fig. 6.4, cross-hatched area, it was found that only 52 firms out of a total of 1400 with 12,884 employees out of a total of 51,892 shipped through the port. When the appropriate

Table 6.8. *Upper limit of employment, wages and salaries, and turnover of port-related dockland firms in 1976, calculated by relating Liverpool shipments/supplies as a percentage of total shipments/supplies to employment, wage and salary bill, and turnover.*

Sector of activity	*Employment*	*Wage & salary bill £m.*	*Turnover £m.*
Food, drink, tobacco	5,108	19·94	248·66
Coal and petroleum products	100	0·40	56·0
Chemicals and allied industries	343	1·40	10·09
Metal manufacture	200	0·40	2·1
Mechanical engineering	476	1·40	7·34
Electrical engineering	57	0·22	1·74
Textiles	145	0·47	3·52
Leather and fur	175	0·75	10·0
Bricks, pottery, glass, cement	83	0·30	5·25
Timber, furniture	72	0·22	2·43
Paper, printing, publishing	210	0·84	3·16
Distributive trades	15	0·06	1·34
Miscellaneous services	415	0·80	4·68
Total	7,399	27·20	356·31

Table 6.9. *Upper limit of employment, wages and salaries, and turnover of port-related dockland firms not already occurring in the shippers section, calculated by relating Liverpool shipments/supplies as a percentage of total shipments/supplies to employment, wage and salary bill, and turnover.*

Sector of activity	*Employment*	*Wage & salary bill £m.*	*Turnover £m.*
Food, drink, tobacco	222	0·12	59·86
Chemical and allied industries	82	0·37	3·07
Metal manufacture	200	0·40	2·10
Mechanical engineering	120	0·32	3·20
Electrical engineering	6	0·02	0·05
Textiles	145	0·47	3·52
Leather and fur	175	0·75	10·00
Bricks, pottery, glass, cement	83	0·30	5·25
Timber, furniture	72	0·22	2·43
Paper, printing, publishing	210	0·84	3·16
Distributive trades	15	0·06	1·34
Miscellaneous services	415	0·80	4·68
Total	1,745	4·67	98·66

Fig. 6.4. The Dockland Zone.

percentages of Liverpool shipments × 100 divided by total shipments were applied to these firms, only 7399 full-time job equivalents (57 per cent of the original figure) can be said to be related to the port. Food, drink, and tobacco is the most important sector accounting for 69 per cent of the total of 7399 employees followed by mechanical engineering with 6·4 per cent and miscellaneous services with 5·6 per cent (table 6.8). £356·3m (65 per cent of the total turnover figure of the dockland firms) in turnover is related to the port, which suggests that firms with high revenues are linked with the port the most, as compared with those with lower revenues but similar employment. Food, drink, and tobacco is again the dominant sector in terms of turnover followed by coal and petroleum products.

However, once double counting in table 6.8 has been eliminated (since the figures duplicate some firms in the 105 shippers) the picture which emerges is shown in table 6.9. If a lower limit figure is produced (by relating Liverpool shipments supplies as a percentage of total turnover to employment, wage and salary bill, and turnover figures), the impact figure is reduced further. A total of 4351 people, a wage and salary bill of £17·17m and turnover of £184·65m can be said to be related to the port and when double counting is eliminated by extracting firms already included in the shippers section, the figures are reduced to 689 jobs, £2·32m in wage and salary bills, and £61·87m in turnover, see tables 6.10 and 6.11. Thus the gross number of full-time equivalent jobs related to/dependent upon the

Table 6.10. *Lower limit of employment, wages and salaries, and turnover of port-related dockland firms in 1976, calculated by relating Liverpool shipments/supplies as a percentage of total turnover to employment, wage and salary bill, and turnover.*

Sector of activity	*Employment*	*Wage & salary bill £m.*	*Turnover £m.*
Food, drink, tobacco	3,512	14·67	130·35
Coal and petroleum products	72	0·29	40·00
Chemical and allied industries	126	0·54	2·44
Metal manufacture	10	0·02	0·10
Mechanical engineering	194	0·51	1·81
Electrical engineering	31	0·12	1·01
Textiles	48	0·16	1·24
Leather and fur	18	0·08	1·00
Bricks, pottery, glass, cement	16	0·07	0·58
Timber, furniture	39	0·11	1·43
Paper, printing, publishing	16	0·06	0·23
Distributive trades	10	0·05	1·01
Miscellaneous services	259	0·49	3·45
Total	4,351	17·17	184·65

Table 6.11. *Lower limit of employment, wages and salaries and turnover of port-related dockland firms not already occurring in the shippers section, calculated by relating Liverpool shipments/supplies as a percentage of total turnover to employment, wage and salary bill, and turnover.*

Sector of activity	*Employment*	*Wage & salary bill £m.*	*Turnover £m.*
Food, drink, tobacco	165	0·85	49·85
Coal and petroleum	0	0·00	0·00
Chemical and allied industries	72	0·33	1·04
Metal manufacture	10	0·02	0·10
Mechanical engineering	35	0·10	0·93
Electrical engineering	1	0·00	1·01
Textiles	48	0·16	1·24
Leather and fur	18	0·08	1·00
Bricks, pottery, glass, cement	16	0·07	0·58
Timber, furniture	39	0·11	1·43
Paper, printing, publishing	16	0·06	0·23
Distributive trades	10	0·05	1·01
Miscellaneous services	259	0·49	3·45
Total	689	2·32	61·87

port in the dockland zone is between 4351 and 7399. Similarly, the wage and salary bill figure is between £17·17m and £27·2m and the turnover figure between £184·65m and £356·31m. These figures will be reduced very marginally once double-counting is eradicated with the suppliers of the port in the dockland zone; this exercise was not done in view of the small degree by which the figures would be affected.

The total impact figures both for UK and for Merseyside by the

Table 6.12. *Total UK impact of the Port of Liverpool in 1976.*

Categories of activity	*Employment*	*Wage & salary bill £m.*	*Turnover £m.*
The port & related	18,300	55·2	98·2
Sample of 100 supplying firms	523	1·9	4·7
Sample of 105 shippers	27,432*–70,897**	116·9*–310·7**	1,196·5*–2,091**
Dockland firms excluding those occurring in shippers section	689*–1,745**	2·32*–4·67**	61·87*–98·66**
Total	46,944*–91,465**	176·32*–372·47**	1,361·27*–2,292·56**

* Lower limit ** Upper limit

Table 6.13. *Total Merseyside impact of the Port of Liverpool in 1976.*

Categories of activity	*Employment*	*Wage & salary bill £m.*	*Turnover £m.*
The port & related	18,300	55·2	98·2
Sample of 100 supplying firms	481	1·6	3·1
Sample of 105 shippers	8,280*–21,632**	39·9*–95·9**	300·3*–574·2**
Dockland firms excluding those occurring in shippers section	689*–1,745**	2·32*–4·67**	61·87*–98·66**
Total	27,750*–42,158**	99·02*–157·37**	463·47*–774·16**

* Lower limit ** Upper limit

Port of Liverpool are summarized in tables 6.12 and 6.13 below. The amount of linkage with local industry supplying the port is not big. The figures might even be over-estimates in view of the assumption of total dependence of seamen and freight forwarders. The numbers are certainly much smaller than was believed by many people. They would be smaller still if it was possible to be sure that any redundancies from a port closure would be swallowed up by alternative jobs elsewhere in either Merseyside or the rest of the United Kingdom. It should not be forgotten, however, that the possible over-estimation has to be balanced against any under-estimation arising from the using of the sample of 105 shipping firms; such under-estimation is, by the inherently soft nature of the entire estimation procedure, conjectural.

One can conclude that the employment impact is likely to be of the order of tens of thousands rather than either of hundreds of thousands or of millions. It might be of the order of only a few thousand.

III

The major deficiencies in the compilation of the results can be summarized under three types, viz:

1. The estimates are, in the main, for one year only but a brief follow-up sample survey for 1979 confirmed our results.

2. The Marshallian ceteris paribus assumption (Marshall, 1920)[19] of not surveying consumption demand multipliers.

3. No account has been taken, in an explicit measurement sense, of the possibility either of the extent to which shippers in total could utilize other ports (it would appear to be fairly high) or of the amount of business suppliers of the port could find as a replacement

in the event of a total port closure. In addition, account has not been taken of the extent to which shippers would need to utilize other port outlets: we have not estimated the extent of vitalness of the trade handled by Liverpool on behalf of shippers. Answers to these questions are impossible to obtain with a complete certainty of accuracy. One can not even rely on the opinions of businessmen involved in this regard for it is difficult, if not impossible, to differentiate wishful thinking from objective realism in the mind of a third party.

The figures, therefore, are in these senses gross figures and not net ones. Net figures, for example, would embody estimates of the likely amounts of alternative employment available if the port were to close. Any such alternatives would diminish the gross figures. We believe the figures to be of high quality in accuracy terms, although we have learnt that an absolutely precisely accurate quantification of this kind of impact is impossible.

NOTES AND REFERENCES

1. The author gratefully acknowledges the generous support for the project of the Leverhulme Trust; the work of Dr Joanna Kinsey, Senior Research Assistant; and comments on previous drafts by Professor A. M. Bourn of the University of Southampton.

2. Kim Yee Chu: *The growth and decline of the major British seaports, an analysis of the pattern of non-fuel cargo traffic 1965–1974,* unpublished Ph.D. thesis. Department of Geography, London School of Economics & Political Science (July 1978).

3. S. Mountfield, *Western Gateway, A History of the Mersey Docks and Harbour Board,* Liverpool University Press (1965).

4. F. E. Hyde, *Liverpool and the Mersey, The Development of a Port, 1700–1970,* David and Charles (1971).

5. TNRUK, *Trade and Navigation Returns for the United Kingdom, 1919–1939,* Board of Trade.

6. Ibid., 1900–1913.

7. A. Redford (ed.), *Manchester Merchants and Foreign Trade,* vol. 2, 1850–1939, Manchester University Press (1956).

8. C. Wilson, *The History of Unilever* (3 volumes), Cassell (1954).

9. J. B. Bibby and C. L. Bibby, *A History of J. Bibby and Sons Ltd., Liverpool,* J. Bibby and Sons Ltd. (1978).

10. TNRUK Ibid., 1949–1950.

11. Ibid., 1950–1960.

12. MDHC (Mersey Docks and Harbour Company), *Annual Reports and Accounts.*

13. H. Gentleman, 'Merseyside: problems of definition in R. Lawton and C. M. Cunningham (eds.), *Merseyside, Social and Economic Studies,* Longman (1970).

14. T. C. Barker, *The Glassmakers, Pilkington: 1826–1976,* Weidenfeld and Nicolson (1977).

15. F. E. Hyde, 'The growth of Liverpool's trade, 1700–1950', in W. Smith (ed.), *Merseyside: A Scientific Survey*, Liverpool University Press (1953).

16. Port of Seattle Commission, *Seattle maritime commerce and its impact on the economy of King County* (1971).

17. M. Brownrigg, 'Industrial contraction and the regional multiplier effect: an application in Scotland', *Town Planning Review,* **51** (2) (April 1980).

18. Central Statistical Office, *Standard Industrial Classification, Revised 1968, Alphabetical List of Industries*, HMSO (1974).

19. Alfred Marshall, *Principles of Economics*, 8th ed., Macmillan, London (1920).

7

Regional policies and industrial development on Merseyside 1930–60

P. H. LISTER

The manifest industrial and economic problems of Merseyside, and the syndrome of social stresses and malaise associated with them, have nourished a formidable volume of academic research and publication and a plethora of current affairs reporting. The region's problems have received recognition and priority at all levels of government from its constituent District and County Councils to national and, indeed, supranational governments. Subsumed within this region of relative disadvantage at the international and national scales of comparison occur localities of more acute deprivation relative to Merseyside as a whole. In consequence the region generally has experienced the commitment of public resources directed towards its economic and social rehabilitation over a prolonged period of assisted area status (fig. 7.1), from a variety of public authorities and in a great diversity of guises. Currently these range from development aids under the regional and social policies of the European Community and under programmes for regional and sectoral assistance of national government, to the vigorous promotional activity of its local authorities. Additional public resources are focused on sub-regional points of stress, particularly within the inner urban areas. These derive from nationally-funded programmes, including urban aid and inner city schemes, recent policy innovations designed to further economic change and development within specific depressed localities, including the creation in 1981 of an Urban Development Corporation acting within the region's docklands and 'Enterprise Zones' established within Liverpool at Speke. Similarly, the dominating philosophy underlying the Merseyside Structure Plan of 1979 is the regeneration of the inner core of the conurbation and of certain peripheral overspill estates experiencing employment and other problems.[1]

Notes and references begin on page 184.

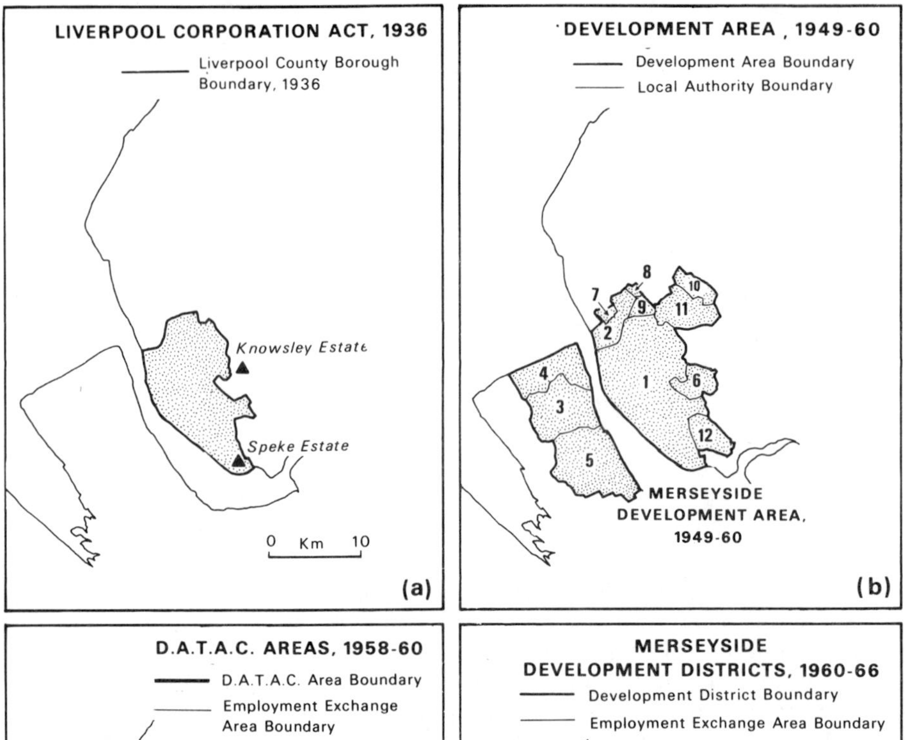

Fig. 7.1. Merseyside assisted area 1936–66.

1(b) The Development Area comprised Liverpool (1), Bootle (2), Birkenhead (3), Wallasey (4) C.B.s; Bebington M.B. (5); Huyton-with Roby (6), Litherland (7) U.D.s; Netherton (8), Aintree (9), Simonswood (10), Kirkby (11), Halewood (12) parishes.

1(c)–(e) Assisted areas comprised Employment Exchange Areas of Crosby (1), Regent Road (2), Bootle (3), Walton (4), Kirkby (5), Old Swan (6), Leece Street (7), Garston (8), Prescot (9), Widnes (10), Wallasey (11), Birkenhead (12), Bebington (13), Neston (14), Ellesmere Port (15), Runcorn (16), Hoylake (17), St Helens (18).

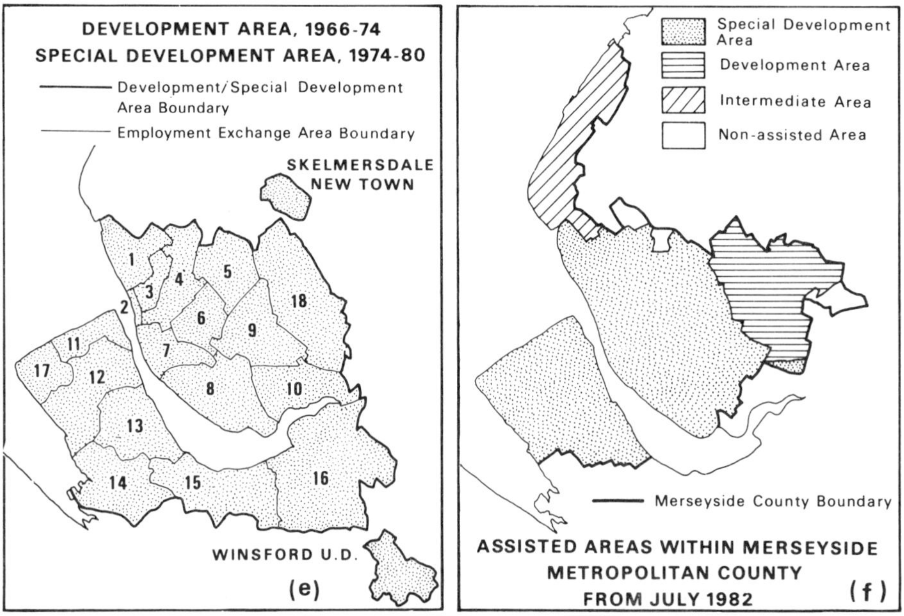

Fig. 7.1 Merseyside assisted area, 1974–82.

1(e) Winsford U.D. downgraded to Intermediate Area status from 2 May 1972; St Helens to Development Area status from 1 August 1980. Peripheral regions received Intermediate Area status from 22 March 1972.

1(f) St Helens downgraded to Development Area status from 1 August 1980. Excepting the Southport coastal region, the Intermediate Areas became non-assisted from 1 August 1982.

This deep public involvement in resolving the problems of Merseyside, including their sub-regional dimension, reflects a serious and persistent disparity between the regional and national levels of welfare which may be measured in varying permutations of social, economic, and environmental indicators. A comprehensive review of the area's problems, and of policy responses to them, is beyond the scope of this chapter. We concentrate, therefore, upon the efforts of national and local government to strengthen the region's economic base. These efforts, dating from the 1930s, have emphasized the attraction to the region of migrant manufacturing industry and, more recently, the encouragement of office employment and of the viability and growth of existing regional enterprises. In consequence the economic geography and employment structure of Merseyside have been transformed although contributory factors have included long-run processes of economic adaptation arising from the commercial decisions and competitiveness of regional industries, the effects of technological change, and the increasing capitalization of productive and distributive methods in the postwar years. These changes have markedly increased the contribution of manufacturing industry to the regional product and employment and changed its intra-regional locational pattern and sectoral composition. This chapter will examine the contribution of public policies to industrial development and spatial change within Merseyside.

An inherent difficulty in such evaluations is the identification of policy-induced changes within the regional economic system given the contemporaneous influence of other processes affecting regional economic adaptation. Approaches commonly adopted to regional policy evaluation include inferential, aggregative modelling and micro-scale behavioural surveys. The former includes the analysis of interregional industrial movement by multiple regression or gravity modelling, incorporating some index of governmental regional policy among the independent variables.[2] Shift-share techniques have compared actual changes in regional employment or patterns of manufacturing movements with those predicted in the assumed absence of regional policy, policy effects being inferred from deviations between actual and predicted outcomes.[3] Micro-scale surveys have identified the influence of regional policies upon the locational choices of business managements, focussing on the characteristics and behaviour of these 'client groups';[4] or have used Factory Inspectorate data on the 'birth', growth, and 'death' of industrial enterprises to infer policy relationships.[5] In all such work an understanding is essential of the nature and efficacy of the instruments and mechanisms of governmental regional intervention, this determining the appropriate index of policy for adoption within statistical modelling and providing the necessary policy framework for an interpretation of both inferential and behavioural analyses. This understanding is constrained by the confidentiality surrounding public policy administration in Britain, constraints exacerbated in regional policy studies by the permissive rather than mandatory nature of enabling legislation, with responsible government departments exercising considerable discretion in the interpretation and implementation of policy. Similarly, regional policy has often relied upon administrative rather than formal, legislative instruments of regional intervention, the nature of policy varying markedly with changes in administrative practices. A comprehension of the role of public policies in the development of Merseyside must therefore depend upon access to the administrative records of government departments and this has confined our review to the period for which documentary materials are either on public record or have been made available on a discretionary basis by departments.[6] We focus, therefore, on the application within Merseyside of regional development programmes from their inter-war inception to end-March 1960, this date concluding a coherent phase of postwar regional legislation with the repeal of the Distribution of Industry

Acts (p. 17). A more direct knowledge of policy administration and processes will facilitate analysis of governmental roles in regional economic change and complement the largely inferential outcomes of aggregative and micro-scale investigations.

I

Merseyside between the wars, in common with other regions, experienced serious economic decline evidenced by falling levels of employment, high unemployment relativities in a period of heavy and rising unemployment nationally, and population losses by net outward migration. Its problems were largely attributable to the decline of port activities and of associated industries, these being the '. . . dominating factor in any consideration of Merseyside's economic structure'[7] creating a gross imbalance between regional and national economies which narrowed its range of occupational types and skills, and largely determined its employment prospects. Compared with Great Britain as a whole, Merseyside was marked by an over-representation of service-sector industries, these contributing 64·9 per cent of the total insured workforce in 1931 compared with 47·9 per cent nationally, the transport and distributive trades alone representing 43·4 per cent relative to 23·5 per cent nationally. Manufacturing and primary industries were markedly under-represented with the latter virtually absent and manufacturing—primarily port-oriented—contributing but 35·1 per cent to regional employment as compared with 52·1 per cent nationally. Reflecting this functional relationship to the port, manufacturing industry was predominantly located on or adjacent to the dock estates within the Port of Liverpool—i.e. docks in Liverpool, Bootle, Birkenhead, and Wallasey—and extending inland along the Leeds-Liverpool canal. Smaller concentrations of manufacturing occurred at the railway dock at Garston, on Unilever's private dock estate at Bromborough, and along the Manchester Ship Canal at Eastham and Ellesmere Port.[8]

Given this narrow economic base Merseyside was vulnerable both to the structural decline of its service and manufacturing specialisms and to downturns in international trade with their exaggerated effects upon port employment. Both occurred between the wars and total insured employment declined between 1924 and 1930 by 31 per cent in river and dock services, 30 per cent in transport, storage, commerce and finance, 27 per cent in ship-building and repairing and by 26 per cent on the railways—industries '. . . upon which the past prosperity of Merseyside was largely built'.[9] Despite compensatory growth in other sectors, the region's unemployed totalled 109,000 in 1932, a rate of 28 per cent relative to 22 per cent nationally, and was reflected in heavy net outmigration.

The response of national governments to Merseyside's inter-war difficulties was muted, attention being focussed on the greater problems of Wales, Scotland, and northern England. Equally, government had yet to accept responsibility for regional balance or full employment and regional policies were hesitant, exploratory and minimalist. Responses to regional economic disparities in the 1920s were varied: limited public works programmes; measures aimed at the revival of trade and industry; the better organization of charitable work and Poor Law relief; and attempts to encourage the voluntary mobility of labour from the depressed areas, furthered in 1928 with the introduction of the Ministry of Labour's Industrial Transference Scheme. Unfilled vacancies in areas of labour shortage were offered preferentially to the unemployed in specified Employment Exchange Areas and financial assistance given towards transfer costs, with separate schemes for adults and juveniles. No Exchange Area on Merseyside was scheduled under the adult scheme although juvenile transference was promoted by scheduling Birkenhead, Wallasey, New Ferry, Ellesmere Port, Liverpool, Bootle, and Waterloo.[10] This differential treatment doubtless reflected the region's low levels of adult unemployment relative to other depressed areas and its greater problems of juvenile employment arising from high rates of natural increase. However, the scheme contributed nothing to industrial redevelopment and but marginally to the relief of unemployment, given nationwide labour surpluses. The unskilled nature of Merseyside's juvenile unemployed handicapped their mobility and the scheme was inherently unpopular.

By 1931 mounting unemployment prompted Board of Trade inquiries into industrial conditions in the depressed areas, including Merseyside,[11] but these produced little response and Merseyside was omitted from further regional surveys by the Ministry of Labour in 1934,[12] a crucial omission given the subsequent scheduling of the reviewed areas under the Special Areas (Development and Improvement) Act, 1934. This Act originated positive measures of regional assistance by central government and focused aid upon four 'Special Areas' in North-East England, West Cumberland, Central Scotland and South Wales and Monmouthshire. Excluded from such regional aid, Merseyside industry was also ineligible for financial assistance provided from 1936 by the Special Areas Reconstruction Association and by the Nuffield Trust for the Special Areas, for rebates of rent, income tax, and rates under the Special Areas (Amendment) Act, 1937, or for remission of national defence contributions under the Finance Act, 1937. Assistance under the original Act of 1934 included the construction of industrial estates within the Special Areas to provide factory premises for rental to migrant industries, the most significant instrument then devised for regional industrial promotion.

These measures placed Merseyside at an increasing disadvantage from the mid-1930s in the attraction of mobile investment capital and the regional policies of national governments exacerbated rather than ameliorated the region's problems. Although the amending Act of 1937 had envisaged the provision of state aid in regions other than the original Special Areas by empowering the Ministry of Labour to create 'certified areas' where 'site companies' with partial Treasury-funding could provide factory premises as inducements for migrant industry and, although a Company for Lancashire was under discussion by March 1938,[13] no action arose. Temporary relief was given by public works schemes including the construction of the Mersey road tunnel from Liverpool to Birkenhead in 1934 and of the East Lancashire Road between Liverpool and Manchester, and by the electrification of the Liverpool–West Kirby railway in 1938.

Government contracts preferences, introduced in 1934, also benefited areas suffering from '. . . the effects of severe and prolonged industrial depression'[14] and firms were preferentially awarded supply contracts given competitive tenders on price, quality, and delivery. Areas eligible were initially those scheduled under the Industrial Transference Schemes although, from early 1936, preference was given in the Special Areas and in 'Depressed Areas' defined as Employment Exchange Areas where adult male unemployment averaged at least 25 per cent over the preceding 12 months, including Birkenhead, Wallasey, and the 'Liverpool Area'.[15] This scheme may have been marginally beneficial for such industries as ship-building and marine engineering, given rearmament expenditure, although the stringent conditions on competitive tendering make it unlikely to have been a prominent locational attraction for mobile industry.

The most significant contribution of national government to industrial development on Merseyside prior to 1945 was the location within the region of wartime productive capacity, reflecting the region's relative strategic safety, manpower resources and, from March 1936, a governmental commitment to locate new manufacturing plant in the Special Areas and Depressed Areas—production, strategic, and economic constraints permitting. This led to considerable manufacturing growth on Merseyside after 1937 with engineering Royal Ordnance Factories (ROFs) in production at Hooton in 1940 and at Fazakerley and Ellesmere Port in 1941 and a shell-filling ROF opening at Kirkby in 1940.[16] Other new factories were operated on an agency basis by private companies, including pre-war 'shadow' factories, while existing enterprises were extended with public finance. Such manufacturing growth included Rootes' shadow airframe plant at Speke, Napier's aircraft engine works at Gilmoss, and factories at Bromborough and Ellesmere Port. The exigencies of war not only reinvigorated the traditional port and ship-building industries of Merseyside but also stimulated a governmental involvement in the area's industrial economy greater than had derived from the specifically regional policies of the period. This injected new manufacturing capacity which, with the exception of the Fazakerley ROF, was to be allocated entirely for post-war civilian production by February 1947. Liverpool Corporation acquired the 1·5m sq. ft. Kirkby ROF for conversion to an industrial estate, Dunlop was allocated the Speke airframe factory (1·3m. sq. ft.) for the manufacture of rubber tyres and footwear, and the Gilmoss factory (1·3m. sq. ft.) was allocated jointly to Napier and English Electric for aero-engine production and electrical engineering respectively. Other government factories were to be utilized for the manufacture of machinery and marine engines at Bromborough, galvanized metal products at Ellesmere Port and construction activities at Hooton. Some 4·5m. sq. ft. of floorspace was added to Merseyside's manufacturing capacity, markedly expanding its contribution to the regional economy. The intra-regional location of this new capacity was peripheral to the conurbation area being concentrated east from Liverpool along the East Lancashire Road (Fazakerley–Gilmoss–Kirkby), at Speke in south Liverpool and on Wirral. War-related growth helped initiate trends towards urban and industrial decentralization which were to be markedly reinforced after 1945.

Given the limited response from central governments to Merseyside's inter-war difficulties the most concerted attempt to restructure its economy came from local government, primarily from Liverpool Corporation under powers conveyed by the Liverpool Corporation Act 1936. This measure primarily concerned the authority's finances, street improvements, public health, water, electricity, sewerage and drainage schemes, and land within St James' cemetery! However, powers were also given for land development and industrial promotion which were then unprecedented for a British local authority and gave the city a unique role in the sponsorship of regional economic adaptation.

The Act must be seen in the light of Liverpool's inter-war physical planning problems and strategies, particularly its acute housing needs. Slum clearance within the central urban area and *in situ* rebuilding at lesser housing densities, albeit often in flatted units, had generated great demands for additional building land to rehouse displaced families, a precursor of serious postwar problems. Extensive suburban council estates were built within the borough boundary, particularly at Norris Green, Walton-Clubmoor, Highfield-Knotty Ash, Fazakerley, and Dovecot. These were generally '. . . cottage schemes . . . built to what is now regarded as very low densities and hence . . . greedy of land, so that they took up much of the virgin agricultural areas suitable for housing which then remained within the city':[17] 45,850 municipal dwellings were completed between 1918 and 1939, including 5838 built on land outside the city boundary. With 26,415 houses completed within the City by private developers, residential expansion brought the town's fabric lapping against its boundaries and produced growing land shortages. In consequence, Liverpool began purchasing rural land within adjacent authorities from the late 1920s for development as overspill estates. In August 1928 the City bought 2216 acres at Speke from Whiston R.D., boundary adjustments incorporating this within the Borough in 1932. The Speke lands were extended farther eastwards in July 1937 by the purchase of 351 acres at Hale, an area which remained within Whiston R.D. until incorporation by boundary changes in April 1952. In January 1932 the City also acquired land adjoining its eastern boundary within Huyton-with-Roby U.D., purchasing Huyton Farm (82·5 acres) and the Knowsley estate (1740 acres) from Lord Derby, adding Bakers Green Farm (49·5 acres) in February 1937 and the Brook House estate (87 acres) in March 1937.[18] The Urban District and Lancashire County Council refused their incorporation by boundary adjustments. The City had acquired 4526 acres of potential building land subject—where not incorporated—to planning consents from the local authorities.

The development of these corporate estates was guided by strategic planning concepts proposed in 1930 by a report of the South-West Lancashire Town Planning Advisory Committee, a non-statutory body of local authority representatives established in 1927. The Committee considered that further development in the Liverpool–Bootle–Litherland–Crosby conurbation area should be restrained and future growth decentralized to satellite townships in peripheral districts, separated from the urban core by open agricultural areas. The Committee's recommendations included an arc of satellite townships from Hightown in the north—via Maghull, Kirkby, Knowsley, Huyton-with-Roby, Halewood, and Hale—to Speke in the south. Liverpool Corporation envisaged the creation of two such townships on its newly-acquired lands at Speke and within Huyton-with-Roby U.D. to receive overspill from its central slum clearance areas, with attendant industrial development, services and amenities to create '. . . a self-contained Community Unit as distinct from a dormitory suburb'.[19]

The Liverpool Corporation Act enabled the City to '. . . lay out and develop . . . the Speke and Knowsley estates of the Corporation and any other lands belonging to the Corporation which adjoin the East Lancashire Road' and gave it power to '. . . erect and maintain houses shops offices warehouses factories and other buildings' and to '. . . sell lease exchange or otherwise dispose of any such lands houses shops offices warehouses factories or buildings', although the

Corporation was obliged to obtain full current market values for any such transactions unless the Minister consented otherwise. In addition powers were taken to promote private investment by granting building leases for developments on Corporation land and the City could '... advance money to the purchaser or lessee of any lands acquired from or leased by them for the purpose of enabling or assisting him to erect buildings on such lands',[20] these advances being limited to two-thirds of the market value of the applicants' interest in the lands when developed and repayable with interest within an agreed period up to thirty years and secured by a mortgage on the building and land. The Corporation was thus able to provide loan finance for private developers at commercial interest rates. The Act allowed a flexible blend of municipal and private finance, of land sales or leases for private development, and of municipal construction of premises for sale or lease. These powers exceeded those of the Special Area commissioners operating in the four Special Areas under the national legislation of 1934, although their financing of industrial estates from 1936 and Treasury assistance to industry under the 1937 Act prompted protests from the City that '... subsidised competition would be created by the Government ... which would seriously affect Liverpool in the efforts being made by the Corporation to attract new industries to the lands which had been acquired, and for which powers had been specially granted by Parliament.'[21]

The principal pre-war outcome of the Liverpool Corporation Act was the establishment of two industrial estates at Speke in the south and at Fazakerley (Aintree) in the north on land adjacent to the East Lancashire Road. In 1936 the Corporation approved the creation of a self-contained 'Community Unit' extending over 854 acres within its Speke estate and across the city boundary in Hale. Its employment needs were to be provided by the large airframe shadow factory and an area of 341 acres zoned to form Speke Industrial Estate. Initially disposing of industrial sites on 999 year building leases, with some mortgage loans for private factory construction, the Speke estate developed rapidly from 1936. By mid-1938 sixteen factories had been attracted to the site, but these developments were transfers of enterprises from other parts of the City to more favourable conditions at Speke, rather than immigrant firms, and contributed to industrial decentralization. This estate continued to expanded during and after the Second World War and by 1952 forty-six factory sites had been leased with thirty-four in production employing 12,500, including 7150 employed by Dunlop within the former airframe factory. Most sites were by then leased and a further land allocation of 101 acres proposed,[22] continuing industrial expansion increasing employment to some 25,000 by 1970. Adjacent sites had also been developed by both Ford and the then Standard Motors and Speke had become one of Merseyside's most important manufacturing districts. Together with municipal residential estates and their associated facilities, built primarily between 1936 and 1957, a major 'satellite township' had been created on Liverpool's south-east periphery. Simultaneously from 1936 a second site of 300 acres was developed at Long Lane, Fazakerley, now the Aintree Industrial Estate. Close to existing commercial and residential areas, this development was not accompanied by extensive municipal housing estates or the planning of a 'Community Unit'. Plots were quickly leased with a reservation policy for 'clean air' manufacturers, particularly food processors, drink, electrical engineering, and printing. By 1952 little space remained with thirty-six sites leased of which twenty-four were in production employing 12,800, rising to some 20,000 by 1970. The engineering ROF opened in 1941 on an adjacent site was acquired by the Corporation on its closure in 1961 and leased to Joseph Lucas for electrical goods manufacture.

The Corporation was unable, however, to develop its Knowsley estate in comparable manner. Since it was located within Huyton-with-Roby U.D. and residentially zoned, planning restrictions precluded industrial development and frustrated the creation of a balanced township. Consequently, Liverpool was negotiating in the later 1930s the purchase of further land within Whiston R.D., adjacent to the East Lancashire Road, to promote industrial employment for its residents at Norris Green and on its out-of-city estates within Knowsley. Negotiations to purchase arable land near Kirkby village, two miles east of the city boundary were aborted in 1939 and the site—some 750 acres between Simonswood Moss and the East Lancashire Road—was developed for Kirkby ROF. Closed in 1946, the land and buildings were transferred to Liverpool Corporation on a 99-year lease. Subsequently made freehold, this site was extended by further land purchases to create, with the agreement of Lancashire County Council, an industrial zone of 2000 acres. Converted to civil use, the ready availability of cheap premises and financial assistance under the 1936 Act attracted many smaller firms from inner Liverpool, especially those displaced by urban renewal, clearance or wartime damage and the ex-ROF provided 'nursery' facilities for new enterprises. As with Speke, Kirkby contributed to the intra-regional re-location of industry and to decentralization from Merseyside's inner core to growth points located on its periphery.[23] Between the opening of the estate on 1 April 1946 and 31 March 1950 the Corporation had completed seventy purchases of land with building leases within the site, including branches of firms moving into Merseyside such as Kodak, BICC, and John Dickinson. In addition, existing buildings were leased to forty-six firms. Total employment on the estate exceeded

5000. Although subject to high closure rates and turnover of leases and tenancies, the original industrial estate at Kirkby proved successful and, from the early 1950s, the estate was extended both south to the A580 and east into adjacent farmlands. This accommodated large manufacturing firms occupying extensive sites, attracted in part under the regional policies of national government following the scheduling of Merseyside as a Development Area in 1949. These included Kraft Foods, Otis Elevator, A. C. Delco, Yorkshire Imperial Metals, and Fisher-Bendix. Typically such firms developed branch establishments of parent organizations based outside the region. By 1970 the Kirkby estate was Britain's largest, its 150 concerns employing some 22,000. As at Speke, the industrial growth of Kirkby was accompanied by extensive residential development. Between 1952 and 1965 some 50,000 people were rehoused in 11,869 dwellings, of which 92 per cent were municipal units built by Liverpool Corporation as overspill reception and Kirkby formed the largest of the city's satellite townships.

The inter-war and war years initiated important trends in the changing industrial structure and geography of Merseyside, stimulated primarily by an innovative local authority and by the demands of a war economy. Many such changes came fully to fruition only after 1945 but there are clear pre-war origins to the growth of the region's manufacturing sector and its industrial diversification and to programmes of inner urban renewal with the attendant decentralization of both population and industry to planned 'Community Units' within and beyond Liverpool's boundaries. Moreover, the development of industrial estates became the principal agent and expression of manufacturing growth. Within Merseyside the major industrial growth points were at Speke and eastwards along the arterial axis of the A580 from the Aintree estate, via Gilmoss to Kirkby. Elsewhere on Merseyside industrial growth was handicapped by the prevailing economic environment, by exclusion from the scheduled Special Areas and by the competitive advantages possessed by Liverpool under its local Act, these working to the detriment of such adjacent local authorities as Bootle, Birkenhead, and Wallasey. Spontaneous manufacturing growth did occur, particularly in Wirral. At Bromborough Lever Brothers developed a private industrial estate close to the company docks, attracting a variety of industries processing imported materials. Along the Manchester Ship Canal at Ellesmere Port growth included grain-milling and paper and at Stanlow Point Shell and Lobitos imported and distributed refined oils. Oil refining and petro-chemicals plants developed subsequently. However, Board of Trade surveys between 1932 and 1938 recorded almost as many factory closures (30) as openings or extensions (39) within the Merseyside region including Ellesmere Port.[24] In June 1938 there remained 80,600 unemployed on Merseyside, a rate of 18 per cent comprising male rates of 22 per cent and 9 per cent for females. The war resolved the region's unemployment problem through conscription, the expansion of war-related industries and an enormous demand for port and shipping services but in 1945, with demobilization and the closure of wartime plant capacity, '... the old problem of finding jobs for unskilled men remained almost as hard to solve as ever.'[25]

II

A considerable expansion of central government activity in regional development occurred from 1945 with policies both to promote industrial expansion in the underemployed areas of Britain and to control industrial growth in South-East and Midland England. Positive measures of regional assistance within newly-defined Development Areas derived from the Distribution of Industry Act 1945 and supplementary Acts of 1950 and 1958, while negative location controls stemmed from building licence procedures and, subsequently, industrial development certificates.[26]

Merseyside was ineligible for statutory regional aids until its designation as a Development Area from 5 April 1949, but the region's initial exclusion under postwar legislation did not present an absolute bar to central governmental promotion of industry within the area and it was the marked beneficiary of preferential administrative action. Merseyside was regarded as one among several regions with lesser degrees of economic difficulty than the Development Areas but sufficient to merit state support. In December 1943 consideration had been given within the Board of Trade to the peacetime needs of the pre-war depressed areas and a policy was announced to give priority to projects locating within 'development areas' in the allocation of building licenses for new factory construction and in the release of surplus government manufacturing capacity. These administrative preferences were precursors of the regional incentives provided by the Distribution of Industry Act. Also, interdepartmental discussions in June 1944 recognized the developmental needs of other regions, termed 'near development areas', although officials were '... anxious that the fact that we are discussing these areas should not get abroad and that they should be retained as a purely inter-departmental administrative arrangement'.[27] In November 1944 a pattern of 'near development areas' was defined—including Merseyside (Liverpool, Bootle, Birkenhead, and Wallasey C.B.s; Crosby M.B. and Litherland U.D.). These areas were to benefit not from legislative measures but from purely administrative preferences including the early release of wartime factory space, sympathetic consideration of building license applications and from official attempts to 'steer' industry to the region when development area locations were rejected by industrialists.[28] Similarly, as unemployment rose with demobilization, the Ministry of Labour was required by Cabinet in February 1946 to identify 'Unemployment Areas' outside the then Development Areas where unemployment rates were 5 per cent or greater and which did not reflect temporary or seasonal factors. Merseyside was included and benefited from other administrative preferences including, in a period of materials shortage and licensing, concessionary allocations of industrial raw materials and the early re-opening of factories closed under wartime concentration schemes.[29] Although in July 1946 '. . . pressure to schedule . . . Merseyside'[30] under the Distribution of Industry Act was still being resisted, its problems were given increased official consideration because of rising unemployment levels and the need to ameliorate the adverse regional consequences of the national financial crisis of Autumn 1947. Acute shortages of steel and other materials had compelled cuts in capital investment programmes for 1947, falling '. . . particularly heavily on industrial investment'.[31] In December 1947 it was announced that 'For a period of at least six months no new industrial buildings or extensions will be started other than a limited number of projects of exceptional importance by reason of their contribution to exports or import saving', and that 'All factory building, including extensions now in progress, which has not yet reached the steel erection stage will be reviewed with the object of postponing at least half'. Within this reduced programme it was conceded that '. . . preferential treatment will continue to be accorded to the development areas' but the Board of Trade was clearly as concerned for Merseyside regarding the effects on unemployment of the ban on new, and review of existing, industrial developments. In January 1948 the Cabinet Production Committee, pressed by the Board, agreed '. . . that Merseyside should be treated as a development area in the application of the revised policy for capital investment, and in the application of any arrangements that may be made for the preferential allocation of resources on a geographical basis'.[33] Also, the Distribution of Industry Committee of Cabinet was invited '. . . to review the effects of revision of the capital investment programme on the Development Areas and Merseyside' and '. . . to consider the possibility of devising schemes for the relief of unemployment in the development areas and Merseyside'. In February 1948 the Committee agreed some easement of cuts in public works schemes on Merseyside although in March the Ministry of Labour brought before the Committee a list of other localities both within and outside the Development Areas '. . . where unemployment was exceptionally high (and) which should be treated in the same way as Merseyside'.[34] These easements were regarded '. . . purely as a temporary stop-gap and not as a substitute for radical and permanent measures'[35] and the public works programmes did not compensate for the loss of capital investment within the region arising from the expenditure cuts of December 1947. In March 1948, of thirty-eight privately-financed building projects under review on Merseyside, valued in total at £1·9m., only fourteen (38 per cent by value) were to proceed while thirteen (35 per cent) were stopped by revoking of building licenses and eleven were suspended (27 per cent). By contrast, 96 per cent by value of equivalent schemes reviewed in the Development Areas were to proceed and, on average, 72 per cent in all other areas. It was clear that 'Compared with the Development Areas, or indeed with other Regions, the cuts have fallen heavily on Merseyside',[36] in part reflecting a slower postwar reconstruction programme with projects caught by the review and the low priority given to warehouse re-building in the region's blitzed docklands.

By mid-1948 unemployment rates of 5·5 per cent on Merseyside exceeded those in the scheduled Development Areas, particularly among males, while '. . . the number of men out of work is still three times the employment expected from the whole of the postwar factory building programme—a most unfavourable contrast with the Development Areas'.[37] It was proposed in October 1948 that Merseyside be scheduled a Development Area and enacted from 5 April 1949 (fig. 7.1) despite reservations from Liverpool which feared the negation of its local powers were the region as a whole to be eligible for assistance under national legislation. This opposition delayed the region's designation and generated considerable friction, particularly in Bootle and Birkenhead given their ineligibility for all but the administrative preferences accorded to the Unemployment Areas.[38] More significantly, Merseyside was effectively precluded from marked material benefit under the Distribution of Industry Acts for, as will be seen, regional programmes were in retreat by 1949 although the region was afforded some administrative priority on its designation given its prominent problem of male unemployment and the protective patronage of the then President of the Board of Trade, a Minister with local constituency associations. The contribution of regional policies to Merseyside's industrial development in the review period 1949–60 in part reflects the volume, pattern, and chronology of governmental expenditure under the Distribution of Industry Acts and in part the nature of official location control policies acting upon industrial investment decisions. We examine these successively.

III

Regional aids under these Acts comprised incentives to promote industrial development and measures to improve the quality of

Table 7.1. *Distribution of Industry Acts.*
Expenditure in Development and DATAC areas 1945/6–1959/60. (£'000).

Year	*Factory building*	*Loans/grants to industry* DATAC	*Board of Trade*	*Basic services*	*Derelict land*	*Key-worker houses*	*Total*
1945/6	565.8 (–)	– (–)	16·7 (–)	69·7 (–)	– (–)	– (–)	652·2
1946/7	5,667·1 (–)	163·3 (–)	0·5 (–)	158·1 (–)	77·7 (–)	– (–)	6,066·7
1947/8	12,540·5 (–)	315·1 (–)	– (–)	798·3 (–)	345·1 (–)	63·1 (–)	14,062·1
1948/9	11,007·3 (–)	511·4 (–)	– (–)	1,009·4 (–)	177·9 (–)	511·9 (–)	13,217·9
1949/50	6,518·5 (NA)	608·4 (–)	2·4 (–)	896·1 (–)	196·5 (–)	242·5 (–)	8,464·4
1950/1	4,974·6 (189·6)	789·7 (NA)	– (–)	1,106·2 (50·0)*	93·5 (–)	287·4 (–)	7,251·4
1951/2	5,033·6 (586·8)	788·6 (NA)	– (–)	1,107·8 (6·3)*	62·0 (–)	146·1 (–)	7,138·1
1952/3	3,593·6 (305·9)	276·8 (NA)	– (–)	1,853·2 (–)	40·0 (–)	78·5 (–)	5,842·1
1953/4	3,039·9 (168·0)	1,061·2 (NA)	– (–)	2,463·9 (–)	5·8 (–)	44·8 (–)	6,615·6
1954/5	4,348·1 (496·0)	1,695·6 (NA)	– (–)	1,787·4 (–)	12·2 (–)	98·8 (–)	7,942·1
1955/6	5,832·0 (302·1)	426·6 (NA)	82·1 (–)	896·1 (–)	1·2 (–)	5·4 (–)	7,243·4
1956/7	4,898·2 (745·1)	267·1 (NA)	– (–)	990·6 (–)	0·2 (–)	20·6 (–)	6,176·7
1957/8	2,713·5 (481·6)	104·3 (NA)	– (–)	615·2 (–)	– (–)	14·8 (–)	3,447·8
1958/9	1,526·5 (126·5)	2,091·8 (NA)	– (–)	599·2 (–)	– (–)	15·0 (–)	4,232·5
1959/60	5,513·0 (166·3)	2,965·3 (NA)	– (–)	480·3 (NA)	65·0 (3·0)*	14·6 (–)	9,038·2
Total GB	77,772·2	12,065·2	101·7 (–)	14,831·5	1,077·1	1,543·5	107,391·2
Total (per cent)	72·5	11·2	0·1	13·8	1·0	1·4	100·0
Merseyside DA	(3,567·9)	(NA)	(–)	(56·3)*	(3·0)*	(–)	

(NA) = not available. ( ) = expenditure within Merseyside D.A. * = approved expenditure. DATAC = Development Areas Treasury Advisory Committee.

Sources: Appropriation Accounts and Board of Trade.

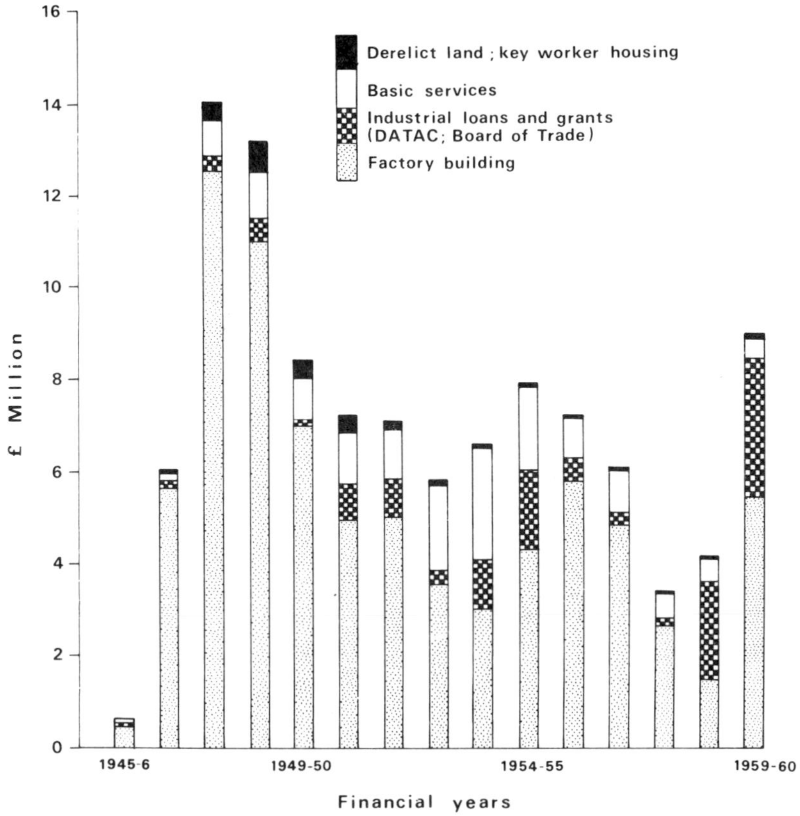

Fig. 7.2. Great Britain: Distribution of Industry Acts expenditure, 1945/6–1959/60.
Note: Excludes residual expenditure from 1960/1 on commitments approved prior to repeal of Distribution of Industry Acts after 31 March 1960.

public services and environmental amenity within the Development Areas. National expenditure totalled £107·4m between 1945/6 and 1959/60, peaking in 1947/8 and declining rapidly to 1957/8 before recovering with the resurrection of regional policies in the late 1950s (table 7.1). Merseyside's late designation is particularly significant in this chronological context. Incentives to industry dominated expenditures. Government-financed factory construction, with associated costs of land acquisition and servicing, absorbed 72·5 per cent of total resources while loans and grants to industry committed a further 11·2 per cent, overwhelmingly of loans approved by the Development Areas Treasury Advisory Committee (DATAC) but also including Board of Trade grants for industry's removal costs. Environmental measures included assistance to local authorities and public utilities for upgrading basic services, grants for clearing derelict land and aids for housing key workers: the former committed 13·8 per cent of expenditures and the two latter 1 per cent and 1·4 per cent respectively. The importance of these several instruments of regional assistance varied temporally (fig. 7.2), the initial postwar dominance of factory building programmes declining from 1948/9 relative to DATAC advances and basic service improvements. This largely reflected the former's more immediate sensitivity to retrenchments in government spending compared with the extended lead times of major DATAC and basic service projects where expenditures often arose years after their initial approval. Increased commitments from 1958/9, however, reflected an invigorated regional programme, particularly DATAC advances within 'DATAC Areas' scheduled under the Distribution of Industry (Industrial Finance) Act, 1958. Given the scale, structure and chronology of total expenditures we now examine the extent to which the several instruments of regional assistance were applied within the Merseyside Development Area. Although data deficiencies preclude a complete identification of the financial resources so deployed, we are able specifically to review the regional allocation of some 89 per cent of these total commitments.

Sections 1 and 2 of the 1945 Distribution of Industry Act authorized the Board of Trade to construct factories in the Development Areas for lease or sale to migrant industry and this dominated regional expenditures in the peak period to 1948/9 but contracted sharply thereafter. The cuts in capital spending imposed in December 1947 had excised 18 per cent of all Treasury-financed factory approvals from 1945 and severely constrained future programmes to the most urgent needs of exporting or import-substituting industries. Similarly, advance-factory construction had formed a significant component within total building but the 1947 cuts and subsequent restrictions on expenditure virtually precluded further approvals. Bar an exceptional treatment of Merseyside, the programme was deferred indefinitely early in 1951 and was not resumed until March 1959. Hence the scheduling of Merseyside in 1949 was inauspiciously-phased and only the most strenuous arguments within Cabinet by the President of the Board of Trade secured the resources required for a nominal programme of factory building within the region.

Essential to this programme was a relaxation of building license controls to release supplies of steel and other resources and Treasury sanction for the expenditure involved. The nationwide ban on factory building had lasted until 22 June 1948 when the Ministry of Supply announced marginal relaxations to permit '. . . cases of exceptional importance by reason of their contribution to exports and import saving'.[39] Despite an administrative preference for projects located in the Development Areas, even here '. . . projects which were capable of providing much-needed employment could often not be sanctioned . . . (if) they did not satisfy the strict dollar earning or dollar saving criterion'.[40] The Board's factory building programmes for 1948 and 1949 had consequently been curtailed and subjected to financial ceilings which prohibited all but the most urgent of new commitments, and which were to be balanced by adjustments elsewhere. Despite such constraints a restricted programme of land acquisition and factory construction was initiated within Merseyside, the Board acting through its agent the North Western Industrial Estates Company. We detail its activities following a review of the resource constraints circumscribing the Company's programmes in the period 1949–60 and the priority afforded to Merseyside relative to other scheduled areas.

In May 1950 the President of the Board of Trade pressed within the Production Committee of Cabinet for relaxations in government expenditure policy to allow additional factory building in Merseyside and in some other parts of the Development Areas, including new advance factory commitments, and for relaxations in the capital investment criteria to encourage private industrial building in selected areas of high unemployment both within and outside the Areas. However, while '. . . prepared to agree exceptionally to three or four advance factories on Merseyside since the area was scheduled so late and something is probably needed to make a start', the Treasury required this programme '. . . be done within the existing ceilings and current criteria of essentiality'.[41] Merseyside was thus given marked priority within regional policies but denied resources to make other than a nominal contribution to its needs, although minor Treasury concessions in July 1950 allowed additional total commitments of £1·25m. for fifteen advance factories of which four were to be located within Merseyside. Continuing Treasury pressures to restrict expenditure led the Board of Trade in March 1951 to restrict even this programme to five units costing £0·45m., including three within Merseyside: two were then under construction at Huyton with a third planned for Cleveland Street, Birkenhead, the Merseyside programme representing some £0·3m. within the total commitment.[42] Advance factory development was then discontinued until 1959 and factory building in the region restricted to the demands of specific applicant firms and subject to stringent budgetary restraints, even the Birkenhead advance unit being shelved.

Merseyside also benefited from relaxations of the capital investment criteria for private industry agreed by the Production Committee in July 1950. Within the Development Areas and other areas of high unemployment firms with factory-building projects providing additional male employment would now obtain building licenses '. . . without regard to the dollar-earning power of the project'.[43] In relation to the Development Areas this relaxation of investment constraints applied only within those districts with continuing problems of male unemployment or a structural dependence upon declining industries, under both of which Merseyside qualified. This more liberal licensing regime for private developments undoubtedly proved beneficial although its advantages were transient given the general relaxation and abolition of building license controls in the United Kingdom in 1953 and 1954 respectively. By then the erosion of such administrative preferences emphasized the importance of specifically regional incentives.

However, Treasury-financed factory building remained at a low level throughout the 1950s and Merseyside's recognized priority weakened relative to other areas by mid-decade. By July 1951 building was largely confined to 'black spots' of localized unemployment within the Development Areas, this classification being determined *ad hoc* as applications for factory premises arose until 1954 when a list was established based largely on the existence over the preceding two or three years of serious unemployment, generally 4 per cent among males or females, or its expectation within a like period. Merseyside was then categorized as among '. . . the outstanding needy Development Areas'[44] where a presumption remained that applications for government factory units would be favourably considered and the volume of approved projects arose in 1954 and 1955. The continuing needs of Merseyside were confirmed in 1955 in a Board of Trade review of the extent and boundaries of the Development Areas. However, following recommendations in 1955 from the Select Committee on Estimates that the Board '. . . should enforce more rigorously their policy of encouraging industrialists to build factories for themselves'[45] and that future building should be of extensions to existing factories rather than for new applicants, the volume of building declined markedly. This had a disproportionately adverse effect upon Merseyside given the relatively small number of enterprises then located within government buildings and eligible for approved extensions. Furthermore, in October 1955 more stringent counter-inflationary policies were introduced, reducing the volume of expenditure on regional aids. The Cabinet decided that no new commitments be made to build new factories or extensions '. . . except in certain special cases', the policy being '. . . something very close to a general ban'.[46] Merseyside ceased to be categorized an unemployment 'black spot', a status reserved for Dundee, Greenock, and South-West Wales. By June 1956 the Board of Trade was refusing approval even for extensions to existing premises within Merseyside[47] and expenditure within the region fell markedly from its peak in 1956/7 both absolutely and relative to other development areas, this peak reflecting earlier approvals (table 7.1). The region had been administratively descheduled for assistance under the Distribution of Industry Acts. However, in February 1959 rising unemployment caused its reinstatement to the short list of areas within which the Board was '. . . prepared to build factories for approved tenants',[48] both of extensions and of new buildings. Also, an experimental programme of three advance factory units announced in March 1959 included a unit of 35,000 sq. ft. within Merseyside at Speke. The region was therefore eligible for Treasury-financed factory buildings under the 1945 Act for only limited periods from April 1949 to October 1955 and from February 1959 to March 1960 and the volume of such activity was severely limited by national economic policies. Related expenditure within the region between 1950/1 and 1959/60 was £3·6m., representing 4·6 per cent of total national commitments.

In the period to end-March 1960 the North Western Industrial Estates Company completed or commenced construction of 1,269,775 sq. ft. of factory premises within the Merseyside Development Area.[49] The one industrial estate at Huyton received 475,343 sq. ft., a group site of three factories at Birkenhead (Beaufort Road) 90,671 sq. ft., with the remaining area on three individual sites at Speke, within Liverpool Corporation's industrial estate, and on single sites at Fazakerley, Birkenhead (Cleveland Street), and Bromborough. The chronology of development reflected the policy considerations examined above, factories constructed to 1954 being almost invariably new units built for specific tenants, excepting two advance factories at Huyton. Commitments peaked in 1950, the building programme declining rapidly thereafter, lesser peaks in 1953 and 1956 almost entirely comprising single new factories for Huntley and Palmer at Huyton (177,550 sq. ft.) and for Kelvinator at Bromborough (313,572 sq. ft.). No new building occurred after 1954 excepting this Bromborough factory and the advance unit built at Speke in 1959, the programme being restricted to extensions. Compared with other Development Areas, government-financed factory building on Merseyside was unusually committed to a few large projects built for specific applicants; four factories, with their subsequent extensions, representing 71·3 per cent of the total area built, i.e. the Huyton and Bromborough units above plus factories for Lockheed at Speke (initially 226,530 sq. ft.) and for Standard Brands at Fazakerley (initially 27,100 sq. ft.). Thirteen new factories had been developed by 31 March 1960 including the Speke advance factory then under construction. Eleven companies tenanted or had purchased these premises, the latter generally on amortized terms. Excepting in Birkenhead their locations were peripheral to the conurbation core with concentrations at Huyton and Speke. Their significance for industrial change was essentially local: by January 1967 employment provided was only 5063 or 0·8 per cent of all insured employees within the original Merseyside Development

Table 7.2. *Development Areas in Great Britain, industrial buildings completed, 1945–58.*

	Floor area completed ('000 sq. ft.) (%)							
	1945–58				*1949–58*			
Development Area	*Government*		*Private*		*Government*		*Private*	
West Cumberland	1,126	(64·4)	622	(35·6)	477	(45·4)	574	(54·6)
Dundee	755	(34·8)	1,412	(65·2)	431	(31·3)	948	(68·7)
Central Scotland	9,223	(34·5)	17,503	(65·5)	6,672	(29·5)	15,968	(70·5)
South Wales	7,244	(26·8)	19,783	(73·2)	4,670	(22·2)	16,373	(77·8)
N. E. Lancashire	392	(24·6)	1,201	(75·4)	392	(25·9)	1,120	(74·1)
North East	6,587	(19·6)	26,989	(80·4)	4,085	(15·4)	22,527	(84·6)
South Lancashire	770	(14·2)	4,638	(85·8)	770	(15·2)	4,299	(84·8)
Highlands	16	(11·0)	130	(89·0)	16	(12·4)	113	(87·6)
Merseyside	1,109	(10·3)	9,705	(89·7)	1,109	(10·9)	9,035	(89·1)
Wrexham	40	(3·0)	1,279	(97·0)	40	(3·1)	1,240	(96·9)
All DAs	27,262	(24·7)	83,262	(75·3)	18,662	(20·5)	72,197	(79·4)

Source: Board of Trade.

Area. Only 55 per cent of this employment was for males and the Treasury-financed factory programme had correspondingly little bearing on the region's main problem. The importance of the government programme relative to private manufacturing investment was less within Merseyside than in any other Development Area except Wrexham. Between 1945 and 1958 the total factory floorspace completed within the region was 10·8 million sq. ft., of which only 10·3 per cent represented government-financed schemes compared with 24·7 per cent for all Development Areas, these proportions being 10·9 per cent for 1949–58 compared with 20·5 per cent in all Areas (table 7.2).[50] In both an absolute and relative sense Merseyside gained little from its eligibility for this form of regional aid.

Other direct assistance to industry under the Distribution of Industry Acts consisted primarily of DATAC loans and grants but the absence of data on their regional and sectoral allocation precludes an assessment of their contribution to the region's development. However, DATAC assistance was regarded by the Board of Trade as of limited value in regional promotion given its availability only for projects unable to obtain capital elsewhere yet, paradoxically, with prospects of commercial viability. Also DATAC facilities were suspended following the recommendations of the Select Committee on Estimates in 1955,[51] expenditure falling rapidly and confined to existing commitments thereafter, again reflecting the penalties arising from Merseyside's late date of designation. In 1958 the Distribution of Industry (Industrial Finance) Act restored DATAC advances within newly-designated DATAC Areas, including Merseyside (fig. 7.1), and these facilities then assumed a prominence in expenditure terms almost equal to that of the factory building programme (table 7.1). It is not possible to identify the contribution of DATAC advances to Merseyside's industrial development, fragmentary data suggesting but a marginal impact in the region up to their withdrawal in the mid-1950s. Of sixty-four loans approved under Section 4 of the 1945 Act by end-October 1952 only six were granted within the Merseyside and South Lancashire Development Areas combined, separate data for Merseyside being unavailable, totalling £0·4m. within total advances of £5·3m.[52] No regional data exist for loans advanced under the 1958 Act. Financial assistance to industry was also provided by the Board of Trade under Section 8 of the 1945 Act and Section 3 of the 1950 Act. The former was irrelevant to Merseyside, allowing remanent expenditure from the pre-war Special Areas legislation, but the latter empowered the Board to make grants to firms '. . . in exceptional circumstances in respect of expenditure or loss arising in connection with the establishment of an industrial undertaking in a development area'.[53] This theoretical eligibility of immigrant industry for grant aid proved of no value as Section 3 was invoked only once, in North-East England.

Besides direct aids to industry, the Distribution of Industry Acts furthered regional development by measures to raise the quality of public services and environmental amenities but the application of such policies within Merseyside was minimal, again largely reflecting the region's late designation and the chronology of policy administration.

The most significant such measure of the 1945 Act was the power given to a Minister under Section 3 to give loans or grants for the improvement of basic services within a development area where adequate provision had not been made by the local authority or statutory undertaking for services '. . . on which the development of the area . . . and in particular of industrial undertakings therein, depends'.[54] These provisions were quite freely used between 1945 and 1951, particularly for water and sewerage schemes, but economies in public expenditure from late 1951 culminated in the Ministry of Housing and Local Government, responsible for such schemes in England and Wales, announcing in June 1952 '. . . that grants under Section 3 of (the) Act . . . shall not be made in future'[55] and that grants provisionally approved, but where no contracts or expenditure commitments had been made, would lapse. An amendment to this ban in November 1952 authorized aid for new schemes '. . . of quite exceptional industrial urgency'[56] but this latitude was exercised only once, for the Tees Valley Water Scheme, prior to a general relaxation of the policy in 1959.

Continuing high levels of expenditure under Section 3 through the 1950s reflects advances for schemes approved before 1952 and for the Tees Project. Given this financial environment, the value to Merseyside of aids for basic service improvements was negligible. Prior to the ban of June 1952 approval was given by the Ministry of Housing and Local Government for grant aid to two schemes of water supply; grants of £50,000 being approved in 1950/1 and of £3200 in 1951/2, these grants being 17·9 per cent and 30 per cent respectively of total approved costs. In addition, one road scheme within Huyton-with-Roby U.D. was given grant approval of £3106 (40 per cent) by the Ministry of Transport in 1951/2. The ban on Section 3 assistance was reviewed in February 1959, the Cabinet Employment Committee agreeing in March to resurrect grant aids for new water and sewerage schemes within those parts of the development areas then experiencing high levels of unemployment, defined as DATAC Areas scheduled under the 1958 Act, these including the whole of the Merseyside Development Area. Although unknown, it is unlikely that any such expenditure arose within the region in 1959/60 and Merseyside thus received but 0·4 per cent of total assistance under Section 3 of the 1945 Act by end-March 1960.

Furthermore, virtually no benefit derived to the region from Section 5 of the Act which authorized Board of Trade grants to local authorities for costs of clearing derelict land, either for '. . . enabling the land to be brought into use or for improving the amenities of the neighbourhood'.[57] Classified by the Board as 'amenity' schemes, land so reclaimed was used primarily for recreational, housing and educational needs. The Board was also able to finance such clearance by itself on land it acquired under the Act, although these projects were classed as 'industrial' schemes on land intended for development within the Board's factory building programmes. Grants to local authorities for amenity schemes, initially at the rate of 100 per cent approved expenditure, were widely used in the early postwar years. However, the scheduling of Merseyside in 1949 had been preceded by Treasury pressures severely to curtail the Board's expenditure on derelict land clearance, the Chancellor requesting in January 1949 that the programme for 1949/50 be reduced and confined to existing commitments.[58] Industrial schemes were suspended from September 1949 but the President specifically obtained a margin of expenditure for new amenity schemes likely to arise from the scheduling of Merseyside although official opinion saw limited need for clearance as dereliction within Merseyside was seen '. . . more in the form of "blight" for the clearance of which there are specific provisions in the Town and Country Planning Act of 1947. A few schemes will qualify for help from us but the majority will have to be dealt with by the Ministry of Town and Country Planning as part of the general development of the area'.[59] Local authorities within Merseyside were requested in April 1949 to submit schemes for approval but tightening budgetary constraints limited the programme for 1950/1 '. . . to an irreducible minimum' while in 1951/2 grant payments ceased to be at 100 per cent costs and clearance was confined to schemes '. . . of special urgency'. In November 1951 new commitments were refused and existing grants rescinded unless work had already started. Derelict land clearance in the development areas was suspended and no provision made for exceptional cases, approval having been given for the clearance of thirteen industrial and forty-five amenity sites, primarily within Scotland, Wales, and North-East England. None was within Merseyside. However, policy on derelict site clearance was reviewed in November 1958 and Ministers agreed that grant aid be restored up to 75 per cent of costs and subject to work being completed by 31 March 1960. All schemes, amenity and industrial, were to be undertaken by local authorities who were invited on 12 March 1959 to submit grant applications.[60] No restrictions were published confining grants to areas of high unemployment within the Development Areas although these were applied administratively and Merseyside qualified. The new policy was intended specifically to generate a limited volume of feasible schemes but an embarrassingly large number of applications led to the approval of forty-seven projects with total grant authorizations of £1·7m. Only one was located within Merseyside: the reclamation for recreational use of 'Webster's Pits' in Kirkby U.D., for which a 75 per cent grant of £3051 was made. This was the only benefit under the derelict land clearance provisions of the Distribution of Industry Acts.

Board of Trade financing of housing for key workers necessarily moving to the Development Areas with migrant enterprises was authorized by Sections 1 and 3 of the 1945 and 1950 Acts respectively. Housing for non-managerial key workers was normally provided either by local authorities or by the employing firms but larger dwellings required by managerial and executive personnel could be financed by the Board and such provision was made in South Wales, North-West England, and Central Scotland. Given the inability of certain local authorities fully to meet the housing needs of non-managerial staffs, the Board's programme was extended in 1947 to all grades of personnel, although primarily used for managerial housing. Expenditures peaked in 1948/9, falling rapidly to residual proportions given restrictive regimes of public expenditure and the progressive easing of the private housing market with the abolition of building licenses by 1954. No expenditure arose in Merseyside.

The financial aids nominally available for environmental improvements in the Development Areas under the Distribution of Industry Acts therefore had scant influence upon the physical infrastructure of Merseyside and did little to promote the region's industrial base prior to 1960. Given the limited direct assistance to industry under this legislation, the positive elements of regional policy, involving incentives and aids for fixed-capital formation within the region, were of scant value. Similarly, little benefit derived from two further elements of regional assistance effected by administrative action rather than under legislative provisions, i.e. contracts preference policies and the dispersal from central London of government office employment.

Contracts preference for firms located in specified areas, introduced in 1934, continued after 1945 within the scheduled Development Areas and, from 1950, in Unemployment Areas defined periodically by the Board of Trade. Merseyside firms were eligible from 1949 under this 'general preference' given competitive tenders to government purchasing departments and, from 1950, the nationalized industries. Also, a 'special preference', introduced in 1950, provided for '. . . manufacturers in Development and Unemployment Areas who are underbid in the initial competitive tendering to be offered up to a quarter of all suitable contracts at the price established by competition',[61] there being no price preference but an opportunity to take up contracts otherwise lost. The value of contracts preferences is unknown but the schemes were officially regarded as of '. . . more political than practical value'.[62] By 1956 the special preference was '. . . now more honoured in the breach than the observance'[63] and the Board believed '. . . that the bulk of the contracts would in any event be secured by the firms concerned as a result of normal contract procedure'.[64] There is little reason to believe that industrial development in Merseyside was more than marginally so influenced.

The dispersal of government work from central London was initiated during the Second World War and continued in peacetime with proposals drawn up by the official Committee for the Dispersal of Government Departments under Treasury chairmanship. By August 1948 agreement had been reached on the transfer to 'the provinces' of some 50,000 jobs from the Headquarters establishments of twenty departments, often involving substantial local recruitment.[65] Surprisingly, the Board of Trade was not represented on this Committee despite the potential importance of the dispersal programme for employment generation within the Development and Unemployment Areas, and the proposed locations of dispersed staffs were overwhelmingly within south-east and southern England: only 3750 posts were to be transposed to the Development Areas of the 46,800 for which a specific location had been adopted provisionally in 1948. No moves were proposed to Merseyside, then an Unemployment Area, although 800 jobs were involved in a move to Southport of the General Register Office's work on the National Register. By 1949 the Board of Trade was represented on the Committee and a greater consideration of regional interests attempted within final location decisions and for departmental moves not as then determined. Specific pressure was exerted to effect dispersals into the Merseyside

Development Area, including 2000 War Office jobs to various proposed locations in North Merseyside, Huyton, Kirkby, or Southport, and the proposed expansion to 2800 posts of existing units of the Ministry of Supply in Liverpool by the transfer of Divisions involving contracts, accounts, technical publications production, storage, and administration. Both schemes were opposed by their respective departments and by the Ministry of Town and Country Planning which cited strategic and planning objections, particularly the area's blitz record, housing problems, and the exacerbation of physical congestion given office growth in the central area. Neither dispersal occurred and the 1948 programme generally was subject to prolonged delay and amendments. Although the General Register Office was relocated in Southport, within commuting distance of the Merseyside Development Area, the effect of the 1948 scheme was actually a net loss of government work given the transfer of 450 jobs within the Departmental Claims branch of the Inland Revenue from Liverpool to Cardiff in 1950! Dispersal policies were pursued throughout the 1950s, both in implementation of the 1948 programme and for other cases arising periodically. The Committee agreed in principle that locational priority be given to the Development Areas or, in reducing preference, locations within the Unemployment Areas, the New Towns and expanded towns beyond the London Green Belt and, finally, the London periphery.[66] Achieved dispersal was limited, however, and the Board experienced difficulty in persuading departments to undertake long-distance moves on regional policy grounds, disagreeing with many decisions favouring intra-regional mobility within the South-East Region. Some proposals were advanced for dispersals to Merseyside or adjacent localities. The Committee decided in 1955 to relocate the Post Office's National Savings Certificate Division into Southport, involving some 3–4000 jobs, and in 1956 both Liverpool and Southport were considered for the Post Office's new Premium Bond Division. Neither dispersal occurred due largely to the lack of local office accommodation. The former decision was in abeyance until 1957 when it was rescinded given the impending availability of existing premises in Lytham St Annes. Similarly, neither of the latter locations was chosen for the Premium Bond Division, Liverpool's case being weakened by the availability of office accommodation only within premises owned by Littlewoods, the football-pool promoters. This raised '. . . grave political objection . . . Ministers would not welcome the association of the Premium Bond undertaking with the main football-pool enterprise in the United Kingdom'![67] Dispersal policies had little consequence for Merseyside in the review period although the region was more positively considered for relocation purposes from 1959 following recommendations by the Sub-Committee on Local Unemployment of the Cabinet's Economic Policy Committee. The dispersal programme was reviewed given rising regional unemployment and the reinvigoration of regional policies, a factor underlying the location in Liverpool of an Inland Revenue PAYE provincial centre in 1960.

IV

Complementing the role of governmental incentives for regional development throughout the post-war period were policies for the national control of industrial location. Given the very limited contribution of the former within Merseyside we now consider the extent to which private industrial investment may have been induced in the area by prohibitions on investment elsewhere. Controls were exercised from 1945 by building licence procedures. Introduced to canalize scarce materials into essential war production, these were retained given continuing supply difficulties in peacetime to control the volume and sectoral allocation of resource use. An administrative preference was given in the granting of building licences by the Ministry of Works to industrial developments located within the Development Areas with restrictive licencing regimes elsewhere, particularly in the South-East and Midland Regions of England. From 1 July 1948 building licences were replaced by industrial development certificates (IDCs) under Section 14(4) of the Town and Country Planning Act, 1947. The erection of industrial buildings above 5000 sq. ft. in floor area, whether a new building or an extension, required the prior approval of the Board of Trade as being consistent with '. . . the proper distribution of industry'[68] before an application for planning permission could be considered by the appropriate local authority. This gave the Board an apparently powerful negative control over the locational choice of private industry, the general intention being to restrict industrial growth in areas experiencing scale diseconomies and pressure on labour resources and to induce interregional mobility of industry in favour of the Development Areas. However, the effectiveness of IDC controls depended on the extent to which they statutorily embraced the developments to be controlled, the willingness of governments to reject applications incompatible with regional considerations, and the interpretation by governments of their powers and responsibilities under the Act—in particular of what constituted the 'proper' distribution of industry. Not defined in the Act, this represented a policy-decision which might properly vary with national and regional economic circumstances, and with the political perspectives and priorities of Ministers. An evaluation of the significance of location control policies for industrial development within Merseyside requires consideration of their general nature and administrative record. It will be apparent that controls as applied from 1949 were largely in abeyance or avoided, at least until 1958, and the region benefited to a much lesser degree than the Development Areas scheduled earlier under very different location control regimes.

Prior to 1 July 1948 applications for building licences for industrial developments were considered by 'Panel A' of the Official Committee on the Distribution of Industry, an interdepartmental body of officials representing the Board of Trade, Scottish Office, and the then Ministries of Labour, Town and Country Planning, Production, and of Supply, and responsible *inter alia* for the review of individual industrial projects within the context of regional policies. Building licences were allocated by the Ministry of Works on the recommendations of Panel A, approval by the Panel depending on the circumstances of the proposed location and the nature and national importance of the project and product. Approval by Panel A did not guarantee the award of a building licence, which depended on the volume of capital investment permissible within the national economic context. The quantity of applications necessitated the restriction of reviewed projects to those of 5000 sq. ft. floorspace or over, but including new buildings, extensions, the conversion of existing premises, warehouses, and the replacement of war-damaged buildings. As will be seen the remit of location control was wider under building licencing than under IDC mechanisms and location approval was subject to a wider range of departmental considerations, the spatial policy perspectives of the Ministries of Labour and of Town and Country Planning in particular supplementing those of the Board of Trade. Considerations of regional balance markedly influenced the decisions of Panel A, the country being divided into four regional categories for the consideration of applications. Severely restrictive licencing regimes were applied in 'congested' areas, including Greater London, Greater Birmingham, and Leicester with lesser restrictions in 'neutral' areas; while licencing assistance was given to projects within the Development Areas and, to lesser degree, in 'other expansion areas' which were basically equivalent to the Unemployment Areas and which included Merseyside.[69]

These administrative arrangements proved a potent locational influence on manufacturing industry and the Development Areas, with 17·5 per cent of the nation's insured employees, received 52·4 per cent of the total floor-space approved within Britain in the period 1 January 1945–30 June 1948. By contrast, Greater London and Greater Birmingham with 28·1 per cent of insured employees, received only 10·7 per cent of approved floor-space[70] and it must be concluded that restrictive licencing policies, complementing the availability of incentives within the scheduled areas, contributed markedly to the successful prosecution of regional policies in this period.

However, from 1 July 1948 building licence procedures were replaced by IDC policies. These proved markedly less potent in effecting a pattern of industrial investment consistent with regional policy considerations. This reflected the narrower imposition of controls under the legislative provisions of the Town and Country Planning Act and changes in administrative and political circumstances attending the transfer from building licence to IDC mechanisms. The bearing of IDC constraints upon industrial location decisions was weakened relative to building licensing by their legal framework. Certain classes of development were explicitly excluded from control, primarily all non-industrial buildings, including office and warehouse developments, and industrial buildings up to 5000 sq. ft. floor area.[71] By 1950 the Board of Trade, given responsibility for location control policies under the 1947 Act, was aware that the exploitation of the 5000 sq. ft. exemption was proving '. . . a very big embarrassment to distribution of industry control'[72] and this was compounded by other loopholes permitting uncontrolled building.[73] For example, Section 14(4) linked IDC procedures to the development control responsibilities of local planning authorities: IDCs were required only in support of an application for planning permission to them for the prescribed categories of development. However, under the 1947 Act, such responsibilities were not given to local authorities for a wide range of developments, thereby excluding them from location control. These included the development of land with existing use rights under the 1947 Act, the reconstruction of buildings damaged or destroyed during the war and the change of use of existing buildings. The most significant of such loopholes was probably the exclusion from control of changes in use of existing buildings, combined with the explicit exclusion of non-industrial buildings. These facilitated, for example, the construction of warehouse premises to be later converted for industrial use subject only to local planning consents and building licence availability. Similarly, no control could be exercised over the re-occupation of vacant existing industrial premises '. . . even though it created a new industry which could be positively detrimental to the proper distribution of industry'.[74] Given these loopholes, the efficacy of location controls within the new legislative framework was inherently weakened, facilitating extensive industrial and commercial growth in non-Development Area locations.

The introduction of the IDC system from 1 July 1948 had removed location control responsibilities from the interdepartmental Panel to the Board of Trade which was responsible for considering whether the application might be considered 'proper' on distribution of industry grounds. Recommendations for building licences were made separately by 'sponsoring' government departments on production criteria alone, the strength of their production support being conveyed to the Board of Trade. These changes in the administration of location control policies weakened the considerations of employment and physical planning previously bearing directly upon location approvals, subjecting policies to the narrower horizons of a department whose historical functions had been concerned primarily with the promotion of exports and of national industrial growth and efficiency. In practice, the Board proved reluctant to deny location consents for projects contributing to the export drive or to increased industrial competitiveness and import substitution. Concerned for the potential loss to productive capacity if an IDC refusal resulted in a decision to postpone or cancel investment rather than the desired diversion of the project to a Development Area or other approved location, the Board was particularly reluctant to refuse an IDC for a proposal with strong production support from its sponsoring department, taking this as indicative of its national importance. Few such were rejected on location grounds, the Board commenting that '. . . the national need for increased production, efficiency of production and exports may lead to the issue of an IDC in cases where other factors would indicate refusal'.[75] Some supported projects were indeed refused IDCs, the Board accepting the possibility of their loss as they were almost automatically replaced by additional approvals then permissible within the aggregate investment ceilings established by building licenses: no net loss to capital investment arising. In fact, the volume of IDC approved projects in the 'congested' areas considerably exceeded the volume permitted for construction by building licensing. By March 1953 when licencing of industrial schemes was relaxed, the Board had approved some thirteen million sq. ft. of factory floor-space within Greater London but which lay in abeyance pending receipt of building licences, with a further eight million in Birmingham.[76] An IDC rejection was not synonymous, therefore, with net restriction on productive expansion within these regions and the restraint on growth in the South-East and Midlands derived more from the aggregative restrictions of building licences than the regionally-motivated constraints of IDCs. Indeed, a disproportionate number of IDC rejections related to applications which lacked departmental production support and which were therefore unlikely to proceed given the consequential unavailability of building licences. The Board had fewer inhibitions in these cases as aggregate productive investment was not diminished and IDC rejections were academic. An apparently restrictive policy was in practice unlikely to generate interregional mobility of industry. For example, in the period 5 April–4 October 1949, IDCs were refused for only 8 per cent of the 193 applications supported by production departments but 81 per cent of the sixty-three unsupported cases were rejected.[77] Location control policies were largely cosmetic exercises in damage limitation compared with the control mechanisms which preceded them. Even disregarding such nuances in rejection policy, the absolute scale of refusals was limited. For the two years to June 1950 only thirty-eight IDCs representing 1·4m. sq. ft. of factory floor-space were refused in the Midland Region, compared with 817 approvals totalling 16·7m. sq. ft., although within Great London between 1 July 1948 and 31 December 1949, 618 IDCs were approved and 192 rejected. However, of these latter, twenty-four were subsequently allowed on appeal, twenty-two were replaced by alternative proposals approved elsewhere in the area and 127 were abandoned. Only one rejection resulted in relocation outside Greater London, that being in Brighton![78] This weakening of location control policies was recognized by the Ministry of Labour within an interdepartmental study-group on distribution of industry policy in 1949[79] and evidenced circumstantially by the marked reduction from July 1948 in the proportion of factory building approved for the Development Areas.[80]

The Board of Trade's view of the impropriety of denying location consent to industrial developments supported by the production departments was reinforced by the relaxation of building licences in 1953 and their abolition in 1954. Within this new context of unrestricted capital investment a project abandoned following an IDC refusal for its preferred location was not, as hitherto, replaced by another project within finite investment ceilings but was deemed a net loss to the economy. The achievements and future of IDC policies were reviewed in April 1953, the Board's Regional Controllers confirming that the policy bore restrictively upon but 5 per cent of all applications in 1951 and 1952, being '. . . popularly regarded as far more effective than it really is'.[81] Approval was given by the President of the Board of Trade in December 1953 for IDC rejections to be limited to proposals in London and other congested areas by '. . . new industry coming from other parts of the country and for expansions so large that they altered the whole scale of the business'.[82] These limited restrictions were further eroded by July 1954 following Board approval of major expansion programmes by Ford Motors in London and by Vauxhall at Luton and Dunstable, decisions which were taken in the interests of national production and export potential irrespective of regional considerations. Given these cases, the President considered '. . . the stage had now been reached where the IDC Control could no longer be effective as a compulsory power . . . (and) . . . he would not feel able to refuse IDCs save in the most exceptional cases'.[83] Regarding '. . . almost every proposal for new development as being *prima facie* desirable' Ministerial agreement was reached to limit refusals to those firms wishing to move into congested areas from other parts of the country and to rely on persuasion and the use of incentives to effect industrial mobility in favour of the Development Areas, Northern Ireland, and the Unemployment Areas. IDC rejections declined to residual proportions, falling in the Midland Region, for example, from sixty-five in the period 1950–2 to four in 1954–6.

Simultaneous with national economic pressures and political decisions almost to abandon restrictive IDC policies, regional policy was further weakened by the competitive demands for new employment of the London New Towns and expanded towns and London County Council 'out-country' overspill estates then under construction. By 1953 the Greater London area was receiving 36 per cent of approved new factory floor-space, excluding extensions, with 16 per cent approved for the New Towns and LCC estates alone, this exceeding the 15 per cent approved for all Development Areas combined.[84] Estimates in January 1954 suggested the annual demands for 'steerable' industrial jobs for the overspill communities within Greater London by 1957 would total 14,000, this being '. . . of the same order as the total available supply throughout the country'[85] with a further 1000 required for provincial overspill needs. The attractions to mobile industry of New Town and expanded town locations within South-East England suggested the Development Areas faced a serious competitive challenge for available industry. The Cabinet's Economic Affairs Committee considered these conflicting programmes and the Board attempted to relate the scale and rate of New Town construction to the availability of mobile industrial jobs and the continuing needs of the Development Areas. The Committee agreed in March 1954 that projects capable of going to Development Areas, or originating outside Greater London, should not be considered for the New Towns and that the Development and Unemployment Areas retain their priority within the Board's industrial 'steering' activities. However, given the Board's reluctance to wield IDC powers negatively, the inherent difficulty in demonstrating the suitability of a Development Area location, the eligibility of the New Towns for moves originating within Greater London, and reductions in the level of available incentives under the Distribution of Industry Acts, regional policies and New Town programmes were doubtless incompatible—to the disadvantage of the former.

Location control policies were administered '. . . persuasively rather than coercively'[86] until mid-1958 when rising levels of regional unemployment prompted a review of IDC policy. In July the President announced the strengthening of controls by a more restrictive certification of both new factory buildings and extensions in Greater London and Greater Birmingham and other areas of low unemployment. With the restoration of regional incentives discussed above, this undoubtedly increased the ability of the Development Areas, particularly those parts also scheduled as

DATAC Areas, to attract industrial investment. Merseyside was a major beneficiary of these more rigorous IDC mechanisms given the consequential induced mobility of the motor vehicles industry. In 1959 the major motor vehicles producers were independently proposing large expansions to productive capacity, raising '. . . important issues for distribution of industry policy'.[87] By October 1959 the Board had held discussions with four companies—Ford, British Motor Corporation, Standard Motors, and Vauxhalls—and was aware of other expansions proposed by the Rootes Group, Chrysler, Rover, and some major components producers. Strong locational pressure, including the refusal of IDCs, induced a remarkable locational shift to regions of high unemployment. Merseyside was a striking beneficiary with the establishment after 1960 of factories in Liverpool by Ford at Halewood, and by Standard Motors at Speke, by Vauxhall at Ellesmere Port, and by the British Motor Corporation at Kirkby—this latter a domestic appliance factory for the company's Fisher and Ludlow subsidiary.[88] Although these developments were effected beyond our review period their origins lie clearly in the resurrection of regional policies from mid-1958 and represent the most significant outcome of such policies as deployed within the Merseyside Development Area.

This review suggests that national location control policies prior to 1958 were of considerably less significance for industrial promotion in Merseyside from 1949 than in the context of the original Development Areas between 1945 and 1948. The number of companies developing within the region following the refusal of IDCs for their preferred location is unknown, although some were clearly so influenced or were responding to the anticipated rejection of IDCs or the provision of locational information and the persuasion involved in the 'steering' activities of the Board of Trade's regional and headquarters' officials. IDC restrictions were probably most influential in diverting industry to Merseyside between 1949 and 1954 and after mid-1958. Known instances include the factories established by Cadbury at Moreton following rejection of their application to expand on their preferred Bourneville site in 1952, and by A. C. Delco at Kirkby following a rejection at Luton. However, the attraction of industry to the region from *c.*1954 owes perhaps as much to its inherent locational and resource advantages, as to the positive benefit deriving from its assisted area status, and these factors were of doubtless significance throughout the review period. Of particular importance were the region's labour resources relative to South-East and Midland England, the availability of serviced industrial sites and existing buildings and the continuing application by Liverpool of its local Act.

The complex behavioural factors underlying the volume, chronology, and geographical origins of industrial movement into

Merseyside makes any evaluation of the contribution of regional policies to industrial immigration inherently hazardous. However, a Board of Trade survey provides useful detail of inward moves by new industries to November 1954,[89] a convenient date to review the impact of regional policies given their limited subsequent role. By then sixty-one new enterprises had entered the Development Area since the end of the war, including fifty branches of firms based outside the region, six complete transfers, four new firms and one acquisition of an existing business by takeover. Of these entrants, twenty-eight were in production in September 1949 and regional policy may be assumed to have had little or no bearing on their locational decisions excepting any administrative preferences preceding the formal scheduling of the area, although continuing application by Liverpool of its 1936 Act attracted many firms to Kirkby and Aintree. These early entrants provided 67 per cent of total employment created by all new firms by November 1954. Twenty-two had entered existing buildings, including reallocated wartime factories, and only six had built new premises, emphasizing the importance of the region's vacant building stock in attracting inward investment. Of the remaining thirty-three firms, for whom regional policy may have been a locational factor, nineteen had utilized existing buildings, nine built factories privately, and five occupied government-financed premises, generating in total some 10,600 jobs by late-1954, or 33 per cent of all employment created by postwar industrial immigration. Probably a substantial proportion of this represents the outcome of spontaneous investment decisions uninfluenced by regional policy considerations particularly among firms entering existing premises. However, on the heroic assumption that all moves into the Development Area were policy-induced after September 1949, the employment so created comprised but 1·7 per cent of the region's insured employees, although a potential contribution of regional policy also came from the expansion of existing industry given the advantages of raw materials, building licence, and contracts preferences, the availability of IDCs and the possible use of DATAC loans. From 1954 the extreme weakness of location controls and financial incentives suggests an even more limited governmental contribution to Merseyside's industrial growth and diversification until the policy changes at the end of the decade.

Given these reservations, the scale and chronology of factory construction by new and existing firms within the Merseyside Development Area from 1945 (fig. 7.3 and table 7.3) provides inferential evidence of an impact of regional policy, despite the relative insignificance of government-financed factory programmes relative to private development. The region's changing share of the total volume of industrial building approved within Development Areas generally and within Great Britain is instructive: an appor-

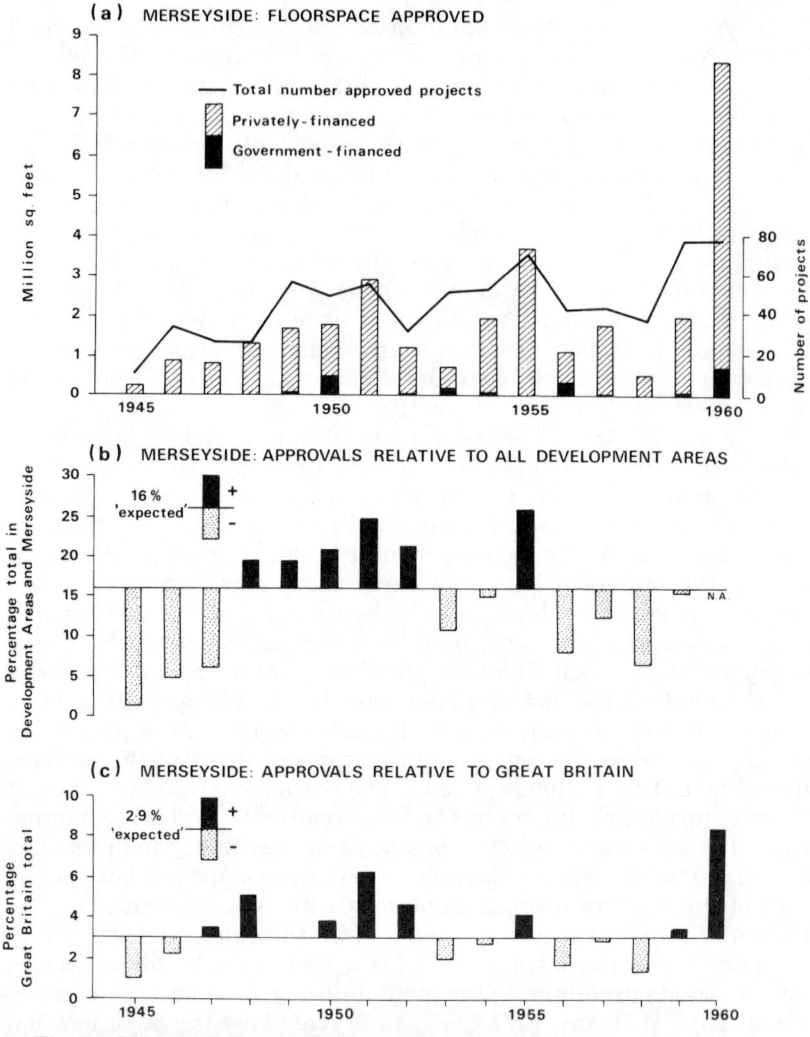

Fig. 7.3. Merseyside Development Area: industrial buildings approved 1945–60.

Note: Data refer to new factories and extensions exceeding 5000 sq. ft. by manufacturing industry.

(b) Floorspace approved in Merseyside relative to total approved in Development Areas and Merseyside for period 1945–48; Merseyside relative to total in Development Areas including Merseyside from 1949. (NA = not available).

tionment of such building relative to numbers of insured employees suggesting a 'fair' share for the region of some 16 per cent of annual Development Area approvals and 2·9 per cent of the national total. On this criterion of 'expected' approvals the area clearly under-achieved relative to the Development Areas between 1945 and 1947;

Table 7.3. *Merseyside Development Area, industrial buildings approved, 1945–60.*

	New factories and extensions in manufacturing industry (over 5000 sq. ft.)			
			% total area approved	
Year	*No.*	*Area ('000 sq. ft.)*	*Development Areas**	*Great Britain*
1945	12 (–)	235 (–)	1·4	0·9
1946	35 (–)	904 (–)	4·9	2·2
1947	27 (–)	868 (–)	6·1	3·5
1948	27 (–)	1,361 (–)	19·0	5·1
1949	61 (3)	1,685 (93)	19·6	2·9
1950	50 (8)	1,724 (514)	21·0	3·8
1951	56 (–)	2,911 (–)	24·8	6·3
1952	32 (1)	1,235 (12)	21·5	4·7
1953	52 (4)	750 (219)	10·9	1·9
1954	53 (5)	1,931 (120)	15·0	2·7
1955	71 (–)	3,707 (–)	26·0	4·1
1956	43 (2)	1,108 (339)	8·1	1·6
1957	44 (1)	1,752 (14)	12·4	2·8
1958	38 (–)	549 (–)	6·5	1·2
1959	78 (3)	1,984 (106)	15·4	3·4
1960	78 (3)	8,379 (725)	NA	8·4

( ) Government-financed schemes within total.
* Development Areas plus Merseyside 1945–48.
Sources: Hansard, Written Answers, 19.4.1962; Board of Trade; English Industrial Estates Corporation.

it received a disproportionately large volume of approvals relative to all Development Areas and the national total from 1948 to 1952, but again generally under-achieved from 1953 until 1958. This pattern is then reversed in 1959 and 1960. This chronology is at least indicative of a regional policy effect when considered in relation to the administrative record of location controls and financial incentives. The concentration of national productive investment in the original Development Areas is reflected in the low level of factory projects approved for Merseyside until 1947. Interestingly, the marked increase from 1948 in the region's share of approvals relative to the Development Areas precedes its formal scheduling from April 1949 perhaps reflecting administrative preferments outside the legislative framework of regional policy proper and Liverpool Corporation initiatives. The priority given to Merseyside after its designation is suggested by its continuing high level of approvals relative to all Development Areas until 1952, although this priority is then generally ceded until the late 1950s and the weakening of IDC controls from 1953 is suggested by the low relative level of approvals within Merseyside to 1959—the high levels of approvals in 1955 perhaps reflecting the attraction of its labour resources in a period of rapid industrial expansion and acute labour shortages elsewhere. The impact of the motor vehicles projects is apparent in the dramatic increase in Merseyside approvals in 1960. It appears probable, on the evidence, that any such regional policy effects derived more from location control mechanisms than from the more tangible instruments of regional intervention provided by the Distribution of Industry Acts, which had but marginal and localized impact as applied within the region in the review period.

NOTES AND REFERENCES

1. Merseyside County Council, *Merseyside Structure Plan: Written Statement* (1979).
2. D. Keeble, *Industrial location and planning in the United Kingdom* (1976); B. Moore and J. Rhodes, 'Regional economic policy and the movement of manufacturing firms to Development Areas', *Economica* (1976), 17–31.
3. B. Moore, J. Rhodes, and P. Tyler, 'The impact of regional policy in the 1970s', *CES Review,* no. 1 (1977), 67–77; B. Moore and J. Rhodes, 'Evaluating the effects of British regional economic policy', *Economic Journal* (1973), 87–110; J. Marquand, 'Measuring the effects and costs of regional incentives', *Government Economic Service Working Paper No. 32,* Department of Industry (1980); R. D. Rees and R. H. C. Miall, 'The effects of regional policy on manufacturing investment and capital stock within the UK', *Government Economic Service Working Paper No. 26,* Department of Industry (1979); G. Coleman, 'Regional development policy: The Merseyside experience, 1949–1966', ch. 16 in A. D. M. Phillips and B. J. Turton (eds.) *Environment, Man and Economic Change* (1975).
4. M. F. Batty, 'Merseyside—a successful development area', *The Three Banks Review,* **86** (1970), 23–40.
5. P. E. Lloyd, 'Industrial change in the Merseyside Development Area, 1949–1959', *Town Planning Review* (1964–5), 285–98.
6. We are grateful for the help of officials within the Department of Industry and the Treasury in facilitating access to documentary materials and to the Social Science Research Council and the University of Liverpool for grant aid towards research costs.
7. Board of Trade, *An industrial survey of Merseyside* (1932), p. 10.
8. W. Smith, *The Distribution of Population and the Location of Industry on Merseyside* (1942), p. 43.
9. Board of Trade, op. cit., p. 50.
10. *Royal Commission of the geographical distribution of the industrial population, Minutes of Evidence,* Appendix IV, HMSO (1938), pp. 323–4.
11. Board of Trade, op. cit.
12. Ministry of Labour, *Reports of investigations into the industrial conditions in certain depressed areas,* Cmd. 4728 (1934).
13. Public Record Office, file LAB 8/17.
14. HMSO, op. cit., p. 268.

15. Ibid., op. cit., p. 335. The 'Liverpool Area' is not defined but may have included Bootle and Waterloo.
16. Ministry of Labour, *Statement relating to Special Areas,* Cmd. 5386 (1937), p. 7; personal communication, Ministry of Defence.
17. *Liverpool Builds, 1945–1965,* Public Relations Office, City of Liverpool (1967), p. 19.
18. HMSO, op. cit., p. 827.
19. HMSO, op. cit., p. 832.
20. *Liverpool Corporation Act* (1936), 26 Geo. 5. and 1 Edw. 8., 1935–6, chap. cxxii, ss. 26–27.
21. HMSO, op. cit., p. 832.
22. *Development Plan: Report of Survey,* City and County Borough of Liverpool (1952), p. 55.
23. H. Gentleman, 'Kirkby industrial estate: theory versus practice', ch. 13 in R. Lawton and M. Cunningham (eds.), *Merseyside Social and Economic Studies* (1970).
24. 'Industrial development in 1932', *Board of Trade Journal,* (29.6.1933), iii–xv; also *Survey of industrial development,* annually (1933–38), HMSO (1934–9).
25. J. E. Baines, 'Merseyside in the British economy: the 1930s and the Second World War', ch. 3 in R. Lawton and M. Cunningham (eds.), op. cit. (1970), p. 70.
26. G. McCrone, *Regional policy in Britain* (1969).
27. Public Record Office, file HLG 71/1104 (1944–5).
28. Second report from the Select Committee on Estimates, Session 1946–7, *The administration of Development Areas*, HMSO HC97 (1947), p. 12.
29. Board of Trade, file LP(DI)(46).
30. Ibid., file LP(DI)(46).
31. *Economic survey for 1948,* HMSO, Cmd.7344 (1948), p. 39.
32. *Capital investment in 1948,* HMSO, Cmd.7268 (1947), p. 12.
33. Board of Trade, file DI(48).
34. Ibid., file (DI)(48).
35. Ibid., file DIR14339 G.
36. Board of Trade, file DI(48).
37. *Distribution of industry,* HMSO, Cmd.7540, (1948), p. 30.
38. See Hansard, *House of Commons Debates* (30.3.1949), cols. 1343–82; (19.3.1952), cols. 2408–11.
39. Minister of Supply, *Board of Trade Journal* (3.7.1948).
40. President of Board of Trade, *Board of Trade Journal* (5.8.1950), p. 290.
41. Board of Trade, file 1261/1950.
42. Ibid., file 1261/1950.
43. Ibid., file 1261/1950.
44. Ibid., file IM6 1768 (1954).
45 Second report from the Select Committee on Estimates, Session 1955–6, *Development Areas,* HMSO, HC139 (1955), p. xxv.
46. Board of Trade, file DIR260 (1956).
47. *Hansard,* Parliamentary Debates, Written Answers (5.6.1956).
48. Ibid. (24.2.1959).
49. Based on information provided by English Industrial Estates Corporation.

50. Board of Trade, file DIR26691, P/Part II.
51. HMSO (1955), op. cit., p. xxv.
52. Board of Trade, file DIR42/P.
53. *Civil Appropriation Accounts, Report of the Comptroller and Auditor-General,* HMSO (1955–6), p. xi.
54. *Distribution of Industry Act* (1945), 8 and 9 Geo.6., ch. 36, s. 3.
55. Ministry of Housing and Local Government, *Economies in local government services, Circular No. 54/52* (1952).
56. Board of Trade, file DIR42/P.
57. *Distribution of Industry Act* (1945), op. cit., s. 5.
58. Board of Trade, file DIR14339/G.
59. Ibid., file DIR14339/G.
60. *Distribution of Industry Act, 1945, Circular 22/59*, Ministry of Housing and Local Government (1959).
61. Board of Trade, file DIR7671/P, Part I.
62. Ibid., file DIR12523 G/II.
63. Ibid., file DIR577, 1956.
64. Ibid., file DIR7671/P/Part I.
65. Ibid., file DIR3365/1949.
66. Ibid., file DI6040, G1–9.
67. Ibid., file DI6040, G1–9.
68. *Town and Country Planning Act* (1947), 10 and 11 Geo.6., ch. 51, s. 14.
69. Board of Trade, file DIR4568/1946.
70. Ibid., file DIR7665/P/1956.
71. *Town and Country Planning (Erection of Industrial Buildings) Regulations*, S.I. No. 1025, HMSO (1949).
72. Board of Trade, file DIR114/P/1950.
73. A. E. Holmans, 'Industrial development certificates and control of the growth of employment in South-east England', *Urban Studies* (1964), 138–52.
74. Board of Trade, file DIR114P/1950.
75. Ibid., file DI&R125/P/1950.
76. Ibid., file DIR7665/P/1956.
77. Ibid., file DIR125/P/1950.
78. Ibid., file DIR114/P/1950.
79. Ibid., file DI&R17/P/1949.
80. T. Balogh, 'The distribution of industry: the reform of the control of industrial location, *Bulletin of the Oxford University Institute of Statistics* (1949), 107–9.
81. Board of Trade, file DIR7665/P, 1956.
82. Ibid., file DIR7665/P, 1956.
83. Ibid., file DIR7665/P, 1956.
84. Ibid., file IM6 166, 1954/Part I.
85. Ibid., file IM6 166, 1954/Part I.
86. Ibid., file DIR 12706 P/1958.
87. Ibid., file DIR26691, P/I, 1963.
88. J. Salt, 'The impact of the Ford and Vauxhall plants on the employment situation of Merseyside, 1962–1965', *Tijdschrift voor Economische en Sociale Geografie* (1967), 255–64; 'The motor industry on Merseyside', *Geography* (1968), 320–2.
89. Board of Trade, file DIR5722/R.

8

The development of transport on Merseyside since 1945*

J. S. DODGSON

I

A number of operators provided public transport services on Merseyside at the end of the Second World War. Liverpool Corporation operated tram and bus services in Liverpool and Bootle, while Birkenhead, Wallasey, St Helens, and Southport Corporations provided bus services in their respective areas. Birkenhead and Wallasey Corporations also operated cross-river ferry services, while other bus services were provided by non-municipal operators, in particular Crosville Motor Services and Ribble Motor Services.

Liverpool's tram system had been partially modernized in the 1930s, with extensions to the system of reserved track routes in the suburbs and construction of new modern-design cars. However, by 1945 half of the fleet was still of slow and obsolete design, while 72 per cent of the route network consisted of street track, mostly in the central and inner-city areas. The system created congestion for other road traffic, and hazard to passengers, who had to cross to the middle of the road to board cars. These factors, coupled with the high cost of renewing and maintaining existing track and overhead line equipment, the high capital cost of new tramcars compared with that of new buses, and the operational inflexibility of the system, led to a sensible early postwar decision for a phased abandonment of the system. This commenced in 1948 and was completed on schedule in 1957.[1]

In terms of traffic the most important local railway services were the electric services of the independent Mersey Railway between Liverpool and Birkenhead, which had been opened in 1886 and electrified in 1903, and the connecting Wirral line services of the London Midland and Scottish Railway, which had been electrified in 1938; the electric services of the former Lancashire and Yorkshire Railway to Southport and Ormskirk; and the electrified Liverpool

Notes and references begin on page 213.

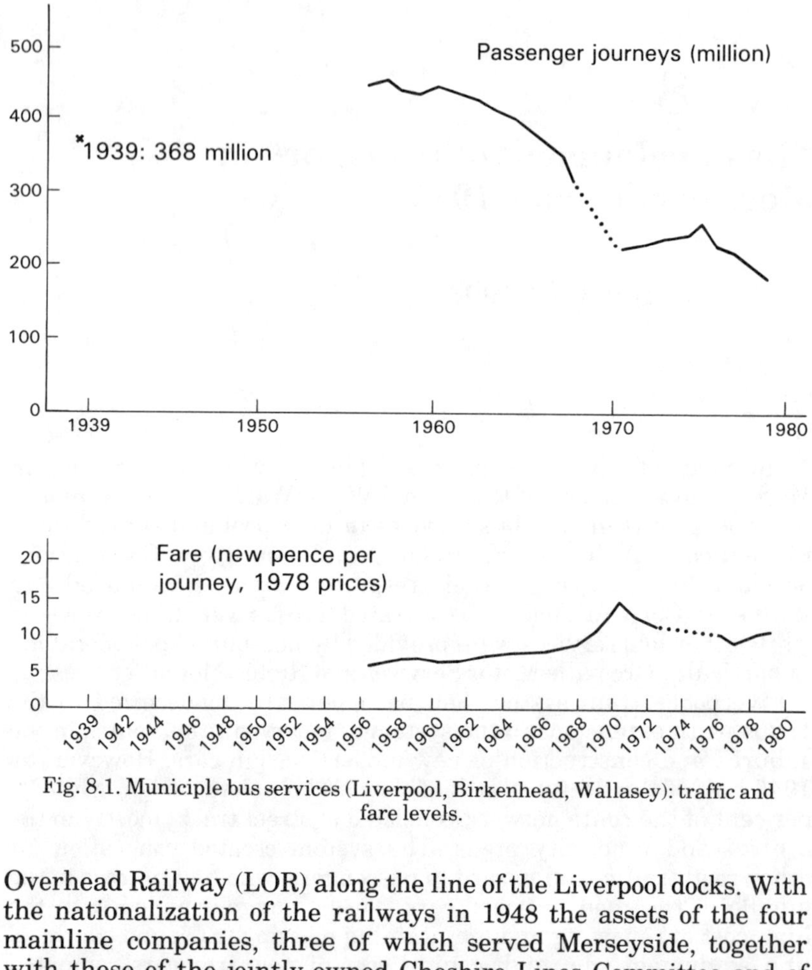

Fig. 8.1. Municiple bus services (Liverpool, Birkenhead, Wallasey): traffic and fare levels.

Overhead Railway (LOR) along the line of the Liverpool docks. With the nationalization of the railways in 1948 the assets of the four mainline companies, three of which served Merseyside, together with those of the jointly-owned Cheshire Lines Committee and of the Mersey Railway, were invested in the newly-formed British Transport Commission.[2]

The LOR retained its independence, but closed at the end of 1956. Traffic on the railway had averaged 6·4 million passengers per annum in the 1930s, and then climbed to a wartime peak of 13·9 million in 1944. Thereafter decline was slow though more or less continuous to 9·0 million in 1956. However, revenue still covered working expenditure and the reason for the closure was not the loss of traffic but the need for extensive reconstruction of the steel decking carrying the tracks. Rather than incur the heavy expenditure required, the directors of the Company decided in 1955 to terminate operations. Though attempts were made to keep the line

Table 8.1. *Car ownership rates per head of population, County Boroughs.*

	1951	*1961*	*1966*	*1971*
Birkenhead	0·03	0·07	0·12	0·16
Bootle	0·01	0·05	0·08	0·10
Liverpool	0·02	0·07	0·09	0·12
St Helens	0·02	0·07	0·10	0·14
Southport	0·06	0·12	0·18	0·24
Wallasey	0·03	0·08	0·13	0·18

Sources. Registrar-General, *Census of Population*, 1951, 1961, 1966, and 1971; Ministry of Transport, *Mechanically propelled vehicles returns*, 1951; Ministry of Transport, *Road Motor Vehicles*, 1961.

open, the fears about the inadequacy of the replacement bus service generally proved to be unfounded. The subsequent substantial decline in the dock labour force referred to in chapter 6 would, in any case, have deprived the system of much of its traffic had it continued in operation.

Declining traffic levels also affected municipal bus services, traffic reaching a post-war peak in both Birkenhead and Wallasey in 1950, and declining in Liverpool from the mid-1950s onwards after some increase in the early 1950s with the extension of outer-area housing estates and the closure of the LOR. Fig. 8.1 shows trends in bus journeys on Liverpool, Birkenhead and Wallasey municiple services from 1956/7 onwards.[3] By 1967/8 traffic in Liverpool was down by 25 per cent from its 1956/7 level, that in Birkenhead down by 39 per cent and that in Wallasey by 53 per cent (Figures for 1968/9 are not shown because the year was affected by an eight-week bus strike in Liverpool). The non-municipal bus operators on Merseyside also suffered some decline in traffic. In 1962/3, 49 million passenger journeys were made on Crosville bus services in the Merseyside conurbation (excluding Southport, Formby and St Helens) and 46·5 million on Ribble services. Traffic on these Crosville services had declined by 18 per cent over the previous ten years, though that on Ribble services had remained more-or-less stable with a slight decline at the end of the period.[4] (The bulk of both of these companies' routes lay outside Merseyside. For example, in 1962/3 roughly three-quarters of Ribble's total traffic and vehicle-mileage was outside Merseyside. Ribble's total traffic had reached a peak of 216 million journeys in 1955/6. By 1968 this total had fallen to 140 million, and by 1978 to 77 million, only about one-third of the 1955/6 peak).

This decline in public transport usage, mirrored elsewhere in the country, reflected rising car-ownership levels, changed location patterns, and the impact of road congestion on bus journey speeds.

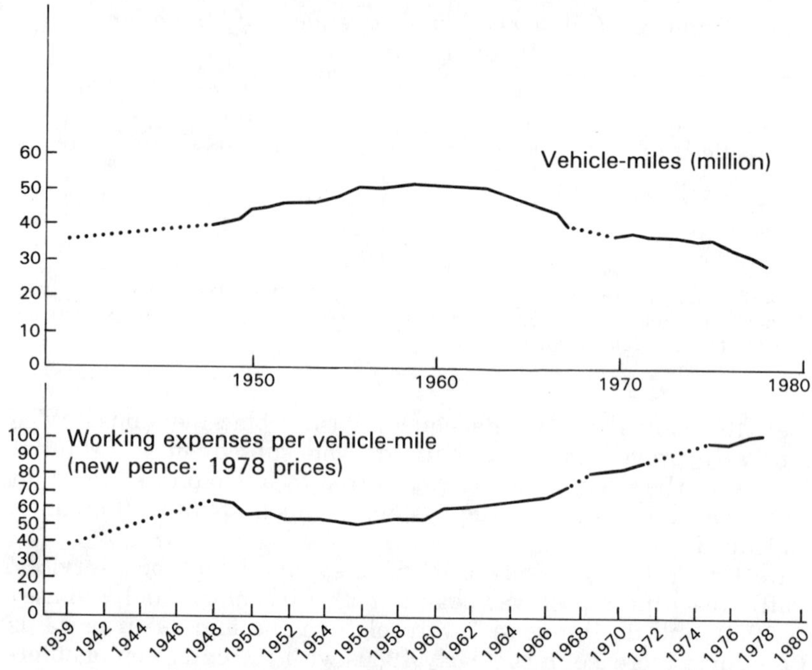

Fig. 8.2. Municiple bus services (Liverpool, Birkenhead, Wallasey): vehicle-miles and working expenses per vehicle-mile.

Table 8.1 shows the growth of car-ownership rates per head of population in the six former County Boroughs of Merseyside. By 1971 the *total* number of cars in the six boroughs was 4½ times greater than it had been in 1951. There is evidence, too, that rising income levels also increase the average annual mileage that each vehicle is driven. In these circumstances it is hardly surprising that there has been a fall in the use of public transport services.

A major problem with bus services is the difficulty in reducing capacity in line with demand. Thus, as fig. 8.2 shows, municipal bus-miles operated continued to increase up to 1959 and, while the number of journeys fell by 32 per cent between 1956/7 and 1967/8, bus-miles operated were only reduced by 21 per cent. If capacity cannot be reduced in line with traffic then, other things being equal, fares must be raised in real terms to keep revenue in balance with costs. Fig. 8.1 shows how real fares at constant 1978 prices, as measured by the rather crude index of real revenue per journey, have changed on Merseyside. This shows a general upward trend in fare levels through the late 1950s and 1960s as a result of relatively infrequent fare revisions. These fare increases would themselves have contributed to the traffic reductions, as would the decline in

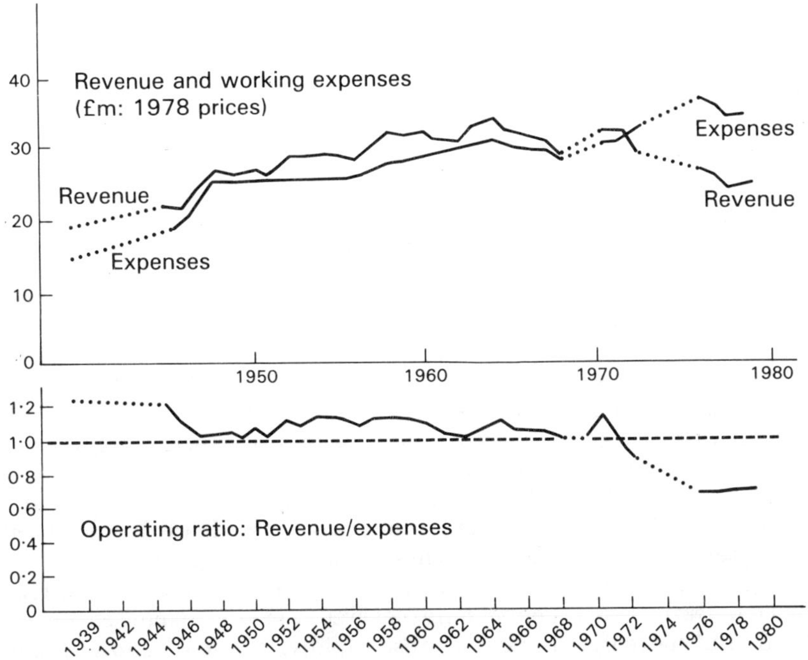

Fig. 8.3. Municiple bus services (Liverpool, Birkenhead, Wallasey): revenue and working expenses.

service standards caused by the fall in vehicle mileage after 1958/9. Considerable empirical evidence is now available on the impact of real fare changes, and of changes in service levels, on urban bus patronage in Britain. Typical results reveal absolute real fare elasticity values of the order of 0·3 (so that increases in fares increase total revenue), while bus mileage elasticities take somewhat higher absolute values.[5]

The overall impact of traffic and fare changes on revenue at constant 1978 prices is shown in fig. 8.3. Traffic growth in the late 1940s and early 1950s, together with the increase in real fares, led to a general upward trend in revenue up to 1963/4. Thereafter the accelerating decline in traffic led to a reduction in real revenue by 1967/8. Working expenses at constant prices also exhibited an upward trend. Working expenses per vehicle-mile are shown in fig. 8.2. There was a general decline up to 1955/6 caused by tramway abandonment in Liverpool. Working expenses per vehicle-mile on Liverpool Corporation bus services were only two-thirds of expenses per car-mile on the tram system, and so as the proportion of tramcar miles to total vehicle miles for the municipal systems fell from 48 per cent in 1947/8 to zero by 1958/9, so working expenses per vehicle-mile fell despite increases in real per unit labour costs. The net result of these factors was that total working expenses rose in the late 1940s, fell between 1948/9 and 1949/50 and between 1950/1 and 1953/4 as tramway abandonment got under way, and then rose from 1954/5 and up to 1963/4, even though vehicle-mileage had peaked in 1958/9. Thereafter declining vehicle-mileage counterbalanced the increased costs per mile, and total working expenses in real terms began to fall.

As fig. 8.3 shows, revenue exceeded working expenses in every year up to 1968. This was so in every year in Birkenhead and Wallasey, and in every year except 1948/9 in Liverpool. The Liverpool tram system failed to generate enough revenue to cover costs from 1946/7 onwards, and consequently operating losses on the tram system were cross-subsidized by operating profits from Liverpool's expanding bus network. The relative size of the overall gap between revenue and working expenses is shown in fig. 8.3 by the 'operating ratio' between revenue and working expenses, which fell as low as 1·01 in 1948/9, 1950/1 and 1967/8. Thus, in many years revenue would have been insufficient to cover realistic depreciation and interest costs on the capital assets used by the operators.[6]

Financial problems were much more serious on the railways. British Railways' revenue only covered working expenses up to 1956, and thereafter the deficit rose rapidly. The most unprofitable passenger services were stopping trains, and the BTC continued the former pre-war companies' policy of a gradual withdrawal of services. On Merseyside, the Bootle branch service between Lime Street and Alexandra Dock was withdrawn in 1948; the Aintree–Bootle service in 1951; the Aintree Central–Southport Lord Street service in 1952; the West Kirby–Hooton service in 1956; and the Aintree–Gateacre and the Bidston–Seacombe service in 1960. These were all lightly-used routes. Nationally the service withdrawals and the massive investment sanctioned in the 1956 Modernization Plan failed to restore profitability, and in the 1962 Transport Act the BTC was abolished and replaced by a separate British Railways Board.

A major report published in 1963 (the Beeching Report) presented an analysis of the profitability of different parts of BR's business and network and proposed very much more widespread closures. Many, but by no means all, of these were implemented but further service closures on Merseyside consisted of desirable cost-saving rationalizations of duplicated facilities rather than real reductions in service quality. Birkenhead Woodside terminus closed in 1967 and services terminated at Rock Ferry; Liverpool Riverside station, used only by boat trains, closed in 1971 with the decline of deep-sea travel; Liverpool Central high level terminus closed in 1972 though most services had been diverted to Lime Street in 1966;[7] Liverpool

Exchange terminus closed in 1977 with the opening of the city-centre link line; and the infrequent Southport–Lime Street diesel service was withdrawn in 1978 following the completion of stations on the loop line which gave connections to the direct Liverpool–Southport electric route.

Decline in public transport usage, rising operating costs, and the associated financial problems of public transport operators were accompanied by increased road congestion as a result of the increased car-ownership levels noted above. This was particularly serious in the Liverpool–Birkenhead road tunnel, where peak-hour congestion led to delays to other traffic in the city centre areas around the tunnel entrances. As fig. 8.4 shows, traffic through the tunnel, which had been opened in 1934, grew very rapidly in the postwar period from 2·6 million vehicles in 1944/5 to 12·6 million in 1959/60 and 18·8 million by 1967/8.

There were a number of responses to these problems of increased traffic congestion and declining public transport usage. In the early 1960s the solution was seen to lie mainly in extensive investment to cater for demand, rather than in terms of more effective traffic management or different types of pricing policy. A series of studies were therefore instituted to determine investment priorities for Merseyside transport. The first such major study was the Merseyside Conurbation Traffic Study of 1962. A Steering Committee on Merseyside Traffic and Transport was appointed of representatives from local authorities on Merseyside and from transport operators. The Steering Committee appointed three Technical Committees; a Highways and Traffic Committee to plan highway improvements; a Transport Committee to consider co-ordination and improvement of public transport services; and a Mersey River Crossing Committee to consider cross-river road facilities. Detailed traffic surveys of highways, bus, ferry, and rail use were carried out in September 1962.

The River Crossing Committee and the Transport Committee submitted Interim Reports in November 1963.[8] The River Crossing Committee recommended construction of a Liverpool–Wallasey tunnel, rejecting a 1961 consultants study which favoured a bridge between Liverpool and Birkenhead. Parliamentary powers for the tunnel were obtained in August 1965. The tunnel is a twin-bore tunnel linked to the M53 mid-Wirral motorway via the route of the closed Bidston–Seacombe railway. The first bore was opened in June 1971 and the second in February 1974.

The final reports of the Committees were presented in 1965.[9] The Highways and Traffic Committee proposed massive road investment to cater for the traffic growth which it forecast would have occurred by 1982. The road investment proposals included substantial urban motorway construction, including both an inner-city circular motorway and a middle-city circular motorway between the inner-city circle and the Queens Drive ring road, plus radial motorways along the dock road, between Anfield and Maghull, and between the docks and the M62. The cost of these schemes over the period 1965–82 was estimated at £1020m. at 1978 price levels.

The basis for these proposals was a crude projection of traffic levels. Existing traffic flows were derived from the 1962 surveys and were then projected to 1982 on the basis of 1982 population forecasts and forecasts of the differential growth-rates in car ownership in different areas of the conurbation. Predicted flows between each origin and destination were then assigned to routes on the basis of minimum time paths. Clearly such traffic projections will depend upon the underlying population and car ownership forecasts, but in addition the pattern of trips cannot be expected to increase pro rata in line with the expected growth in these area-specific variables. The investment proposals themselves were based purely on that investment which was judged likely to be able to carry the forecast traffic levels without undue congestion; there was no consideration of whether the benefits to traffic would be sufficient to cover the construction and environmental costs involved.

The Transport Committee's report recommended the setting up of a unified authority to be responsible for all forms of cross-river traffic. This authority would not only operate the road tunnels but would also take over operation of the Mersey rail tunnel from BR. The Committee had considered the case for a unified authority for all public transport in the Merseyside conurbation, echoing proposals that had been made in the 1930s,[10] but had been unable to reach agreement; it appears that some local authority representatives were in favour but that BR, Ribble, and Crosville were opposed.

The other main recommendation of the Transport Committee was to improve rail services in central Liverpool by construction of a one-way loop on the former Mersey Railway line and of a link line between the Southport and Ormskirk lines, Liverpool Central low level, and the Garston/Gateacre line and the Wapping Tunnel line to Edge Hill. The loop line, together with a burrowing junction at Hamilton Square Birkenhead, was regarded as necessary to cater for a forecast increase in traffic on Mersey Railway line services. The September 1962 rail survey had shown that morning peak-period traffic on the Mersey railway exceeded seating capacity (but not fully-loaded capacity), and a rough estimate was made that there would be an increase of traffic suitable for rail conveyance of the order of 2½ per cent per annum. In addition, surveys of ultimate destinations of rail passengers showed that most were heading for a destination close to their rail terminal and that there was a reluctance to walk far within the city centre area. The loop scheme would both increase capacity and improve city centre distribution of rail passengers to four instead of two Liverpool stations, while link construction would provide rail access to the south side of the city centre for commuters from north of the city. Construction of the link would be made possible by vacation of the existing Central low level platforms by cross-river trains after construction of the loop. The Liverpool City Corporation also proposed in an independent report that services over the link should be extended over newly-electrified but existing rail routes to provide a continuous outer circle service over the Garston–Gateacre–West Derby–Walton route of the former Cheshire Lines Committee.[11]

The whole premise on which all these schemes were based was thus the forecast undercapacity on the Mersey Railway. However, the forecast increase in rail traffic is inconsistent with the road traffic forecasts produced by the Highways and Traffic Committee. Peak hour road traffic to Central Liverpool was forecast to grow by 2·3 times between 1962 and 1982, and while some of this increase would be due to population growth, much would come from the forecast increase in car ownership. But the increase due to car ownership would be likely to be balanced by a reduction in public transport use. Indeed rail traffic figures in the Transport Committee's report show an actual reduction in Mersey Railway use between 1957 and 1962. Thus even assuming population growth in the Merseyside conurbation, the case for increasing MR capacity (on which all the other rail schemes depended) was not proven, particularly since no estimates were made of the economic benefits of any of the rail improvements.

The early 1960s were a period of rapid development and improvement of traffic prediction and evaluation methods, with the spread of comprehensive land use/transportation studies from North America throughout the world. Already, in January 1965, it had been decided to undertake such a major study on Merseyside to remedy acknowledged faults of the 1962 traffic studies. The final report of the MALTS study (Merseyside Area Land Use and Transportation Study) was completed in 1969.[12] As with land use/transportation studies for other UK conurbations, the study surveyed existing land use and private and public transport traffic levels; developed models which synthesized the existing traffic patterns; and then forecast future traffic demand in a 'design-year' (1991) on the basis of these traffic models, a chosen land-use plan for the design-year and forecasts of socio-economic variables such as population and employment.[13] Alternative methods of catering for the traffic forecasts by means of alternative road and public transport improvements were then subjected to a form of economic evaluation.

MALTS forecast that population in the MALTS area (the Merseyside conurbation, excluding Southport and St Helens) would grow from their estimate of 1·4 million in 1966 to between 1·8 million and 2 million in the early 1990s, while employment would grow from 665,000 to 767,000. Since a population of 1·8 million would have required an employment of 784,000 to support it, whereas the estimated employment lay below this, MALTS also made some allowances for a lower population growth to 1·6 million, though this does not appear to have had much impact on the proposals in the final Report. To cater for the increased population, alternative land use plans were compared in terms of their differential impact on development costs, land drainage and public service costs, highway and public transport capital costs, public and private transport operating costs, travel time costs, accident costs, and the sources and availability of finance. The extent to which the schemes satisfied a number of planning goals was also considered, and, on these bases, a preferred plan was chosen. This plan, referred to as the Eastern Radial Plan, envisaged the main new development being around rail links to the East of the Conurbation.

The socio-economic implications of this land-use plan were then used to produce traffic forecasts for 1991, and a transport system was designed to carry the traffic. As a lower limit it was considered that the network should be able to handle all off-peak traffic without congestion: this was referred to as the 'restrained network'. A more extensive network which could also handle all peak movements by those who wished to use their cars was referred to as the 'choice network'. The recommended networks for these two situations were estimated to cost £847m. and £945m. respectively at 1978 prices, plus £100m. to meet environmental standards and a further £160m. to include schemes in a wider study area (broadly corresponding with the present Merseyside County). The two schemes were therefore similar, and both included substantial urban motorway and new arterial road construction, together with a 6-lane Aigburth-Bromborough bridge across the Mersey.

MALTS also considered the case for improvement of city centre rail services, and concluded both that they would be justified and that they should have priority over the road improvements. Its priority rail recommendations for the 1970s were the construction of the loop, link, and burrowing junction, together with electrification from Rock Ferry to Hooton and from Liverpool Central to Hough Green, and for demonstration projects on car/rail and bus/rail interchange. The report doubted whether the Outer Rail Loop or a proposed Aintree–Bootle scheme would be justified. The total cost of all the recommended rail schemes was estimated at £36m. at 1978 prices.

II

By the time the final MALTS report appeared, the unified passenger transport authority for Merseyside debated by the Transport Committee had come into being as a result of national policy changes. The then-Labour Government had instituted a comprehensive review of all aspects of transport policy which culminated in the passing of the 1968 Transport Act. By this Act Passenger Transport Executives responsible for all aspects of public transport in their area had been set up in the four largest English conurbations outside London. The PTEs were charged with the task of securing or promoting 'the provision of a properly integrated and efficient system of public passenger transport'. To this end they were to take over municipal bus operators in their areas (in Merseyside; Liverpool, Birkenhead, and Wallasey Corporation Passenger Transport Departments); to negotiate agreements concerning service and fare levels on local bus services provided by non-PTE operators (in Merseyside, the Crosville and Ribble subsidiaries of the newly formed National Bus Company); and to assume responsibility for the fares, service levels and frequency, but *not* operation, of local BR rail services in their areas. The professional PTE was responsible to a Passenger Transport Authority made up of elected representatives of the local authorities in the Merseyside conurbation. To aid the improvement of urban public transport, Section 56 of the 1968 Act provided up to 75 per cent central government grants for approved capital expenditure projects.

The Act also revised financial arrangements for BR. It was recognized that many local rail services which were unprofitable also provided social benefits sufficient to outweigh the financial losses from their provision. These services were to be identified and a specific subsidy paid to cover each service's loss. Services within PTE areas would be subsidised by the PTEs, with Central Government assistance, under Section 20 of the Act, while others would be subsidized directly by Central Government under Section 39 of the Act. Although the framers of the Act had intended that social cost-benefit analysis would be used to determine which services justified subsidization, in the event this was not done and many services providing low levels of social benefit continued to be operated.[14] Figures of costs and revenues for individual services in 1971, 1973, and 1974 indicate that, of services wholly or partly subsidized by Merseyside, the New Brighton/Birkenhead–Wrexham line certainly did not justify subsidization on social benefit grounds.[15]

Following the priority recommendations in MALTS for the loop and link lines, the Merseyside PTE applied to Central Government for Section 56 grants. The Department of the Environment approved a grant for the two mile loop in April 1971 and one for the $1^1/_8$ mile link in January 1972. Contracts for construction were let, and both loop and link lines were opened in April 1977. The line to Kirkby was also electrified, in April 1977, as was the closed Liverpool Central to Garston line, which was re-opened in January 1978.

The 1968 Transport Act had required each PTE to produce a plan describing its proposals for the future development of the passenger transport system of its area. That for Merseyside was published in March 1972.[16] The plan proposed that rail services based on the loop and link would form the backbone of public transport services on Merseyside. Bus services would be re-organized to feed passengers into the rail network at interchange points. Interchange imposes a time and inconvenience penalty on passengers, and following the MALTS priority recommendation, the impact of this was investigated in an important series of interchange experiments on Merseyside financed by the PTE and the Department of the Environment.[17]

The early 1970s were a period of economic growth and of growth in public expenditure, and central government had shown itself willing to help finance major public transport improvements. In addition, the 1960s solution of massive urban road investment was now seen to be unworkable both for financial and for environmental reasons. Consequently the 1972 transport plan proposed further rail investment in electrification of rail routes and re-instatement of closed passenger services. These were appraised on the basis of traffic forecasts from an updated version of MALTS which made some downward adjustment to the original MALTS population and employment forecast for 1976. Alternative plans were compared with a base plan which included the loop and link and other MALTS priority rail schemes. The base plan itself was not appraised, but a cost-benefit study was made of the relative advantages of the different alternatives. It was on the basis of this that further rail extensions were proposed, including North and South loops using the CLC outer circle line, which would have been connected to the direct Lime Street–St Helens line at Broadgreen, and an underground link between Liverpool Central and the St Helens line at Edgehill. However, the explanation in the report of the cost-benefit study methodology is unclear, and it appears that different types of effects of proposals (such as impact on construction costs, operating costs, travel costs, accessibility, convenience, comfort, needs of the old, environmental effects, and accidents) were weighted against each other in an arbitrary manner, so that the final proposals probably reflect optimism about government finance rather than a proper economic evaluation.

The 1972 Local Government Act reorganized local government boundaries and led to the enlargement of the PTE area. From April 1974 the new Merseyside Metropolitan County Council became the

Passenger Transport Authority for its area, discharging those duties through its Passenger Transport Committee. The enlarged County area now includes the former Southport and St Helens County Boroughs, whose municipal bus services were transferred to the PTE. At the same time a significant change was made in the system of central government finance for local transport expenditure. Formerly central government assistance for highway and public transport services was provided at different percentage rates. This was alleged to lead to biases against types of expenditure which attracted lower rates of central government assistance. In addition, County Councils were not required to consider their transport expenditure as a whole.

Under the new system each County Council must submit an annual Transport Policy and Programme (TPP) setting out the objectives of its transport policies and detailing its planned expenditure over a five-year period. On Merseyside the TPP is prepared by the County Council's Joint Transportation Unit.[18] On the basis of the TPP submission central government approves a total level of expenditure, which attracts Rate Support Grant. In addition, Transport Supplementary Grant (TSG) is paid on all eligible expenditure over a minimum threshold. The percentage rate at which TSG is paid is fixed each year, and all eligible expenditure attracts support at the same rate. Some items of transport expenditure, most notably concessionary travel payments and new bus grants, are not eligible for TSG though they attract some element of Central Government assistance through the Rate Support Grant or, in the case of new bus grants, via grants under Section 32 of the 1968 Transport Act. In addition losses on the Mersey Tunnels are capitalized, and trunk road expenditure is financed wholly by central government. Once central government has approved a total level of expenditure and determined its own contribution, the County Council has autonomy in allocating its actual transport spending as it sees fit (though implementation of a programme not consistent with the original TPP submission might lead to a response by central government in the following year's TPP negotiations).

By the early 1970s it had been realized that most of the MALTS recommendations were no longer relevant for Merseyside's transport needs. One major weakness of land use/transportation studies was dependence on the forecasts of future land use, population, employment, and other socio-economic variables on which the transport use forecasts depended. Relatively little effort was put into deriving these land use forecasts and allowing for the possibility of divergences from the predicted population and employment trends. This proved to be the downfall of MALTS, because of the slowdown of population growth and economic growth on Merseyside. Thus work

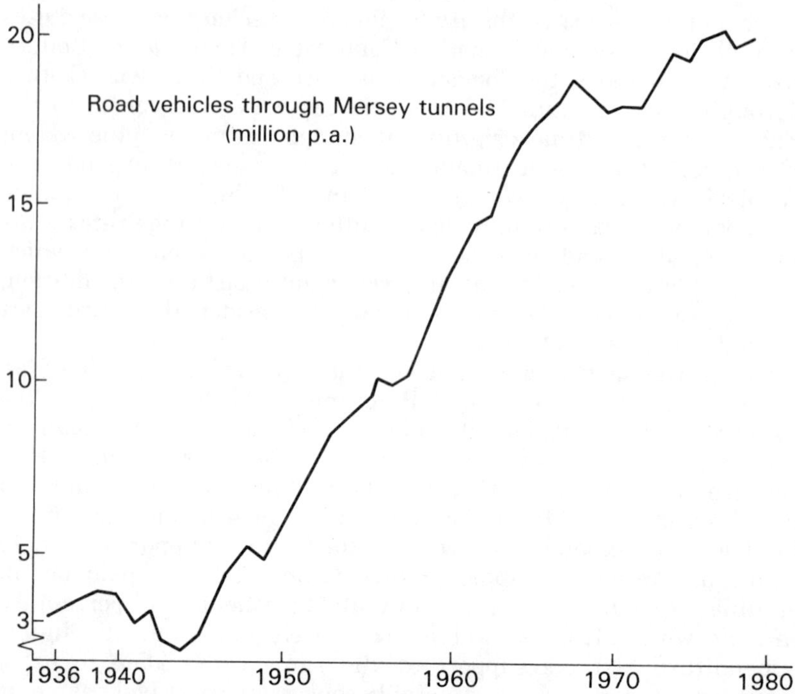

Fig. 8.4. Mersey Tunnels: road traffic.

trips to Liverpool city centre fell from 158,000 per day in 1961 to 92,000 in 1971. As fig. 8.4 shows, traffic through the Mersey Tunnels has not expanded rapidly in the 1970s; from 18·8 million vehicles in 1967/8, the annual total had only reached 20·2 million in 1978/9. The current expectation is that, far from increasing, Merseyside County's population will decline from 1·58 million in 1976 to what the Merseyside County Council's Draft Structure Plan describes as 'best guesses' of 1·51 million in 1981 and 1·48 million in 1986.[19] The current policy is to renew existing built-up areas rather than expand the size of the conurbation as envisaged in MALTS.

With the downturn in national economic growth and reaction against urban motorway construction, the MALTS forecasts of the availability of government finance for capital expenditure also proved to be greatly over-optimistic. Because, like other similar studies elsewhere, MALTS had based its recommendations on a transport system designed for a year far in the future, with little consideration of the best policies in the intervening period, or of short-term measures to achieve the best use of existing assets, it suffered from what has been termed the 'long-range planning syndrome', and with the collapse of its under-lying assumptions the approach was not flexible enough to provide adequate advice as to what should be done in the changed economic and financial climate.

Financial stringency has therefore been a major feature influencing transport planning in Britain in the latter part of the 1970s. The annual TPPs have therefore had to balance conflicting demands for transport expenditure against limited resources. One major requirement is for maintenance of the existing highway network. Table 8.2 shows expenditure accepted by central government for Transport Supplementary Grant for 1978/9 in different County Councils, plus the value of concessionary travel. Highway maintenance accounted for 31 per cent of this expenditure on Merseyside and, although the proportion varies from County to County, the expenditure per head was roughly similar in all the conurbations, lying between £7·26 and £10·67 per head at 1978 prices.

A second major requirement for finance has been to support operating losses and capital charges on bus services. Figure 8.3 shows that while revenue had covered working expenses on Merseyside bus services up to 1971, after 1971 working losses were incurred and in the period from 1974/5 to 1977/8 revenue only covered 75 per cent of working expenses, leaving the remaining 25 per cent, plus all capital charges, to be met by subsidy. In the first years of PTE operation, 1970 and 1971, deficits were avoided by very substantial increases in real fares, as fig. 8.1 shows. After 1971 fare increases failed to keep pace with inflation, partly as a result of government price restraint, so that real fares fell and although there was some recovery in bus traffic up to 1974/5 this was insufficient to prevent real revenue from falling as shown in fig. 8.3. Figure 8.2 shows that vehicle-miles operated remained relatively stable up to 1975/6 and this, coupled with increased real costs per vehicle-mile, led to the increases in total working expenses at constant prices shown in fig. 8.3.

The main response to these financial problems was to rationalize bus services. PTE bus mileage fell by 17 per cent between 1975/6 and 1978/9. The mileage operated by NBC companies on behalf of the PTE also fell by a similar proportion because the agreement under which Crosville and Ribble provide services within Merseyside specifies that they should operate a fixed proportion of the total bus mileage in the area. Real fares also fell slightly, and passenger numbers continued to decline.

While rationalization reduced the total bus subsidy on Merseyside by 32 per cent in real terms between 1975/6 and 1978/9, the total public transport subsidy only fell by 10 per cent because of a 40 per cent rise in the subsidy to rail services, largely due to increased capital costs associated with the loop and link and with rolling stock replacement. By 1978/9 bus services accounted for 63 per cent of the

Table 8.2. *Transport expenditure in English conurbations 1978/79 (1978 prices).*

		Proportions of total (%)				*Expenditure per head of 1977 population (£)*			
	Total (£m)	*Highway maintenance*	*BR revenue support*	*Bus + other revenue support*	*Capital*	*Highway maintenance*	*All revenue support*	*Capital*	*Total*
Merseyside	43·9	30·6	22·0	38·3	9·2	8·60	16·94	2·58	28·12
Greater Manchester	61·5	31·6	13·7	34·1	20·6	7·26	10·99	4·71	22·96
Tyne and Wear	91·0	12·1	2·8	18·0	67·1	9·39	16·12	52·07	77·58
West Midlands	62·2	38·2	5·4	40·4	16·1	8·69	10·43	3·65	22·77
South Yorkshire	34·2	40·7	3·9	40·7	14·6	10·67	11·69	3·83	26·19
West Yorkshire	49·7	43·8	10·0	26·9	19·2	10·50	8·84	4·61	23·95
Greater London	239·9	29·6	0	34·1	36·3	10·19	11·74	12·49	34·42

Notes. Transport expenditure includes transport expenditure accepted by Central Government for TSG, *plus* value of concessionary travel. The figures for Greater London exclude Central Government subsidy for BR rail services in London; GLC subsidies for London Transport underground services are included under 'bus and other revenue support'.

total public transport subsidy, rail services for 32 per cent and ferries for 5 per cent. While Merseyside is the conurbation outside London and Glasgow with the greatest rail use—in 1971, 17 per cent of commuters to the city centre arrived by rail, compared with 14·5 per cent in Manchester, 8·5 per cent in Newcastle, and 8 per cent in Birmingham—the rail subsidy does appear high in relation to that for buses. Thus in 1978/9 the subsidy per journey was 5 pence by PTE bus, 10·8 pence by NBC bus, 27·5 pence by rail, and 40·6 pence by ferry. The subsidy per passenger mile was 1·7 pence by PTE bus, 3·7 pence by NBC bus, 4·8 pence by rail, and 40·6 pence by ferry.

The poor value-for-money provided by ferry services has led to attempts to withdraw them. The ferries carried 26·2 million people in 1945 and 31·1 million in 1950, but by 1977/8 the annual total was a mere 3·2 million. In 1974 a study commissioned by the PTE to recommend policy concluded that withdrawal of services would minimize the financial loss and that other cross-river modes could cope with the diverted traffic.[20] Withdrawal of the Birkenhead ferry is complicated by the PTE's inheritance of an ancient royal charter. A Parliamentary bill was promoted to release the PTE from its obligations under this charter, but was talked out. Consequently, the ferries remain, although, as the Merseyside Structure Plan correctly notes, they 'are no longer essential for cross-river traffic'.

Table 8.2 shows that revenue support per head of the population for public transport services is high on Merseyside compared with most other conurbations. (The London figure is not directly comparable because it excludes central government subsidies for BR services in London). In these circumstances capital expenditure has been squeezed, with investment only accounting for 9 per cent of expenditure on Merseyside in 1978/9. Most of the rail electrification and extension schemes proposed in the PTE's 1972 Transport Plan have been abandoned. Only the electrification extensions to Hough Green and Hooton are under consideration, with the possibility of a spur line through the Wapping Tunnel to Edge Hill, where services would link into the St Helens line whose electrification on the 25 kv a.c. system depends on BR plans to electrify connections from Liverpool to the main London–Glasgow line. As we have seen, the population and employment projections in MALTS proved incorrect, as were the forecasts of undercapacity on the Mersey Railway. Instead of increasing, rail traffic under the Mersey fell in every year between 1969 and 1977. By 1979 the number of trains in the busiest hour on the loop, a major justification of which was to increase capacity, was 18, compared with 24 per hour in 1975 before the loop was opened. Neverthless, the rail extensions do appear to have arrested the decline in rail traffic, with a 25 per cent increase in weekday central area rail passenger arrivals between March 1977 and March 1979.

Though many of the rail improvements proposed in MALTS were implemented, the highway investment plans were not. With capital expenditure limited, it is important that those schemes which are approved be those with the best returns. The Merseyside Structure Plan states that priority should be given to maintaining and improving existing roads, with the aims of helping commerce and industry, reducing accidents, improving the environment, helping the operation of buses, and reducing excessive traffic delays. Of £80m. proposed for road investment by Merseyside between 1978/9 and 1985/6, £36m. is accounted for by one scheme, the Liverpool inner ring road. However, the justification for this scheme is flimsy in the extreme. Botham and Herson have shown that on the basis of the figures and forecasts presented in the Feasibility Study and Technical Reports on the road there can be no doubt that the economic benefits, in terms of savings in vehicle operating costs, savings in time, and reduction in accident costs, will be insufficient to cover the capital costs of the scheme.[21] Furthermore, the road will lead to serious environmental effects. Finally, as I argue in the following section and as the consultants' report on the ring road scheme concluded, the impact of road investment in stimulating economic activity is not likely to be significant. (Indeed a number of factories will actually have to be demolished to make way for the ring road, with consequent loss of employment). The only reason for the County Council proceeding with the scheme appeared to be the willingness of central government to provide most of the finance, and the questions of whether the expenditure would actually increase net social benefits or of whether alternative road schemes might yield better returns have not been considered.

One of the objectives of the TPP system was that County Councils should compare different types of transport expenditure, whether for public or private transport or for current or capital expenditure, and achieve the best balance between them. In practice this has not happened because short-term exigencies and inherited obligations have been the major factor determining the split between different types of expenditure. One problem on Merseyside has been the vacuum in economic appraisal left by MALTS. MALTS took a long-term view of requirements, and there was a failure to develop effective economic techniques to monitor and appraise existing operations and minor improvements. This failure is only now being remedied. (At the same time, a broader comparison of the benefits of different types of expenditure within a multi-criteria analysis framework might be helpful in determining whether the current balance between different types of expenditure is the best one.)[22]

A second problem is the lack of clearly-specified objectives. While successive transport plans and policy statements have listed objectives in physical terms, the lack of ways of trading-off benefits of different kinds has meant that, where different objectives were inconsistent with each other, the appropriate policy was not clear. In 1978 the PTE adopted as its objective the maximization of passenger-miles, subject to financial and other constraints. This objective was first developed by London Transport, but so far the objective appears to have had little impact on policy on Merseyside.[23] The figures of subsidy per passenger-mile quoted above show that, in terms of passenger-mileage from a given subsidy, PTE bus services are more effective than NBC bus services, rail services or ferry services, though the scope for improving on achievement of the objective depends on the marginal subsidy per passenger-mile rather than on these average figures.

One problem in implementing the PTE's objective is lack of data. Historically, bus companies did not develop proper costing systems,[24] and, although a Service Costing/Revenue Analysis and Monitoring (SCRAM) system came into operation in 1981, Merseyside PTE was relatively slow in remedying this omission. This has meant that, despite passenger surveys, bus service cuts have not always been based on the fullest information since the PTE was not fully aware of the cost implications of cutting different services. Thus the present pattern of bus services is not necessarily optimal, and with SCRAM operational it would be sensible to carry out a further review of services. A more comprehensive approach to service revision is that being implemented elsewhere in the country by NBC subsidiaries. While traditional methods of revision modify the existing pattern of bus services, these Market Analysis Project studies survey passenger needs and try to design an optimum bus network around them. Preliminary results of implementation of NBC studies show that significant cost savings can be achieved without the passenger loss that often accompanies blanket service reductions.[25]

In conclusion, there have been major changes in public transport on Merseyside since 1968, particularly with the development of the rail system. With interchange facilities, marketing and zone ticketing the PTE have been innovative, and have gone far to achieve integration of public transport in the physical sense. Unfortunately, while the priority public transport improvements recommended in MALTS have been implemented, the changes in the Merseyside economy have meant that the improved system will carry much less traffic than originally forecast. Increased energy prices are unlikely to change this situation. The 1979/80 TPP submission notes that when the price of petrol more than doubled in 1973/4 there was no noticeable increase in public transport patronage. A detailed monitoring study of the effects of this fuel price increase on rail commuting on Merseyrail's Northern Line found some evidence of a short-term switch to rail, with a road-to-rail cross price elasticity of 0·3. However, the transfers from car to rail were lost with subsequent rail fare increases, and the study concludes 'significant substitution to the use of public passenger transport in the longer-term, consequent upon increases in petrol prices alone, does not appear to be a very probable development'.[26]

Given the decline in population and city centre employment, it is now questionable whether the social benefits of the major rail improvements will justify their cost. Furthermore, while the real improvements in the quality of many public transport services can help to arrest the decline in ridership, the future is likely to see continuing financial problems. The Structure Plan proposed that bus mileage be stabilized at its 1979 level. With fare increases planned at the rate of increase in earnings, this meant that total public transport revenue support in real terms was forecast to increase from £20m. in 1978/9 to £32m. by 1985/6.

In the present economic climate such an increase may simply be unrealistic. If finance were not available for greater operating subsidies then, because cuts in bus costs are easier to achieve than cuts in rail costs (both because of the more fixed nature of railway costs and because costing of rail services is under the control of BR and not of the PTE), there might be reductions in the quality of bus services to finance the more expensive rail services inherited as a result of MALTS. Consequently, travellers in those areas, often with lower than average levels of income and car ownership, not directly or through interchange indirectly served by rail services would be further disadvantaged.

In such circumstances the alternative of more rapid increases in public transport fares may be preferable. But there does appear to be an unfortunate and widely-held view that escalating public transport subsidies are inevitable, and cannot be avoided except by such fare increases or by cuts in service quality. Acceptance of such a view by local politicians leads to provision of an open-ended subsidy, which is itself dangerous because it can lead to managerial inefficiency.[27] It is important that services be operated as efficiently as possible, and a strict cash limit on the size of the subsidy can help to achieve this. One important area where significant savings in manpower could be achieved (though it would probably take strong central government pressure to do this) is in the operation of rail services, for example through one-man operation of trains and through reductions in ticket checking staff. A further area may be in the operation of bus services. It should be a matter of considerable concern that, over ten years after the formation of the PTE, the PTE was only at the end of 1981 beginning to be able to cost and monitor revenue on individual bus services. What is now needed is a comprehensive review of services, on the lines of the NBC's Market

Analysis Projects, with attempts to determine criteria (for example in terms of minimum number of passengers or in terms of types of areas served) to judge where bus services should be provided on social grounds. In addition, it would be desirable to instigate a thorough review by a body independent both of the PTE and of the County Council, to monitor the efficiency with which the PTE is utilizing its manpower and capital resources in the provision of bus services. It is only by operating those public transport services with the greatest patronage per £1 of costs, and operating them as efficiently as possible, that subsidy escalation, and reductions in service quality can be avoided in the 1980s.

III

Inland freight traffic in Great Britain has increased considerably since the war. In 1954, 44,000 million ton-miles were hauled, 48·5 per cent by road, 50·8 per cent by rail, and the remaining small proportion by canal and pipeline. Total traffic increased to 58,000 million ton-miles in 1964 and to 81,000 million in 1977. By 1977 the road share of the total had increased to 75·6 per cent and the rail share declined to 17·6 per cent. Thus over the period from 1954 to 1977 total road freight moved increased by 184 per cent, while total rail freight moved declined by 37 per cent. While total inland ton-miles increased by 23 per cent over the ten years from 1968 to 1977, the greatest *tonnage* lifted was in 1968. Since then total annual inland tonnage has fluctuated around a declining trend, and the increase in ton-miles has been due to an increase in the average length of haul. By 1977 inland tonnage lifted was 15 per cent below its 1968 peak (with road responsible for 85 per cent of total tonnage and rail for 10 per cent).[28] The major cause of this national decline in tonnage has been the fall in the output of the mining, quarrying, and building construction industries. The increased length of haul is not simply due to this changing composition of traffic. Major causes have been such factors as changes in distribution systems, the relative growth of large retail outlets, and increasing use of less direct but faster motorway routings.[29]

Detailed statistics of freight transport movements at a local level are collected infrequently, so it is not possible to determine in full the trend of freight transport movements on Merseyside over the whole period covered by this chapter. However, statistics are available to present a detailed picture of road and rail movements in the mid-1960s. In 1962 the Ministry of Transport conducted a survey of the origins and destination of goods moved by road. Chisholm and O'Sullivan updated this information to 1964 to make it compatible with origin and destination information for rail movements derived from a BR survey conducted in that year. The resultant information

Table 8.3. *Freight transport on Merseyside*, 1964 (million tons).*

Commodity group	*Originating tonnage*			*Terminating tonnage*			*Balance: originating minus terminating tonnage*
	Road	*Rail*	*Total*	*Road*	*Rail*	*Total*	
Coal and coke	4·0	1·9	5·9	4·7	4·7	9·5	− 3·6
Iron ore	0	1·9	1·9	0	0	0	+ 1·9
Steel and scrap	1·7	0·1	1·9	2·5	0·6	3·1	− 1·3
Oil	5·0	1·1	6·1	3·5	–	3·5	+ 2·7
Building materials	11·0	0·5	11·5	13·3	1·4	14·7	− 3·1
Chemicals	4·0	0·5	4·5	3·5	0·5	4·0	+ 0·5
Other crude	5·3	0·6	6·0	4·1	0·6	4·8	+ 1·2
Food	21·8	0·4	22·2	19·2	0·2	19·4	+ 2·8
Manufactures	6·2	0·1	6·4	6·9	0·3	7·1	− 0·8
Miscellaneous	4·3	–	4·3	4·2	–	4·3	–
Total	63·4	7·2	70·6	62·0	8·3	70·3	+ 0if-021.3

Totals may not always add due to rounding errors.
— less than 0·1 million tons.
* Merseyside is here defined by the following local authority areas: County Boroughs, Birkenhead, Bootle, Liverpool, St Helens, Southport, Wallasey; Municipal Boroughs, Bebington, Crosby, Ellesmere Port, Widnes; Urban Districts, Formby, Hoylake, Huyton-with-Roby, Kirkby, Litherland, Neston, Ormskirk, Prescot, Rainford, Runcorn, Wirral; Rural Districts, West Lancashire, Whiston.

is available for 13 commodity groups and for 78 zones of Great Britain.[30]

Table 8.3 presents a summary of this information for the Merseyside area. This table shows that 70·6 million tons of traffic originated on Merseyside while 70·3 million tons terminated. (Goods imported through Liverpool docks are counted as originating on Merseyside, while goods exported are treated as terminating). The Merseyside region was a net 'importer' of coal and coke; steel and scrap; building materials; and manufactures. The region was a net 'exporter' of iron ore; oil products; chemicals; other crude materials; and foodstuffs. Rail carried 10 per cent of originating tonnage, ranging from 100 per cent for iron ore (the flow from Bidston Dock to Shotton steelworks), to 33 per cent for coal and coke, down to less than 2 per cent for food products, manufactures, and miscellaneous products. BR carried 12 per cent of terminating tonnage, ranging from 50 per cent of coal and coke movement down to less than 1 per cent of food stuffs and of miscellaneous products.

The detailed information on origins and destinations of flows reveals the short distance nature of most flows. An analysis of the 1962 data in MALTS showed that 45 per cent of the tonnage was internal to the region, both originating and terminating there.[31] Only 26 per cent of total tonnage on Merseyside travelled over 50 miles and only 10 per cent over 100 miles. There is a tendency for rail to handle relatively more longer distance traffic than road.

Thus 51 per cent of road tonnage on Merseyside was carried less than 10 miles, but only 3 per cent of rail tonnage. 21 per cent of road tonnage was hauled over 50 miles and 8 per cent over 100 miles whereas 64 per cent of rail tonnage travelled over 50 miles and 23 per cent travelled over 100 miles. Nevertheless, of *all* tonnage hauled over 100 miles, road and not rail handled the larger proportion, namely 71 per cent.

Generally, the longer the distance hauled, the greater the average vehicle load. This means that a much higher proportion of trips than of tonnage is accounted for by internal movements. The MALTS survey of goods vehicle movements found that in 1966 250,000 goods vehicle trips were made on Merseyside on an average weekday, and of these 86 per cent were internal trips. Because external trips are of a longer average length, internal trips accounted for 61 per cent of goods vehicle mileage in the MALTS study area. The average length of trip within the area was as short as 2·1 miles for light vehicles, namely those under about 2 tons unladen weight, and 3·4 miles for heavy vehicles. This indicates the importance of short-distance movements in considering transport improvements to aid freight traffic.

The MALTS study also indicated the relative importance of freight movements for the total demand for roadspace. The study estimated goods vehicle movements at about 25 per cent of the total daily vehicle movement on Merseyside. Conversion to a passenger car unit basis to allow for the greater roadspace required by goods vehicles increases this proportion to about 33 per cent, although goods vehicle trips occur more-or-less evenly throughout the working day, and so do not take up this high a proportion of the peak-hour demand which often determines the need for extra capacity. Nevertheless, the benefit of a road improvement to a goods vehicle is likely to be higher than the benefit to a car user who is travelling in leisure time. Most *inter*-urban road investments in Britain are appraised by cost-benefit analysis using the COBA computer programme. An official estimate of the importance of different types of benefit indicated that, on average, time savings to leisure travellers accounted for 29 per cent of benefits; time-savings to car travellers in working-time for 26 per cent; time savings for goods vehicle drivers for 22 per cent; time savings to bus crews for 3 per cent; and accident cost savings for 20 per cent. (While there might sometimes be some savings in operating costs, these are often offset by increases due to increased mileage or to higher speeds.)

The benefits to commercial vehicle traffic have therefore been an important component of the measured benefits of inter-urban road investments. The 1960s and early 1970s saw substantial improvements in the British inter-urban road system, particularly with construction of the motorway network. This grew from the opening of the Preston by-pass in 1958 to 473 miles in 1967, 1037 miles in 1972 and to 1423 miles in 1977. Merseyside is linked to the network via the M62 cross-Pennine motorway which links into the M6 and which reached Liverpool in 1976; the M53 mid-Wirral motorway; the M56 North Cheshire motorway; the M57 outer ring road from the M62 to Aintree; and the M58 from Aintree to the M6 near Skelmersdale . Other new roads have also improved communications on Merseyside. These include the Runcorn–Widnes bridge, opened in 1961 and replacing the inefficient Transporter Bridge; the Wallasey Tunnel and link road to the M53; the A41 Rock Ferry by-pass; the A561 Speke–Runcorn road; and the A5036 Aintree–Seaforth Docks road. Other existing roads, including the A580 East Lancashire Road opened in the 1930s and a pioneer in its day, have been widened and improved.

Priorities for road construction have not been based only on economic appraisals, but also on a belief that new road construction can foster industrial development in depressed regions. Hence the 1975 government report on roads could note that 'compared to many other areas of the country, the North-West has benefited from a more dynamic road construction programme in previous years and as a result is now relatively well-provided with motorways and high-quality trunk roads'.[33] The extent to which road construction does enhance regional economic growth is however not clear; though patently it is not sufficient to prevent industrial decline. The problem is in determining cause and effect, that is in determining how an area would have fared in the absence of a road improvement. Indeed road improvements could conceivably harm an area's industries by making it more economic to supply that region's consumers from outside the area. After surveying the evidence on transport investment and regional growth, the 1978 Leitch Committee on trunk road investment appraisal concluded 'at the national and regional levels all the evidence points to the conclusion that improvements to the trunk road system can only have a limited effect on industrial location and growth'.[34]

My own work on the impact of the M62 motorway is consistent with this view. I estimated that the M62 would reduce industrial road transport costs in Merseyside by 2½ per cent on the Liverpool side of the Mersey and by 2 per cent on the Wirral side. While the transport cost savings themselves are important, their overall impact on employment levels would be likely to be small, though in precise terms.[35] The County Council have also recently carried out a detailed study in St Helens of the value of road improvements to freight transport. Although there were some localized problems, the study concluded that the network in general operated at a satisfactory level, and that even very substantial road improvements would lead to only small time savings and to savings of less than 0·5 per cent in operating costs. The study concluded that there was little to suggest that road improvements aimed at speeding up goods vehicle movement would have any influence in attracting new development to St Helens.[36]

All of this implies that appraisal of the impact of road investments on freight transport should concentrate on the measurable savings in costs, much of which, as we have seen, will accrue to local traffic, and should ignore any magic, and in practice illusory, benefits which road investment might be supposed to have on industrial regeneration.

While the road network and road freight traffic have been expanding, rail freight has been taking a declining share of the market. Total BR rail freight tonnage was 273 million tons in 1948, rose to 289 million tons in 1953, and then declined, being 171 million tons in 1978. Loss of traffic in the 1950s and early 1960s was reinforced by the Beeching Report, which proposed the rationalization of goods services by the closure of many little-used depots, the development of trainload movements of block loads between private sidings, and the transfer of traditional wagon-load movements to a newly developed rail container network.

In 1971 the Liverpool Division of BR, which includes Merseyside together with Wigan, Warrington, and an area of North Cheshire extending as far South-East as Northwich but excluding Chester, dispatched 9 million tons of freight, earning a revenue of about £30m., or £3.30 per ton, at 1978 prices. By 1978 the tonnage figure had reduced slightly to 8·4 million tons, earning revenue of £19m., or £2.26 per ton. A part of the reduction in real revenue per ton is due to a change in the composition of traffic and increased use of privately owned wagons. In 1978 81 per cent of the originating tonnage was carried in full trainloads, and bulk commodities made up much of the tonnage. Oil and petroleum products, mostly from the Stanlow complex on the south bank of the Mersey, accounted for 2·7 million tons; coal movements from the Lancashire coalfield for 1·8 million tons; chemicals, mainly from North Cheshire, for 1·8 million tons; iron and steel, largely iron ore for Shotton, for 1·5 million tons; and earths and stones, particularly rock salt from North Cheshire, for 0·4 million tons. The chemical movements include oxygen and nitrogen from British Oxygen's Widnes plant to distribution depots at Wembley and Sheffield; wet salt from Middlewich to South Wales; caustic soda liquor from Runcorn to Holywell, Grimsby, and Whitehaven; chlorine from Ellesmere Port and Runcorn; and fertilizers from Ellesmere Port. The other major originating freight traffic is of car components from Ford's Halewood plant to Dagenham and Harwich, and of finished cars from Speke to distribution depots.

Inward traffic to the Division also consists largely of bulk flows.

In 1978 major traffic included limestone (2 million tons) from Derbyshire to mid-Cheshire for the chemical industry; coal to Fiddlers Ferry power station, to Garston docks for export (½ million tons) and to domestic distribution depots (¼ million tons); cement (¼ million tons) to Widnes; soda ash, sand, and oil for the St Helens glass industry; and inward traffic to Fords.

The concentration on the major bulk flows, which are the traffics most suited to rail haulage, has been accompanied by a reduction in individual wagon-load movements. Thus, the volume of domestic coal transported by rail has been halved over the last seven years and the traffic is now handled at only three rail concentration depots instead of at a large number of local coalyards. With the exception of some general cargo at Birkenhead Docks, conventional rail traffic at the docks has almost entirely disappeared. The Mersey Dock and Harbour Board had handled over 4 million tons of rail traffic in Liverpool in 1944, but by 1972 this was down to about 175,000 tons, and rail facilities were withdrawn entirely from the Liverpool docks system in 1973. The large number of individual railway-owned freight terminals which forwarded and received conventional freight traffic from individual customers has been reduced to two, at Canada Dock and Spekeland Road, and most rail traffic is now handled at private sidings.

However, some general rail traffic is containerized and handled by Freightliners, a BR subsidiary. Freightliners started operations in 1965 and the Garston terminal in Liverpool was opened in June 1966. The terminal handled 19,500 containers in 1967 and this increased to 88,000 in 1973. Traffic was lower in 1974 and 1975, but about 80,000 containers per year were dealt with in 1976, 1977, and 1978. Of this traffic about half is domestic business within the UK, and the other half is maritime traffic. Some of the maritime traffic now passes through a rail terminal at Seaforth docks which was opened in 1980.

Overnight services are operated to other Freightliner terminals in Britain, and road collection and delivery takes place mainly within a radius of about 20 miles from Garston. Major domestic commodities handled include beer, steel products, chemicals, bricks, edible oils, and salt. In addition, Freightliners perform trunking operations both for the National Freight Corporation's parcels subsidiaries National Carriers Limited and Roadline UK Ltd, and for the Post Office. The total tonnage handled at Garston is very roughly ½–1 million tons per annum and while this is a small proportion of total freight transport on Merseyside it is a much larger proportion of long-distance traffic, since Freightliners are only competitive with road haulage for the longer distance flows because of the double-handling involved in road-rail transfers.[37]

Other rail container traffic is handled at the inland port at Aintree

Containerbase, services being operated in 1979 to Southampton, Tilbury, and Coatbridge (Glasgow). These services therefore provide a facility for maritime container traffic originating or terminating on Merseyside but passing through the other main UK ports.

In summary, rail transport makes an important contribution to freight handling on Merseyside, although it should be noted that much of the tonnage in the Liverpool Division is handled outside the Liverpool/Birkenhead/Wallasey urban area, and particularly in North Cheshire. The future of rail traffic is very much bound up with the fortunes of the basic industries served and, while rail does have some environmental advantages compared with road, the specialized nature of rail haulage means that any significant transfer of traffic from road to rail is impossible for both practical and economic reasons. Nevertheless, some government assistance is available under Section 8 of the 1974 Railways Act, which provides a 50 per cent grant to firms for construction of new private sidings and privately-owned rail wagons where carriage of traffic by rail is expected to confer environmental advantages. On Merseyside such grants had, by the end of 1979, been awarded to Aintree Containerbase, to a firm of steel stockholders in Birkenhead, and to the Seaforth Docks container terminal.

Growth of road traffic can be expected to depend upon the prosperity of the UK and Merseyside economies, and on trends in average vehicle size. Official Department of Transport projections published in 1978 forecast that nationally vehicle-miles of goods vehicles over 1½ tons unladen weight would increase by between 20 per cent and 33 per cent between 1976 and 1990, and that ton-miles hauled would increase by between 28 per cent and 51 per cent, depending on the assumed rate of growth of the economy. However, it has been argued that the assumptions about the growth in the numbers of largest size vehicles which underly these forecasts may be too low.[38] Furthermore, even the lower range of national income forecasts looks rather optimistic in the light of recent UK economic performance. Consequently it is possible that total goods vehicle-miles will fall, although total ton-miles and vehicle-miles by lorries in the largest size category will rise. Merseyside's share of the changes which actually do occur will depend upon the health of the Merseyside economy, though even if Merseyside's share of total road goods traffic declines there is still likely to be an increase in the numbers of the largest size vehicles on Merseyside's roads.

NOTES AND REFERENCES

* I have benefited considerably from discussions with a number of individuals and organizations concerned with the provision of transport services on Merseyside and I should particularly like to thank the following

for their assistance: Mr H. Dalton, British Rail, Liverpool Division; Mr F. G. Plumb, Freightliners Ltd.; Dr L. Lesley, Liverpool Polytechnic; Mr J. J. Milne, Merseyside County Council, County Engineer's Dept; Mr P. Burnell and Mr B. Duffey, Merseyside County Council, Joint Transportation Unit; Mr S. Rihani, Merseyside Passenger Transport Executive; and Crosville and Ribble Motor Services Ltd. I must stress that none of these individuals or organizations necessarily agree with any of the views expressed in this chapter, and that I alone am responsible for any errors or omissions.

1. For more details see R. E. Blackburn, *Liverpool Tramways 1943–1957*, Light Railway Transport League (1968).

2. For a general discussion of the development of rail services on Merseyside see G. O. Holt, *A Regional History of the Railways of Great Britain*, Newton Abbot (1978). For individual local services see N. N. Forbes *et al., The electric lines of the Lancashire and Yorkshire Railway*, Electric Railway Society (1976); C. E. Box, *The Liverpool Overhead Railway 1893–1956*, Hampton Court (1962); G. W. Parkin, *The Mersey Railway* Lingfield, n.d.; Campbell Highet, *The Wirral Railway*, Lingfield (1961); R. Prys Griffiths, *The Cheshire Lines Railway*, Tanglewood (1947).

3. The total number of passengers carried in 1938/9 had been 368 million, but figures on a consistent basis are not available for Liverpool from 1939/40 to 1955/6. Figures in Figs. 8.1, 8.2, and 8.3 are taken from the *Annual Reports and Accounts* of the Birkenhead, Wallasey, and Liverpool County Borough's Transport Departments and, for figures after 1969, from the *Annual Report and Accounts* of the Merseyside Passenger Transport Executive. Financial figures have been converted to 1978 purchasing power using the retail price index.

4. *Merseyside Conurbation Traffic Survey 1962 Report of the Transport Committee*, Steering Committee on Merseyside Traffic and Transport (1965), p. 97 but see also p. 9.

5. See, for example, *Passenger Transport; Effect of fares increases on passenger demand and network viability*, Chartered Institute of Public Finance and Accountancy, London (1976).

6. The actual provisions made by local authority transport departments for capital charges were often inadequate, and are not explored further here.

7. The Liverpool Central to Gateacre service was also withdrawn in 1972, although a much-improved service was restored as far as Garston in 1978.

8. *Interim Reports: The Mersey River Crossing Committee, The Transport Committee*, Steering Committee on Merseyside Traffic and Transport (1963).

9. *Merseyside Conurbation Traffic Survey 1962*, Steering Committee on Merseyside Traffic and Transport (1965).

10. H. J. Dyos and D. H. Aldcroft, *British Transport: An economic survey from the Seventeenth Century to the Twentieth*, London (1974), p. 381.

11. W. G. Bor, *Outer Rail Loop, Feasibility Study*, Liverpool City Planning Department (1965). This scheme had a precedent in parliamentary powers taken out in 1903 to construct a railway from Seaforth Sands on the LOR to Sefton on the CLC. This line, together with a proposed connection between the south end of the LOR and the CLC in South Liverpool, would have provided an outer circular electric service over the LOR and the CLC.

12. *MALTS Final Report A*, Traffic Research Corporation, Liverpool (1969).

13. A description and critique of such studies can be found in M. J. Bruton, *Introduction to Transport Planning*, London (1970).

14. For full accounts of this see R. W. S. Pryke and J. S. Dodgson, *The rail problem*, London (1975); and J. S. Dodgson, 'Cost-benefit analysis, Government policy and the British railway network', *Transportation*, June (1977), pp. 149–70

15. See J. S. Dodgson, op. cit. Merseyside PTE has since withdrawn its subsidy for this service, and the loss on this line is now met by Central Government and Clwyd County Council.

16. *A Transport Plan for Merseyside*, Merseyside Passenger Transport Authority and Passenger Transport Executive (1972).

17. *Passenger Interchange on Merseyside: demonstration programme results and recommendations*, Peat Marwick Mitchell & Co. (1973).

18. The JTU is formally independent both of the PTE and of the County Council's highways engineer's department, and is responsible to a directing group of three, consisting of the Director-General of the PTE, the County Planning Officer and the County Engineer. The JTU was also responsible for developing the transportation component of the Merseyside Structure Plan.

19. *Merseyside Structure Plan: Draft Written Document*, Merseyside County Council (1979).

20. J. W. Perdue and J. Hale, *A Study of the Future Need for Surface Transport Facilities across the River Mersey*, Centre for Transport Studies, Cranfield (1974).

21. R. Botham and J. Herson, 'From rationality to rationalisation: or motorway madness in Liverpool', *The Planner* (September, 1980).

22. A multi-criteria analysis framework was suggested for road investment appraisal by the Leitch Committee (*Report of the Advisory Committee on Trunk Road Assessment*, Department of Transport, HMSO, 1978); and for comparing road and rail expenditure by Sir Peter Parker (P. Parker, *A Way to Run a Railway*, Haldane Memorial Lecture, Birkbeck College, London, 1978).

23. On the advantages of the objectives see C. A. Nash, 'Management objectives, fares and service levels in bus transport', *Journal of Transport Economics and Policy* (January, 1978).

24. J. Hibbs, *The Bus and Coach Industry: Its economics and organisation*, London (1975), pp. 108–14.

25. *Annual Report 1978*, National Bus Company, p. 16.

26. D. Maltby, K. A. Lawler, and I. G. Monteath, *A Monitoring Study of Rail Commuting on Merseyside with Particular Reference to the Effects of Increases in the Price of Petrol*, University of Salford (1976), p. ix.

27. For a summary of the impact of open-ended subsidies on BR, and a survey of the case against public transport subsidies, see Richard Pryke 'The case against subsidies' in *A Policy for Transport?*, The Nuffield Foundation (1977), pp. 47–65.

28. Statistics in this paragraph are from Department of Transport, *Transport Statistics, Great Britain, 1967–1977*, HMSO, London (1979); and Department of the Environment, *Transport Policy: A consultation document*, HMSO (1976).

29. Department of Transport, *Road Haulage Operators' Licensing: Report of the independent committee of inquiry*, HMSO (1978), p. 135.

30. For details of the source of this data see M. Chisholm and P. O'Sullivan, *Freight flows and spatial aspects of the British economy*, Cambridge (1973). I am very grateful to Professor Chisholm for making the original road and rail matrices available to me.

31. Traffic Research Corporation Ltd, *The Development of Goods Vehicle Forecasting Procedure*, MALTS Technical Report 7 (1969).

32. *Transport policy: a consultation document*, vol. 2, Department of the Environment, HMSO, London (1976), pp. 98–9.

33. Department of the Environment, *Roads in England and Wales 1974–75*, HMSO (1975), p. 3.

34. Department of Transport, *Report of the Advisory Committee on Trunk Road Assessment*, HMSO (1978), p. 207.

35. J. S. Dodgson, 'Motorway investment, industrial transport costs and sub-regional growth', *Regional Studies* (March, 1974).

36. Merseyside County Council, *Transport Policies and Programme 1979/80* (1978), pp. 27–8.

37. For more details see R. W. S. Pryke and J. S. Dodgson, *The Rail Problem*, London (1975), pp. 85–9.

38. Ibid., *Road Haulage Operators' Licensing*, pp. 140–2.

9

The ports of Liverpool and the North-West in an age of transport revolution

S. GILMAN

I

To the historic maritime cities their ports were much more than places of employment and cargo transfer. They had a central place in the life of the city, providing the basis for a wide range of commercial and other port related economic activities. This is particularly true of Liverpool where ports and shipping were such an important feature of the city's life and character. Liverpool and London were giants of the general cargo era; until the 1960s they were the premier ports of the nation and it seemed as if nothing could affect their pre-eminence. However, changes in trading patterns and the transport revolutions of the last two decades have had profound effects. They reduced the contribution of port activities generally to local hinterlands and created a need for re-development and re-adjustment which has had to be accomplished within a fiercely competitive environment.

There are a number of works covering the history of the port of Liverpool and its shipping services from their early beginnings. James Bird's *The Major Seaports of the United Kingdom* concentrated on the growth of the dock complex and also provided a historical and geographical model of the development of major ports up to 1960, in the 'Anyport' thesis.[1] The late Francis Hyde's *Liverpool and the Mersey* covered shipping and commercial activities as well as the development of the port from 1680 on.[2] In its final chapters it grappled with the implications of container transport, but the developments were too new for a perspective to be formed. There is also an extensive general literature on modern developments in ports and shipping, whilst the major landmarks in local development have been documented in the press and annual reports of the Mersey Docks and Harbour Board. However, there has been no general review of the impact of the recent transport revolutions upon local

Notes and references begin on page 233.

ports. The aim of this paper is to fill part of the gap by considering some of the major forces which have shaped recent history and which affect current prospects. It deals particularly with the logic of modern transport systems as this affects the attractiveness of calls in Liverpool and other north-west ports. There is also a general review of trading patterns and technological change leading to a discussion of some current issues in port development. Attention is concentrated on the general cargo sector which is the major employer of port resources and is still in the process of completing its adjustment to the revolutions in maritime transport.

II

Throughout the conventional or pre-container era it was considered perfectly natural for coastal and short sea ships (which specialize in port to port services), to sail on long roundabout routes to collect goods from ports close to points of origin and distribute them close to points of consumption, and for deep sea ships to serve many ports in each trading region to achieve the same end. This was partly because of the relatively low cost of sea transport and primitive levels of development of inland road transport. But there were also special factors at work in the form of the network of commercial links between the port and local businesses and in the fragmented nature of maritime transport systems, in which inland costs had a disproportionately strong influence on the overall system configuration. With the improvements in inland transport of recent decades and the development of unit loads and integrated through transport systems, the balance has changed and decisions are now taken more on the basis of through transport costs. As a result of this, new route patterns have been developed and traditional port/hinterland relationships have been weakened.[3]

The main factors controlling the choice between ship and inland transport modes and, therefore, the nature of port hinterlands are:

(a) unit mile costs for ships and inland modes;

(b) overall route patterns and relative marine and inland distances on competing routes and sectors;

(c) the distribution of cargo in trading hinterlands;

(d) transport system organization and pricing structures.

Taking first the question of unit mile costs, a typical short sea ro-ro ship of 80 trailer capacity has costs of about £8 per 100 TEU (twenty foot equivalent unit) miles, a small containership of 100 TEU capacity will be somewhat cheaper at about £6 per 100 TEU miles, and for a large containership at full load costs come down to as little as £2.50 per 100 TEU miles. Against this road transport costs are likely to be of the order of £25 per 100 TEU miles. Clearly if the relationship between marine and inland sector costs was the

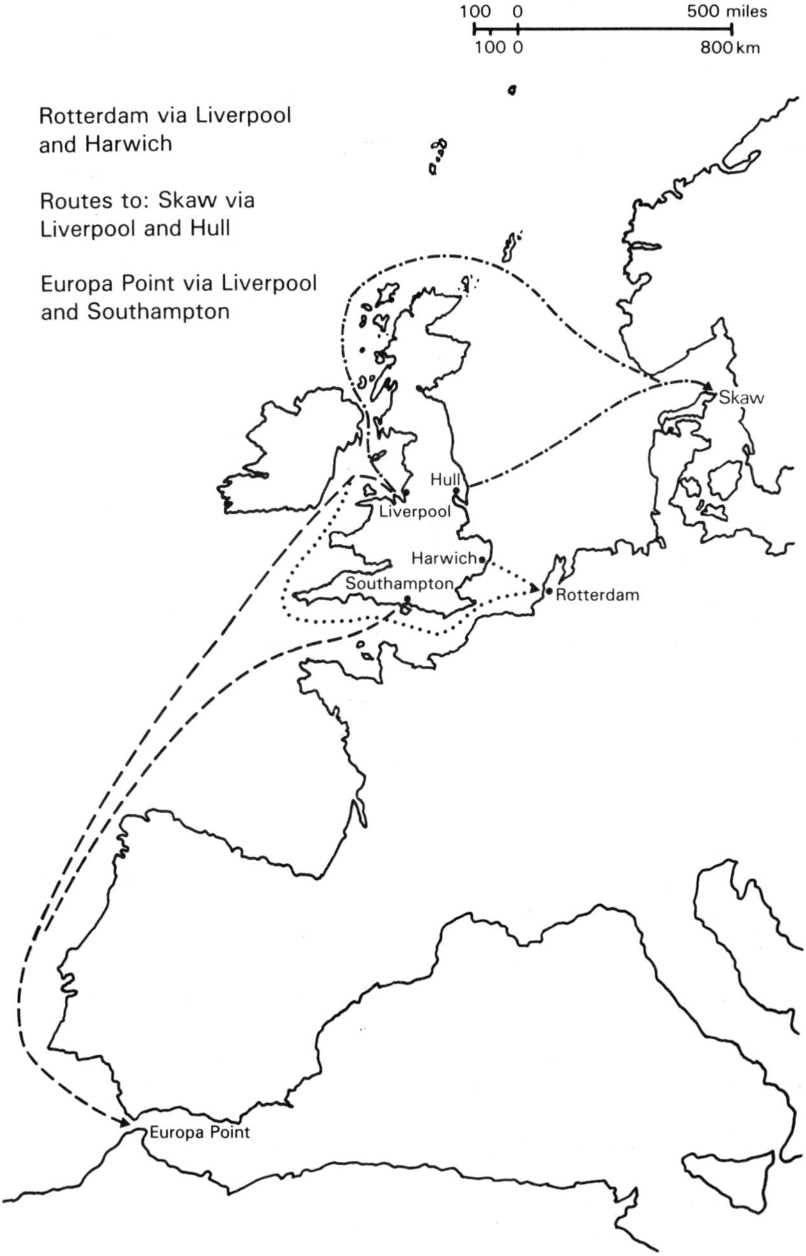

Fig. 9.1. Marine distance comparisons.

dominant factor at work, ships would still be used extensively for local distribution and large containerships would tend to operate on milk runs. However, the other factors can be equally powerful. Marine and inland distances on competing routes are usually very different, the precise relationship depending upon the shapes of land masses and the basic route alignment. In some cases the inland mode can take the more direct route, in others the ship, and these relationships are such that the ratios of distances in competing sectors can easily be up to ten-to-one in either direction. Second, for deep sea ships the consignment to a diversion port may be small (it can range from between say 5 to 25 per cent of the ships' cargo), and this scales down the ratio of inland to competing marine sector costs by a similar amount. Finally, for deep sea ships, transport system organization determines whether the incentive for a local call is to obtain sea freight revenues for cargo dedicated to the port, or merely to save the extra inland transport costs involved in moving it to another port.

This is a basic statement, and the precise modelling of the way these and other subsidiary factors interact in controlling choice of route is beyond the scope of this paper. However, the prospects for north-west ports can be discussed in general terms. Since they vary substantially according to route length, short and deep sea routes will be dealt with separately.

An important characteristic of short sea trades is that ships usually operate on specialized two-port routes. There may be some multi-port itineraries, and individual ships sometimes operate more than one route, but this is comparatively unusual. The reason is that inter-port distances within trading areas are large relative to the trunk distances between them, and such scale economies as could be obtained by using large ships on multi-port itineraries would be outweighed by the losses in average load factor. Secondly, there are enormous differences in relative distances on competing routes. The use of UK west coast ports for Continental traffic involves a long roundabout sea haul and the same would apply to the use of east coast ports in the Irish trades. In spite of this, routes with a convex maritime geography operated quite successfully prior to the development of integrated transport systems. They have now dwindled away and direct routes making more use of inland transport have largely taken over.[4]

Sailing distances from various competing UK ports to major Continental ports and to the entrances to the Mediterranean and the Baltic are shown in tables 9.1 and 9.2 below. From this it can be seen that Liverpool is at a primary disadvantage on routes to the main north Continent and Scandinavian ports, sailing distances being some 400 to 600 nautical miles greater than those from east coast ports. For trades to the Iberian Peninsular and the

Table 9.1. *Sailing distances from UK ports to the north Continent and Scandinavia.*

	Rotterdam	*Hamburg*	*Esbjerg*	*Scaw*	*Gothenburg*	*Copenhagen*
Liverpool	639	946	887	898	943	1050
Middlesborough	273	411	345	442	487	594
Hull	210	383	331	456	501	608
Harwich	123	362	334	480	525	632

Source: B.P. Marine Distance Tables.

Mediterranean Liverpool is quite well placed. Taking Europa Point near the Straits of Gibraltar as a point of reference it can be seen that there are only small differences in sailing distances from the various UK ports to Europa point—the entrance to the Mediterranean. Finally, in the Irish trades, west coast ports clearly have an enormous advantage in sailing distance over those in any other region. In order to assess the importance of these differences they have to be related to inland transport distances and to differences between inland and marine sector transport costs, and in figs. 9.2, 9.3, and 9.4 an approach is made to this.

The method of evaluation is to take the difference in marine distance from Liverpool and a competing UK port to a common point of destination, and to relate this to differences in inland distances in a set of hinterland contours. For example, fig. 9.2 compares Liverpool and Southampton on the route to Europa Point (the entrance to the Mediterranean), in which the sailing distance from Liverpool is 125 miles further than that from Southampton. The contour line '1' represents the path of points which are 125 trunk route miles closer to Liverpool than they are to Southampton, so that the difference in land miles compensates exactly for that in sea miles. The contour line '2' represents the path of points where the distance to Southampton is 62½ miles further than that from Liverpool, so that the difference in land miles would compensate for that in sea miles if land miles were twice the cost. Conversely the contour line '0·5' represents the path of points 250 miles closer to Liverpool than they

Table 9.2. *Sailing distances from UK ports to the entrances to the Mediterranean and the Baltic.*

	Europa Point	*Scaw*
Liverpool	1269	898
Middlesborough	1509	442
Harwich	1297	480
London	1323	553
Southampton	1144	651

Source: B.P. Marine Distance Tables.

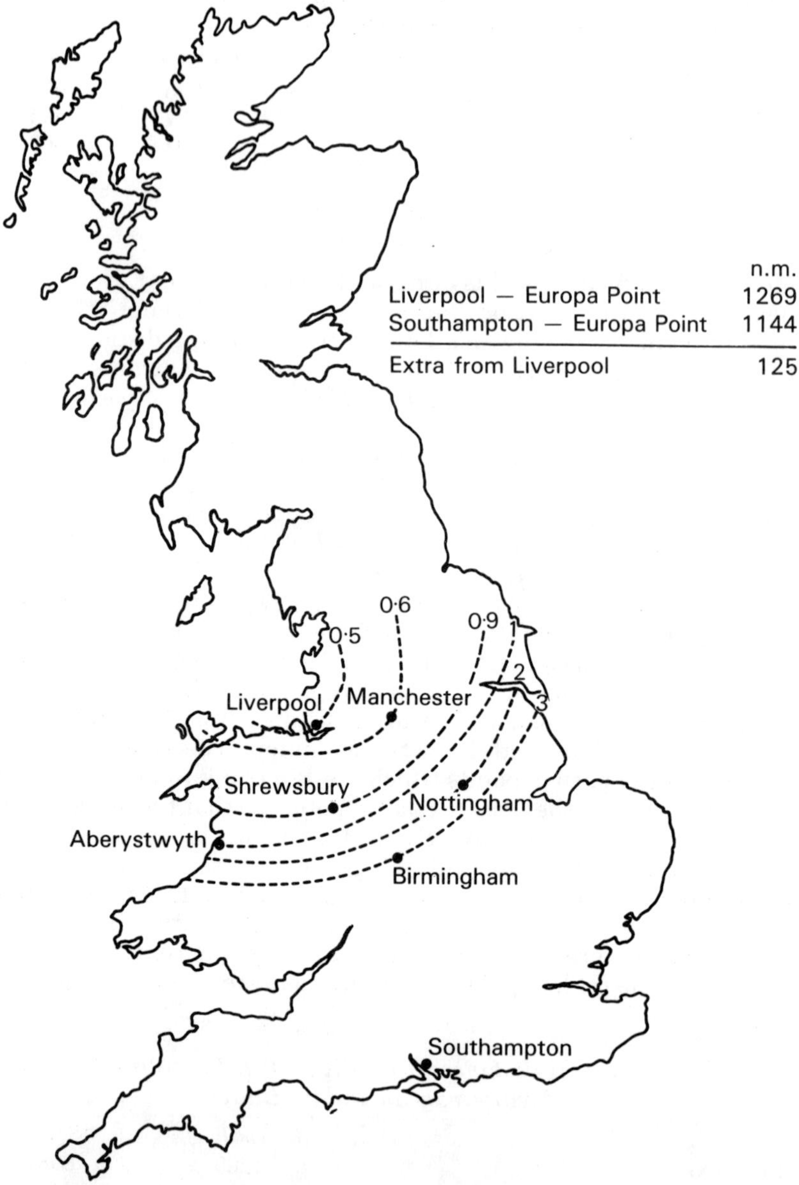

Fig. 9.2. Hinterland contours: Liverpool v Southampton to Europa Point.

are to Southampton, so that even if land miles were only half the cost of sea miles the shipper would still choose Liverpool in spite of the additional marine distance. In fact we know that on short sea general cargo routes land miles are roughly three times the cost of sea miles so that the contour line '3' roughly defines the hinterland of Liverpool, for the route in question, subject to there being sufficient cargo to sustain a reasonably frequent service and to considerations relating to speed and quality of service. We can now interpret the three contour maps. They suggest that for routes to the Mediterranean Liverpool has an extensive hinterland encompassing the main exporting areas of the Midlands. There is much more limited hinterland on routes to the Rotterdam area, and a very tight hinterland on routes to Scandinavia, and in both of these cases there will be a tendency for general cargo traffic to concentrate on east coast ports. Finally, in the Irish and Isle of Man trades, (which are not shown in the figures above), north-west ports can be expected to dominate the trade. The analysis of market shares of Section III below confirms these results.

On deep sea trades a quite different set of forces applies. Because of the length of deep sea voyages economies of size have always been important and in order to employ large ships, whilst still providing the service frequencies required by shippers, cargo liners have typically served wide trading areas. Individual ships called at several ports at each end of the route and in some cases cargo exchanges were quite small.[5]

Towards the end of the conventional era there was an awareness of the waste involved in unrationalized route structures but the strong port/hinterland relationships referred to above sustained the system.

Radical change came as a result of the increase in ship size and changed transport system organization associated with containerization. By allowing cargo to be piled over 100 feet high without need for the tween decks risk of cargo damage, or loss of control of individual consignments, containerization made an increase in ship size technically feasible. It also made it economically possible because the tremendous increase in cargo handling speeds held down time in port. Maximum ship size rose six-fold from the 560,000 cu. ft. of a large conventional liner to the 3m. cu. ft. which a Panamax ship will carry at full load.[6] The very largest ships tend to be used on long routes and out of Europe, these are chiefly those to the Far East, Australasia, and South Africa. But even on somewhat shorter routes like the north Atlantic, ship size has risen substantially. In order to employ large ships, whilst continuing to maintain the service frequently required by shippers it was necessary for services and trade routes to be amalgamated. The general effect of this in Europe was to forge a closer link between the UK and the

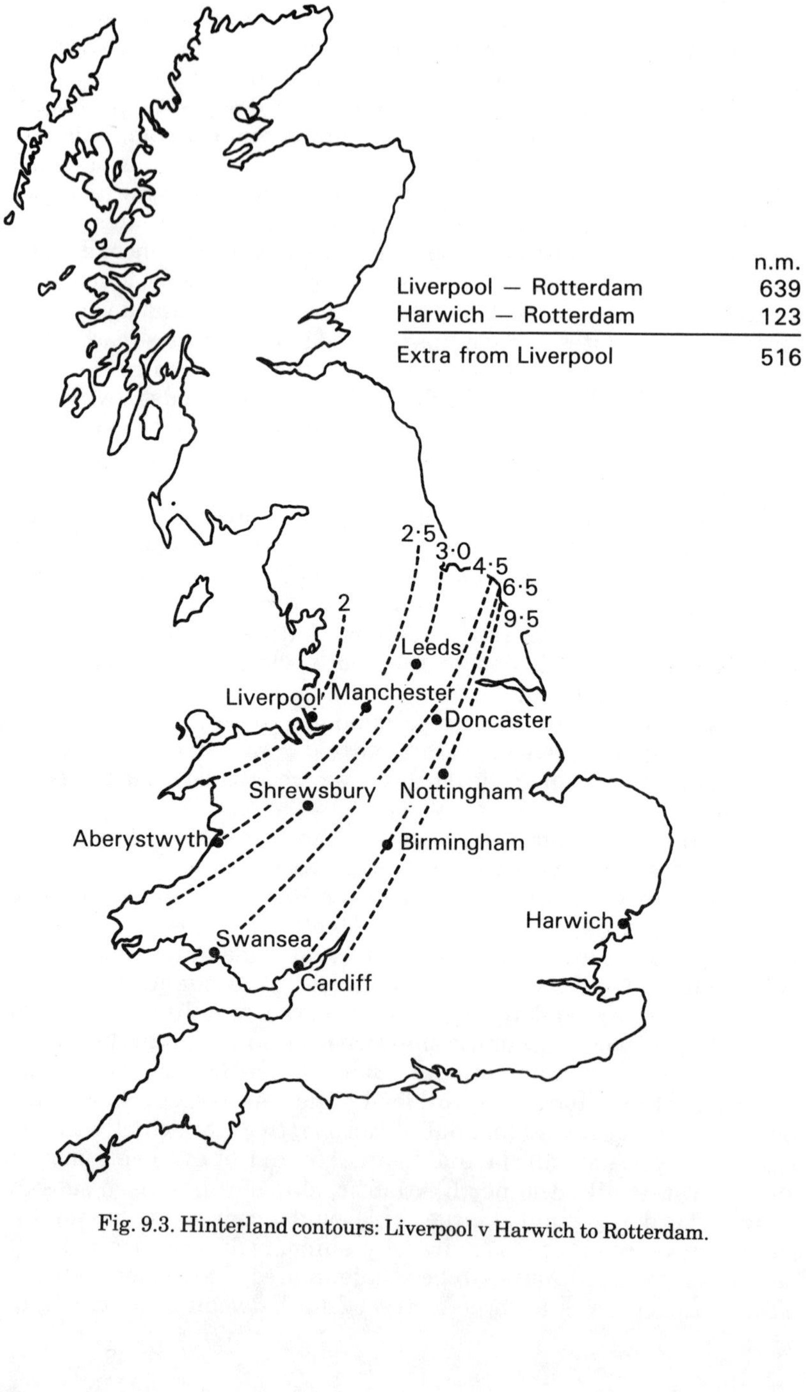

Fig. 9.3. Hinterland contours: Liverpool v Harwich to Rotterdam.

Continent and this has had a quite profound influence. The UK has a south-east to north-west axis of cargo concentration, but for Europe as a whole the major concentration lies in the hinterlands of the Continental ports from Le Havre to Bremen, plus those of the south-east UK. Thus where a line serves Europe as a whole north-west cargo will be diluted to a low proportion of total ship capacity. However, where there is sufficient traffic for a number of services lines will tend to specialize, and the cargo distribution within their ships will reflect areas of regional concentration so that the proportion for the north-west could be much higher. Clearly the extent of cargo dilution is an important factor affecting route economics but equally important is the question of pricing, as it affects the relationship between cargo flows, costs and revenues.

Prior to 1965, shipping companies confined their attention largely to the sea voyage. Freight rates covered only the cost of the ship and its overheads, plus a limited amount of cargo handling (usually stevedoring to and from the ship's rail), the other organizations in the chain, charging separately for their services. Sea-freight rates varied substantially according to cargo type and this has been a subject of great concern to shippers, governments, and maritime economists. However, variations according to port were relatively small and have received little attention although recent developments have shown that this is a matter of the greatest importance in its effects on route structures and port location. Broadly, conferences had three classes of port—main ports generating large cargo flows, which would be included on most itineraries; secondary ports, which would be served at a lower frequency; and 'way' ports which would receive calls only on inducement, i.e. with a certain minimum of cargo and a higher freight rate. For the main ports and most of the secondary ports there was usually a common rate for each type of cargo. There were good reasons for this; first, differences in direct sailing distances would often be quite small; second, once an itinerary serving a group of ports is established its costs are indivisible and unavoidable (in order to provide capacity on that itinerary for the closest ports space has to be carried over the whole of the route); third, equalization of freight rates helped maintain a stable market, whereas differentials could have opened a back door to rate competition.

Under this system shippers tend to minimize their total outgoings by minimizing inland distances and, therefore, choose the closest port. Their choice is made on the basis of relatively small differences in inland transport costs, but for the shipping lines the whole of the sea freight revenue is at stake. It is this which encourages multi-port calling and sustains a system of uneconomic duplication of calls.

With containerization door-to-door services were introduced and

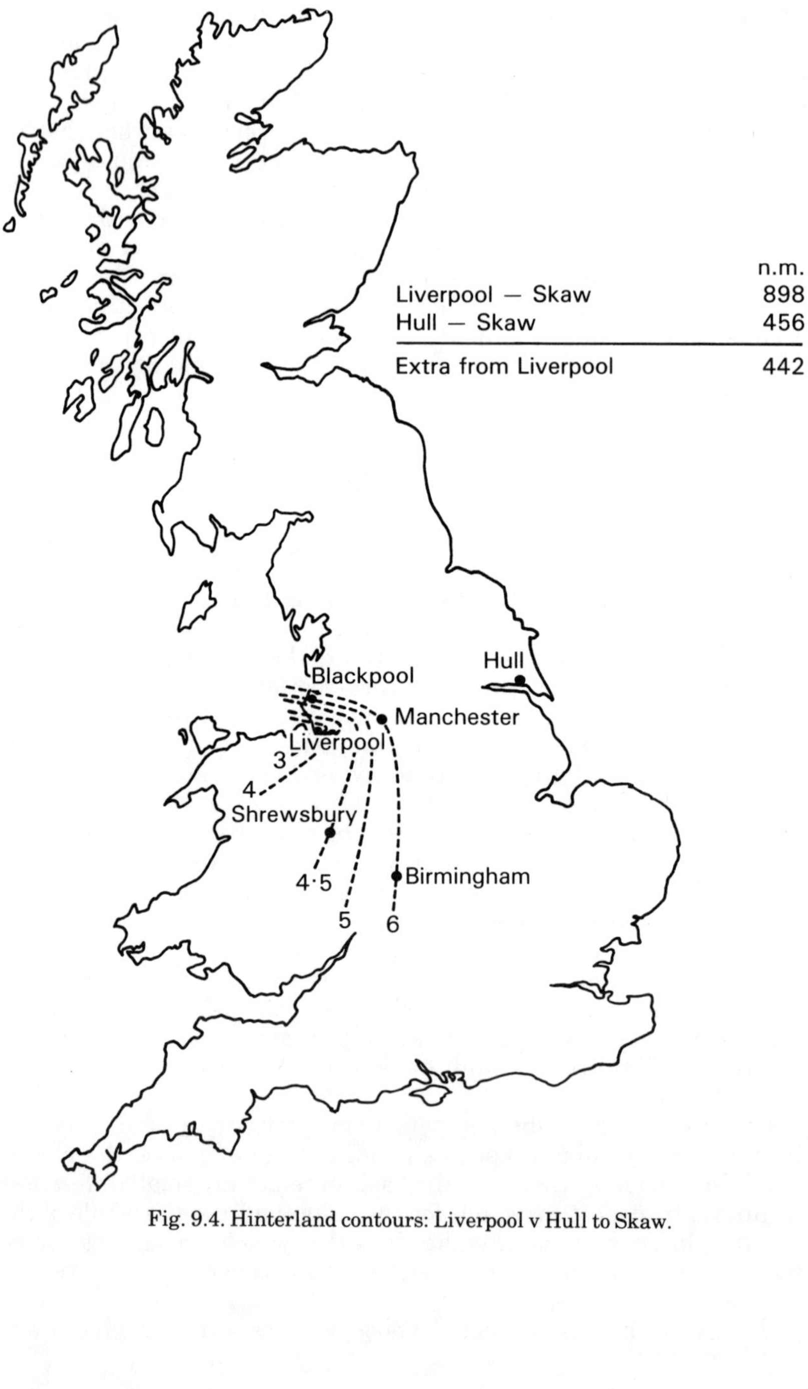

Fig. 9.4. Hinterland contours: Liverpool v Hull to Skaw.

through freight rates were offered, but at the start these rates were built up on the conventional model described above. This placed early container operators in a quandary—sea freight revenue remained a powerful attractive force, but they could not allow their new large containerships to be lured on to a typical conventional type milk run. A solution quite widely adopted in the early years was to use feeder-ships, whose costs could be absorbed by the shipping line, to serve regional cargo concentrations. In the late 1960s American companies in particular adopted this approach and it was responsible for the Sealand and US Lines feeders to Preston and Liverpool which have only recently been abandoned. It was also in part responsible for the super-port concept.[7]

In the late 1960s new integrated pricing structures were developed in which door-to-door freight rates became largely independent of choice of port and length of inland haul, costs being absorbed by the lines. Where this applies shippers are much less concerned with choice of port, and lines can have access to sea freight revenues from large trading areas whilst operating through a limited number of ports. Under these circumstances their decision on which to choose is based largely on the difference between inland transport costs and ship diversion costs.

In total, choice of route is determined by a complex set of interactions, in which cargo dilution, price and cost structures, and route geography are all important. The attraction of a Liverpool call is weakest where a trade is dominated by one service aimed at Europe as a whole and absorption pricing structures are in force. The classic example of this is the Trio service which dominates the north-west Europe–Far East route. Conversely where there are a number of services the north-west is likely to retain a strong position on some of them and this has happened on north American trades in particular.

There have been some factors helping to sustain the port of Liverpool. First the growth of container transport and the increase in competition have given more scope for specialization. Second, there has been a general loosening of itineraries, with more time allowed for operational disturbances, and for additional calls which have marketing advantages. Third, the port which is first call into a hinterland and/or last port out obtains the competitive advantage of reduced transit times. Because of its geographical position and volumes of export cargo, Liverpool has often been last port out. Recently ACL have adopted the strategy of making it first in and last out on the north Atlantic, giving very competitive transit times. The Manchester Liners service on the north Atlantic also transferred from Manchester to Liverpool, when larger ships unable to transit the Manchester Ship Canal were introduced. They were then able to run a 21 round trip to Montreal, whilst most other north Atlantic lines have been operating 28 round trips in recent years. However, following the take-over of Manchester Liners by C. Y. Tung there has been a radical change in the Canadian trade, as Manchester Liners, Dart and C.P. Ships have formed a consortium to run a combined service with large ships serving the Le Havre–Bremen range.

Clearly Liverpool no longer has the specially favoured geographical position that existed in the conventional era. Provided it can maintain a high quality of service it should be able to retain a role in deep sea container trades although this will inevitably be a much smaller one than in the heyday of the conventional era.

So far the argument has dealt with unit load cargoes only and the competing routes all have a common structure. However, there are a number of important bulk and semi-bulk cargoes (chemicals, steel, forest products, etc.), where the destination of the flow is in the port itself as the location of distribution centre or processing plant. In this case a service to the local port may cut out the inland mode completely, simplifying the system and saving two handling operations and a port transit. This is an important advantage and in these trades local ports tend to have a stronger hold. However, even here geographical influences are powerful; they can lead to re-location of distribution facilities and may in time affect the location of industry. Perhaps the classic example of re-location is in the Scandinavian/UK trades in forest products where distribution centres have moved to east coast ports like Hartlepool.

III

The second main set of influences affecting the prospects for Liverpool and other north-west ports concerns changes in trading patterns and the volume of trade. As shown in tables 9.3 and 9.4 below trade in dry cargoes grew by some 21m. tonnes to 108m. between 1967 and 1976. At the same time there were tremendous changes in trading patterns. The main growth was concentrated on trade with Continental Europe which doubled over the period to nearly 27m. tonnes. Some 4m. of this was in foodstuffs, which includes the rather volatile element of food grains, but there was also a rise of 7½m. tonnes in manufactures. This was the single most important development in the overseas trade of the UK during the period and a modest continuation of the trend would make Continental Europe our most important trading partner in manufactures. The second area of growth was in trade with the Iberian Peninsula and the Mediterranean where cargo volumes more than doubled to some 12½m. tonnes: most of this was also in manufactures.

Traditionally the most important component of the trade of the UK was deep sea. In this sector there has been little growth

Table 9.3. *UK foreign trade in manufactured goods and share of N.W. ports (000 tonnes)*[8]

	Irish Republic		*Continental Europe*		*Scandinavia and Baltic*		*Iberia and Mediterranean*		*Deep Sea*	
	1967	*1976*	*1967*	*1976*	*1967*	*1976*	*1967*	*1976*	*1967*	*1976*
Imports										
Total	298	261	3827	8211	3697	5031	943	2353	4280	5141
Liverpool	27	44	139	41	165	18	69	132	904	432
Manchester	6	1	152	379	264	141	27	263	492	392
Others	33	93	18	19	29	—	—	17	—	28
Total N.W.	66	138	209	439	458	160	98	412	1399	852
N.W. share (%)	22	53	5	5	12	3	10	17	32	17
Exports										
Total	519	977	1836	4921	1961	2550	1425	2618	7066	8335
Liverpool	121	154	77	22	49	20	257	135	2333	1703
Manchester	22	68	44	167	271	194	63	267	359	524
Other N.W.	82	319	10	—	6	—	8	31	7	66
Total N.W.	225	541	131	190	326	215	328	433	2699	2293
N.W. share (%)	43	55	7	4	17	8	23	16	38	28

Source: N.P.C. *Annual Digests of Port Statistics.*

Table 9.4. *UK foreign trade in dry cargoes and the share of N.W. ports (000 tonnes).*

	Eire	*Continental Europe*	*Scandinavia and the Baltic*	*Iberia and the Mediterranean*	*Deep Sea*	*Total*
Imports						
UK total 1967	1,814	13,377	21,358	5,810	41,474	87,082
N.W. ports	759	941	2,707	1,560	11,748	18,046
Share of N.W. ports (%)	42	7	13	27	28	21
Exports						
UK total 1976	2,358	26,963	22,924	12,408	43,564	108,216
N.W. ports	1,277	1,435	1,739	2,032	8,905	15,388
Share of N.W. ports (%)	54	5	8	16	20	14

Source: N.P.C. *Annual Digests of Port Statistics.*

although at 43m. tonnes in 1976 it still accounted for 40 per cent of total trade. Although deep sea trades are still the most important in imports of basic materials and foodstuffs they now have only a third of trade in manufactures—about the same as the Continent. There have been substantial changes within this sector with some areas of growth, and some of decline, but the enormous re-development and re-adjustment required as a result of containerization has had to be accomplished in a not particularly strong overall trading environment. This has been the source of great difficulty for those ports which dominated trade in the conventional era.

Market shares clearly reflect the influences in transport geography outlined above. Liverpool and other north-west ports have small shares of the trades to Continental Europe, and to Scandinavia and the Baltic. They have a rather larger share of trades with the Iberian Peninsula and the Mediterranean and some 20 per cent of deep sea trades. Even if there had been no change in shares on individual routes the north-west's share of total trade would have declined, because growth has been concentrated in markets where it is relatively weak. However, with the exception of the Irish trade, where the north-west consolidated an already strong position, there has been some loss of share and total cargo volumes dropped from 18m. tonnes to 15·4m. over the period. As a final comment on these general trends it is clear they have resulted in a shift in favour of short sea trades, and because these are small ship trades there has been lively development among the smaller ports.

All north-west ports except Manchester participate in the Irish trade. Fleetwood is the most important as the new Pandoro service now handles some 125,000 units per annum, whilst Garston and Liverpool also have substantial levels of traffic. In the trades with

Continental Europe and Scandinavia, such traffics as there are tend to concentrate on the Port of Manchester because of the importance of small bulk trades along the ship canal. In trades with the Iberian Peninsular and the Mediterranean there is a more even split between Liverpool and Manchester. Finally, on deep sea trades the Port of Liverpool predominates, although even here Manchester until very recently had a large share of the Canadian traffic.

IV

One of the important trends of the last two decades has been the growing difference between terminals for short and near sea trades and those for deep sea trades. There always was a difference simply because the short sea trades used rather smaller ships, but with the application of new technologies this has become enormously more important.

Near sea services are characterized by small ships operating with great regularity on frequent services, so that there is an even daily load on the facility. Cargo exchanges are of a consistent moderate size, and the fact that there is a complete exchange reduces the complexity of terminal operations. The frequency of service holds down cargo dwell times and in many cases terminals do not carry out a consolidation function, limiting themselves to the processing of full unit loads. These factors combine to limit demands for space and depth of water so that many terminals operate at redeveloped conventional berths, and even where new developments are required they do not usually have expensive requirements for infrastructure.

Deep sea terminals for the major trades have a much more difficult task. The depth of water required is up to about 42ft. and since this is way beyond the limit of the conventional port, new sea access facilities are required. Depending upon the site, this can be very expensive. Extensive areas of land are required for large cargo exchanges combined with relatively long container dwell times. Most terminals provide a multi-user capability and there is often an uneven rhythm to ship arrival patterns which when combined with a lack of regularity or operational disturbance gives rise to severe peaks. The terminal operation is therefore, much more complex, rates of throughput are lower and costs per unit substantially higher. There is, therefore, a clear case for the specialization which has occurred. However, in the search for sites for small terminals it is arguable that one of the most important factors was the desire of operators to avoid the costs and problems of Liverpool and that if the evaluation had been purely on the basis of the merits of the site, Liverpool might well have had more to offer than some of the very limited locations that have in fact been selected. As the long-term limitations of some of these sites become more apparent the question of relocation in Liverpool could arise again; and there are some indications of this in recent demands for a riverside berth at Liverpool for short sea trades. Certainly there may be a case in transport terms and in terms of the best long-term use of the infrastructure of the region, for further consolidation in Liverpool and it will be unfortunate if lack of flexibility prevents the opportunities that this presents from being realized.

V

In the late 1960s, when attitudes to containerization were formed, emphasis was on the opportunities offered, the possibility of superport status in container trades and the need for major investments.

Experience of the last fifteen years shows that this understandable expectation and confidence was in fact misplaced. The ports best placed to take advantage of containerization were those with a stake in the conventional system but with a location appropriate to changing route structures and trading patterns, and Felixstowe is a clear example of this. Ports like Rotterdam and New York, which were well placed to serve the major cargo concentrations have also flourished, although there has been substantial redundancy of old facilities. Liverpool, in common with many other major conventional ports, was in fact facing a very difficult problem. It had to make substantial investments in new facilities, whilst at the same time dealing with the run down of a widely spread old dock complex and a large labour force; and all this had to be achieved in a difficult trading environment.

Liverpool's first bite of the cherry was the ambitious scheme at Royal Seaforth, which includes a large deep sea container complex, a new grain terminal, timber, and meat berths. There have been many difficulties in development of this complex but it has now achieved a substantial level of traffic. A second stage is now required to meet the needs of routes to developing countries as they containerize, and also to take advantage of such opportunities in short sea trades as may exist. This has to be achieved by a piecemeal process of redevelopment and a succession of modest investments achieved within the framework of a coherent overall master plan.

The process of re-adjustment and redevelopment at Liverpool has been a difficult and painful one, but it is clear that a substantial decline in the relative position of the port was an inevitable outcome of developments in trading patterns and container transport geography, whilst the decline in employment per tonne of throughput was an equally inevitable outcome of changing transport technology. Much of the re-adjustment has not been completed and the port has been very much slimmed down in terms of both facilities and the number of jobs it provides. However, it is still a major seaport and there are still opportunities. It is important that these should be taken and that the port should be operated as a viable enterprise and continue to make its contribution to the maritime transport industries and the life of the city.

NOTES AND REFERENCES

1. J. Bird, *The Major Seaports of the United Kingdom,* Hutchinson & Co. Ltd. (1969).

2. F. E. Hyde, *Liverpool and the Mersey.*

3. *Containers on the North Atlantic,* Marine Transport Centre, The University of Liverpool (1977).

4. *The Economics of Short Sea Freight Ferries,* Ibid. (1980).

5. *Containerline Performance and Service Quality,* Ibid. (1980).

6. Panamax containerships are the largest that have so far been built and were tailored to transit the Panama Canal. They are 950 ft. long, 105 ft. beam and 42 ft. draught and can carry 3000 20ft. containers.

7. In the early days some container lines, not wishing to use their new large ships on the traditional milk run, began to use small feeder ships in support, absorbing the costs of these services. Because of this and early somewhat erroneous ideas about the importance and effect of scale economies and the cheapness of trans-shipment, the view became current in the late 1960s that Europe might be served by one or two super-ports, wider distribution being obtained by networks of feeders. London and Rotterdam were both anxious to fulfil this role and other ports also had ambitions. However, the super-port idea fizzled out. Scale economies at the port are not an overwhelmingly powerful influence and in fact in many ways ports and shipping lines find moderate sized container exchanges easier to handle. For the ship itself containers have to be handled somewhere, and although cargo handling is slower in multi-port operations this loss of efficiency is more than counterbalanced by the wider distribution achieved. Many lines now follow the policy of having a moderate number of calls at each end of a long route.

8. Definitions here follow the groupings used in NPC Statistics. Liverpool encompasses Birkenhead, the British Transport Docks Board port of Garston, and the Unilever port at Bromborough. Manchester includes Ellesmere Port and Runcorn.

10

Merseyside's service and office economy

The key to future stability?

P. W. DANIELS

It is now generally accepted that Britain is moving into the post-industrial phase of its economic development (Bell, 1974; Gershuny, 1978). One of the principal symptoms of the transition to post-industrial life is the growing concentration of the country's labour force and its wealth in those industries which are collectively described as the service or tertiary sector of the economy. These industries are distinguished from the manufacturing or secondary sector by the fact that the latter are concerned with the production of a tangible good or product while the service industries are primarily concerned with organizing the transfer of these goods from one place to another, with the marketing of products, with the generation and exchange of a wide range of administrative and scientific information, or with the provision of social, educational, and welfare services (to name but a few) which regularly touch upon our daily lives. The service industries comprise a diverse range of activities which employed more than fifty-five per cent of Britain's labour force in 1971, a position which has been attained as a result of rapid growth since 1945. Technological and social change has accelerated during the last twenty years and has created a wide range of new skills and specialisms in the labour force and many of them have been absorbed by service rather than manufacturing industries which were the cornerstone of the Industrial Revolution.

Urban areas have been the principal recipients of the expansion of service industries and unemployment. Merseyside, with its long-standing dependence on these industries since the nineteenth century, would seem to be particularly well placed to benefit from the recent upsurge in the role of service industries in urban economies. It will become clear, however, that Merseyside has somehow missed out on the service revolution since 1945 and this

Bibliography begins on page 258.

has not helped the task of economic regeneration which has been one of the dominant policy issues in the area since the Depression of the 1930s. After outlining some important characteristics of service industries which may clarify the significance of some of the existing deficiences on Merseyside, the evolution and structural attributes of service industries on Merseyside before and after 1945 will be outlined. This is essential since the legacy from the past has had an important influence on present problems. The next section of the paper introduces office employment into the service industry equation because much of this kind of employment, which is also growing rapidly at national level, is concentrated in service industries and its performance is therefore a good indicator of the strength of Merseyside's service economy. The final section of the paper presents a brief résumé of the spatial distribution of office and service employment within Merseyside before turning to a consideration of how some of the problems and deficiencies which have been identified and which persist might be rectified. The underlying argument in this paper is that a sound service economy which contains a fair measure of 'growth' services is vital to Merseyside's economic health during the last quarter of the twentieth century (see also Goddard, 1979).

I

Service industries include construction, the public utilities such as gas, electricity, and water, insurance, banking, and finance, professional scientific services, a wide range of miscellaneous services, and public administration. Indeed the group is so diverse that it is difficult to make generalizations about trends for the sector as a whole though recent evidence suggests that it is continuing to absorb a growing proportion of the labour force (Central Statistical Office, 1978). The growth of service industries has not been uniform, however, and this is important since it is the biased sectoral structure of Merseyside service industry which has made the transition to a modern service economy so difficult. In this context it is useful to divide services not on the basis of the Standard Industrial Classification (as above), but to distinguish them according to whether they are producer or consumer services. This is a functional division of the service sector: consumer services are final services which are provided directly to customers such as sales of retail goods, legal advice about a motoring offence from your solicitor, or a visit to your doctor or dentist for treatment; producer services are those services provided to other organizations or firms before their products reach the consumer. Therefore these are sometimes called intermediate services. In theory this is a useful and distinction but in practice it is rarely possible to classify any one service activity as exclusively producer or consumer oriented. Many service industries, such as legal services, freight transport, or banking, provide output which goes to both producers and consumers and only a few industries such as market research or management consultancy can truly be classified as producer services. It is not easy to assign the proportion of a firm's output to intermediate and final services but it may be worth attempting to do so because it has been shown (Marquand, 1978) that the location behaviour of producer and consumer services is significantly different.

It has been found that the concentration of producer services increases with the size of urban areas while consumer services are much more evenly distributed in relation to city size (see Marquand, 1978; Hughes and Thorne, 1975). This suggests that the distribution of consumer services is population-related while producer services are employment-related i.e. they tend to be distributed relative to major concentrations of employment such as city centres in metropolitan counties such as Merseyside. The significance of this distinction becomes clearer when it is observed that a large proportion of office or white-collar occupations are primarily, although by no means exclusively, associated with producer services and those which are sometimes classified as 'mixed' services in that they cater for both intermediate and final demand. Many of these office occupations are also contact-intensive managerial and professional jobs which generate demand for a large number of supporting workers in clerical or technical occupations. It is therefore not surprising to find that office occupations also show a tendency towards concentration in large urban areas, particularly city centres and major suburban centres. It should now be clear that the performance of Merseyside's service economy is closely related to the producer/consumer balance of its service industries, the performance of these industries, and their effect on the level of office employment. Care must be taken, however, not to assume that all producer services are subject to the hierarchical effect on their location behaviour; service industries which are subject to government decisions about location such as universities, research establishments, or national government offices reveal a weak relationship with urban status. Some service industries are, in this sense, more 'footloose' than others and this provides Merseyside with a valuable source of additional service employment.

Another characteristic of service industries, which is helpful to an area like Merseyside with high unemployment rates, is that they are less likely to reflect the effects of vagaries in the business or economic cycle on the demand for labour. The demand for football pools coupons, nationwide banking facilities, visits to the local medical centre, or education, remains much the same whatever the state of the economy. But some service industries are very prone to external factors which are beyond their control, such as fluctuations in world trade, and it will be shown that this has been a critical factor in the poor performance of Merseyside's service sector since the War; an experience very different to most other areas of Britain where services have expanded steadily. A thriving service sector provides scope for adequate circulation of income through the urban system, thereby helping to sustain the demand for other service jobs.

There is still considerable uncertainty about the actual contribution of service industries to the economic growth of a city or region. Manufacturing is still considered by many observers to be the main generator of growth and to be largely responsible for a city's material welfare while service industries reflect the consumption of that wealth on less essential luxuries and because of this they can be described as 'parasitic' activities. This idea extends back to Adam Smith (1776) and lends itself to the conclusion that the shift from manufacturing to services typical of recent decades will reduce output and therefore material welfare. If this proposition is accepted, Merseyside's economic past and future cannot be viewed very favourably since services have been of above-average significance in its economy. It is often argued that service activities are always less productive than secondary industries and therefore policies should be biased towards the latter because they lead to a better use of resources. In practice, this argument is difficult to support very conclusively because the measurement of service sector output is elusive since so many of its 'products' are intangible and make labour productivity difficult to gauge accurately. Most measurements of service sector output are based on employment (which is an input) so that it is difficult to show whether the quantity or quality of service provided per man or per hour has changed (see Rostow, 1960; Fuchs, 1968; Smith, 1972; and Marquand, 1978; for a full discussion). Empirically, there is still no clear evidence that a high level of service employment is detrimental to city growth.

This brief sojourn into the characteristics of service industries has been made in the belief that it will help both an interpretation, as well as an appreciation, of the problems which continue to beset Merseyside's service economy. Possible ways of trying to resolve these difficulties may also be highlighted in this way but it must be stressed that the level of knowledge about the factors which determine the location and growth of service industries, especially the critical producer services, is infinitely smaller than that available for manufacturing industries. Local and central government have been slow to recognize and acknowledge the place of service industries in urban and regional development and this has also made Merseyside's efforts to amend the structure of its service economy more difficult than it might otherwise have been. Much research remains to be undertaken and recent initiatives by central government departments and research councils such as the Social Science Research Council suggest that the significance of service industries has finally, if very belatedly, been appreciated.

Against this background it is possible to proceed with an outline of the role of service industries in the Merseyside economy prior to 1945. It should be noted that the term 'Merseyside' is used to refer to different amalgamations of administrative areas such as local authority boundaries or labour exchange areas used for the purposes of individual studies. Throughout this paper the term is used in the context of the contemporary Merseyside Metropolitan County and although earlier Merseysides do not coincide exactly with the area covered by the present local authority an attempt is not made to define the actual area involved in each case since it is not considered that this affects the interpretation of the statistics which are cited from time to time. A more serious difficulty is that service industry definitions have not been consistently applied and this makes the analysis of trends over long periods rather hazardous. Hence, much of what follows is used to illustrate a problem rather than to provide a definitive analysis of trends in Merseyside's service industries during this century.

Two reports completed within ten years of each other in 1932 and 1942 provide a good indication of the status and structure of service industries on Merseyside before 1945 (University of Liverpool, 1932; Smith, 1942). Neither report was particularly concerned with services *per se*, an indication perhaps that the emergence of post-industrial society had not yet been appreciated, but the University of Liverpool (1932) report notes that

> Liverpool is pre-eminently a port, the centre of a great maritime and distributing industry. Out of 381,000 insured workers on Merseyside in 1930 (see table 10.1) no fewer than 193,000, or over one-half, were attached to *(service)* industries associated with Shipping, Transport and Distribution. The proportion of workers so engaged in the country as a whole was less than one-quarter (p. 12).

At this time some 65 per cent of Britain's insured workers were employed in manufacturing while in Merseyside the figure was only 37 per cent of all insured workers in the area. The remainder were employed in distribution, commerce, transport, and various forms of personal or public service. Contrary to the view of services as a stable source of employment, about three-quarters of Merseyside's unemployed in 1930 were in service industries. In a ranking of

Table 10.1. *Insured and employed persons in the service industries, Merseyside and Great Britain, 1930.*

Industries associated with:	*No. of workers* — *Insured* (*Merseyside*)	*No. of workers* — *Insured and employed* (*Merseyside*)	*% of all workers* — *Insured* — *Merseyside*	*% of all workers* — *Insured* — *GB and NI*	*% of all workers* — *Insured and employed* — *Merseyside*	*% of all workers* — *Insured and employed* — *GB and NI*
II Transport and distribution	108,100 (15·8)[2]	91,100	22·3	4·7 (7·9)	17·5	4·0
VIII General service[1]	45,300 (14·0)	39,000	11·3	11·7 (8·4)	13·0	12·6
Total (All industries)	381,000 (21·3)	297,000	100	100 (15·4)	100	100

1. Heterogeneous group which comprises professional workers; insured persons in the service of the Government or Local Authority; engaged in the provision of water, gas and electricity; on trams and 'buses; serving in hotels and cafes, and in laundries.
2. Percentage unemployed of total insured workers in each industrial group.

Sources. University of Liverpool (1932); *An Industrial Survey of Merseyside*, London, HMSO, Tables 1 and 2.

industries on Merseyside according to the numbers employed in 1930, the top five (accounting for approximately 50 per cent of the total number of insured workers) did not include a single manufacturing industry and 'towering high above all the others stands "Distribution", which includes shop assistants of every kind as well as those engaged in wholesale establishments . . . and its rapid and persistent growth since 1924 is a feature no less astonishing than its absolute size' (University of Liverpool, 1932, p. 47).

The paradox is that the undoubted dominance of service industries as a source of employment in Merseyside during the inter-war years was to be a liability rather than an asset in both the short- and long-term despite the trend since 1945 towards a level of national employment in services typical of Merseyside during the inter-war years. The distributive trades contained a significant proportion of population- and income-related consumer services rather than producer services and as the former have steadily declined in parallel with population loss on Merseyside the latter have not provided much growth by way of replacement or compensation. The dependence of the area on port-based service industries made it particularly vulnerable to the depression of the inter-war years as the level of imports and exports through the port fell and so helped to reduce the demand for labour. The 1932 report does note, however, that some consumer and mixed services did grow steadily between 1924 and 1930; entertainment, legal services, accountants, and estate agencies, provided some relief.

Table 10.2. *Importance of service industry groups on Merseyside, 1939 (%).*

Industry group	*Merseyside*	*UK*
Transport	15·0 (52)[1]	6·1
Distribution	19·1 (66)	14·9
Other services	25·3 (87)	25·3

1. Number of insured employed in each industry group (in thousands).

Sources. W. Smith (1942); *The Distribution of Population and the Location of Industry on Merseyside*, Liverpool, Liverpool University Press, part of table.

By 1931/2 the full impact of the depression was evident on Merseyside and, perhaps surprisingly, the recovery of its economy was much slower than for the United Kingdom as a whole. This reflects a structural problem with its service economy in that it was excessively dependent on the port and its activities; the volume of shipping using it, the volume of imports and exports, and the buoyancy of overseas trade affected the demand for producer and to some extent consumer services. But the factors controlling the performance of these activities were external and beyond the control of Merseyside. Thus the 1929 level of employment was not reached again until 1936 on Merseyside compared with 1935 for the United Kingdom as a whole. Employment grew steadily after 1936 and the sharp decline in United Kingdom employment in 1938 was not replicated on Merseyside.

At the end of the 1930s services still occupied a very significant place in Merseyside's economy (table 10.2). Transport, distribution, and other services accounted for 59·4 per cent of the total number of insured employees and it is not surprising that Smith (1942) concludes that the

> structure of manufacturing industry on Merseyside . . . is different from that of the county (Lancashire) as a whole. But it is also clear that manufacturing industry as such is not as important a source of insured employment on Merseyside as in the United Kingdom, the percentages being 40·6 per cent and 53·7 per cent respectively . . . The port rather than the workshop is the primary focus of the economy on Merseyside, now as in the past (p. 43).

As part of his analysis Smith divides the industries and services localized in Merseyside into five main groups and although the terms consumer and producer services are not used, the resulting classification is remarkably similar. Hence in Group 1 are industries and services, but mainly the latter, involved in the working of the port of Liverpool (port-dependent producer services). The other group (Group 4) comprises services which are characteristic of the functioning of a large conurbation (consumer services) and Smith notes that some of these will service other industries while others service the population directly; an early indication of the problem of labelling service industries as producer or consumer oriented.

The port therefore 'had a fundamental influence on the pre-war employment structure of Merseyside' (Department of Economic Affairs, 1965, p. 13) and it had to carry this legacy into the postwar years. Since 1945 the Merseyside economy has gradually been converging with that of Great Britain, so that by 1963 the proportion employed in manufacturing industry was about the same as the national figure although still lower than for the North-West Region as a whole. Service industries did not therefore continue to grow at the national rate and the levels evident in 1939 were much the same in 1953 and 1963 at approximately 60 per cent of the labour force. Some reasons for the static character of service employment during this period are evident from table 10.3 which shows that in absolute terms the number of additional jobs in services (excluding construction) in 1963 was higher than for manufacturing industry but the growth-rate was only half the national average for services. The growth-rate for manufacturing employment, on the other hand, was only just below the national rate.

Neverthelesss, only three out of eight service industry groups actually decreased their total employment between 1953 and 1963 compared with eight out of thirteen manufacturing industries. Construction recorded a marginal reduction of 0·8 per cent but transport and communication (– 8·1 per cent) and miscellaneous services (– 4·2 per cent) revealed more positive declines. The former decreased more rapidly than expected from the national rate (– 6·5 per cent), probably because of the legacy of over-representation from the inter-war years while the decrease in miscellaneous services can be attributed to labour shedding by the football pools industry, for example, for which Merseyside was the national centre in the 1950s (Department of Economic Affairs, 1965). Although the volume of trade through the port of Liverpool increased during the decade, improved cargo handling methods and a shift towards bulk cargoes such as oil, sugar beet, or grain, reduced the demand for dock labour from 17,000 in 1953 to 14,500 in 1963. The sluggish performance of the service sector was compounded by the fact that only public administration managed to grow faster than the national rate (19·8 per cent on Merseyside compared with 11·1 per cent nationally). This group includes civil service departments or local authority functions which as Marquand (1978) shows are least likely to conform to hierarchical effects on their location of the kind typical of intermediate or mixed services in general. The growth of insurance, banking and finance, and professional and scientific services, both of which contain an important element of producer services as well

Table 10.3. *Changes in service employment in the Merseyside area compared with Great Britain 1953–63.*

	Employees in employment on Merseyside		*Percentage change 1953–63*[2]		*Jobs provided by industry on Merseyside 1953–63*	*Changes in indigenous employment between 1953–63*
	1953	*1963*	*Merseyside*	*GB*	*(000's)*	*(000's)*
	(000's)					
All manufacturing industries (III–XVI)	256·9	266·8	+ 7·0	+ 7·6	31·2	− 13·1
Construction (XVII)	46·4	45·8	− 0·8	+ 16·8	–	− 0·4
Gas, electricity, and water (XVIII)	10·0	10·0	+ 3·1	+ 6·5	–	+ 0·3
Transport and communications (XIX)	96·6	88·8	− 8·1	− 6·9	–	− 7·9
Distributive trades (XX)	80·2	102·2	+ 18·1	+ 23·4	–	+ 14·6
Insurance, banking, and finance (XXI)	15·8	18·3	+ 22·1	+ 35·9	–	+ 3·4
Professional and scientific services (XXII)	48·5	66·2	+ 27·8	+ 38·2	–	+ 14·2
Miscellaneous services (XXIII)	68·5	65·4	− 4·2	+ 5·4	–	− 2·9
Public administration (XXIV)	24·5	28·0	+ 19·8	+ 11·1	–	+ 4·7
Total services[1] (XVIII–XXIV)	344·1	378·9	+ 7·6	+ 15·8	–	+ 26·4
Overall total	654·1	695·8	+ 6·4	+ 9·4	31·2	+ 10·5

1. The figures do not include certain seamen and civil servants. The Orders mainly affected are XIX and XXIV.

2. The figures in these columns cannot be derived directly from columns showing absolute employment in 1953 and 1963 because of adjustments made by the Standard Industrial Classification in 1959. The changes shown are thus not simply the result of absolute differences between 1953 and 1963.

Source. Derived from data in Department of Economic Affairs (1965) *The Problems of Merseyside* (An appendix to *The North West: A Regional Study*), London, HMSO, table 7.

as office occupations, only took place on Merseyside at about two-thirds of the national rate.

The problem clearly emerging during the late 1950s and early 1960s therefore revolved around decline of the area's 'traditional' services (many in the producer group) without adequate replacement with those service industries growing most rapidly elsewhere in the country. National growth-rates of 35·9 per cent for insurance, banking, and finance and 38·2 per cent for professional and scientific services were the highest for any industry group in the service sector but this was certainly not the case on Merseyside (see table 10.3).

Some indication of the conflicting attitude adopted towards the contribution of services and manufacturing industry as a source of new employment on Merseyside, which has persisted until very recently, is also provided by table 10.3. It was assumed that services were not mobile, although the Barlow Commission (1940) had made some reference to them, and that new jobs would therefore arise from the movement of manufacturing industries. There were certainly no incentives available of the kind provided for manufacturing industry but despite the absence of statistics in the 'new jobs' column of table 10.3 it seems highly unlikely that Merseyside's service economy was so internalized as to be exempt from the incursion or even attraction of new jobs if only as a result of corporate reorganization, takeovers, mergers, or the movement of service-type employment as a result of the in-migration of manufacturing plants attracted by the regional incentives. The Department of Economic Affairs (1965) summed up the situation in 1963 by commenting that this 'disparity (in the growth of services) is not readily accounted for by the high preponderance of services in Merseyside in 1953 and the growth of service employment is a matter which needs more detailed examination' (p. 20). It has taken another twenty-five years for research workers, local authority officials, and central government agencies to recognize the relevance of this plea and there are only recent signs of a concerted effort to improve our understanding of the factors which influence the growth and location of service industries.

The changes in the structure of Merseyside's service industries between 1953 and 1963 were also contributing to unemployment in a way which would not be expected from the earlier comments about the stability of these activities (table 10.4). Compared with Great Britain, Merseyside's share of unemployment in manufacturing industry was about the same for both males and females but in the service industries the figures for both groups are higher than the equivalent national statistics. The sources of this discrepancy can again be traced to just two industries, transport and communication and the distributive trades. Only the female wholly unemployed in transport and communication comprise a lower proportion of the

Table 10.4. *Wholly unemployed by service industry group, males and females, 1963.*

	Merseyside				*Great Britain*			
	Males		*Females*		*Males*		*Females*	
Industry group	*No.*	%	*No.*	%	*No.*	%	*No.*	%
Manufacturing industries (III–XVI)	7,473	30·5	3,774	38·8	106,502	30·8	42,633	37·1
Construction (XVII)	4,906	20·0	26	0·3	66,478	19·2	513	0·4
Gas, electricity, and water (XVIII)	218	0·9	12	0·1	3,447	1·0	205	0·2
Transport and communications (XIX)	4,418	18·0	135	1·4	26,217	7·6	2,313	2·0
Distributive trades (XX)	2,838	11·6	1,867	19·2	35,293	10·2	19,378	16·8
Insurance, banking, and finance (XXI)	221	0·9	81	0·8	4,986	1·4	896	0·8
Professional and scientific services (XXII)	289	1·2	418	4·3	5,634	1·6	6,540	5·7
Miscellaneous services (XXIII)	1,635	6·7	2,011	20·7	28,083	8·1	20,058	17·4
National and local government (XXIV)	1,162	4·7	116	1·2	19,778	5·7	2,577	2·2
All services	10,781	43·9	4,666	48·0	123,438	35·7	51,967	45·2
All industries and services[1]	24,511	100·0	9,712	100·0	345,666	100·0	115,036	100·0

1. Includes Agriculture, Forestry, Fishery, Mining, and Quarrying.

Source. Department of Economic Affairs (1965), *The Problems of Merseyside* (An appendix to *The North West: A Regional Study*) London, HMSO, derived from tables 25 and 26.

Table 10.5. *Employment structure and location quotients for Merseyside service industries, 1973.*

Industry group	*Merseyside % of total employment*	*Great Britain % of total employment*	*Location quotient Merseyside/ Great Britain*
Manufacturing (III–XVI)	34·4	34·6	–
Construction (XVII)	5·8	6·0	0·961
Gas, electricity, water (XVIII)	1·1	1·5	0·733–
Transport and communication (XIX)	10·1	6·8	1·507–
Distributive trades (XX)	12·6	12·1	1·041
Insurance, banking, and finance (XXI)	4·1	4·4	0·877*
Professional and scientific services (XXII)	14·4	14·3	1·007*
Miscellaneous services (XXIII)	10·0	9·5	1·052*
Public administration	8·2	6·9	0·880*
All services (XVIII–XXIV)	52·9	49·9	–
Total employment (thousands)	663	22,182	–

– denotes service industries declining at national level.
* denotes service industries growing at national level.

Source: Merseyside County Council (1975), *Merseyside Structure Plan: Draft Report of Survey, Economic,* Liverpool, County Planning Department, parts of figs. 21 and 59.

total wholly unemployed than the national proportion. Unemployment in the 'growth' services such as insurance, banking and finance, was below the national level but this cannot be taken as an indication of the stability of these activities because, as already noted, they expanded considerably more slowly on Merseyside than nationally between 1953 and 1963. The low share of unemployed in these services may simply reflect the imbalances in the job skills of Merseyside's labour force at that time with the less skilled occupations associated with many of the port-related services occurring in large numbers but often less amenable to re-orientation towards the office-based work required in the growth services.

By 1973 Merseyside's economic structure had moved even closer to the national average with service industries only accounting for 53 per cent of total employment compared with 50 per cent nationally (table 10.5). Structural problems have persisted, however, and are indicated by the location quotients which indicate the degree to which each service industry group is over- or under-represented on Merseyside relative to its national share of all employment. A value of 1·0 indicates that Merseyside has exactly the share expected while a value below or above 1·0 indicates under- or over-representation respectively. All the service industries, with the exception of transport and communication, are either badly under-represented, such as insurance, banking and finance (0·877), or very marginally over-represented, such as professional and scientific services (1·007). Therefore despite the steady shedding of labour by the transport and communication industries they continue to be the most heavily concentrated service activities on Merseyside (1·507). This occurs even though these industries contracted in employment terms by 45 per cent between 1959 and 1973 compared with nine per cent nationally. Some sectors which have expanded nationally have also showed some growth on Merseyside, but again it has taken place at a slower rate and has contributed to the poor location quotients for the growth services. Closer examination of the minimum list headings (MLHs) within each service shows that those experiencing national growth, such as accounting services or legal services in the professional and scientific services group, are also under-represented on Merseyside.

The most recently available evidence for the period 1971–6 indicates that the trends up to 1973 are continuing (Reeve, 1979). Merseyside's performance in relation to Manchester and other areas in the North-West continues to give cause for concern, particularly when the decline of service industries in central Liverpool is taken into account. Every category has declined to produce an overall change of – 19·1 per cent between 1971 and 1976 compared with 0·7 per cent in Merseyside as a whole. The equivalent figures for Manchester are – 4·5 per cent and 10·5 per cent and three industry groups, professional and scientific services, miscellaneous services, and public administration all increased their employment in Manchester city centre. The significance of these intra-regional and intra-urban differences in the performance and location of service industries may become clearer if attention is now devoted to the relationship between office employment and service industry on Merseyside.

II

It has already been mentioned that the expansion of service industries since 1945 has often been viewed as synonymous with the equally rapid growth of office occupations. Since some 65 per cent of these occupations are in the service sector it is reasonable to expect a connection with the performance of service industries on Merseyside. It has also become clear in recent years that office employment is an important, and growing, component within the manufacturing sector and this should be recognized when trying to identify suitable policies for office activity in general (Crum and Gudgin, 1977; Morris, 1978). In 1971 over 25 per cent of Britain's employees were engaged in office occupations and between 1961 and 1966 alone the number of office workers in the North-West increased by 10 per cent but, in common with services in general, Merseyside failed to conform with the regional growth-rate.

The reason can again be traced to the structure of the service sector which, as we have seen, is still dominated by transport-related services. The office work generated by shipping offices or by the offices of import/export agents has tended to be primarily in the clerical grades rather than in administrative, managerial, or professional/technical occupations. As with services in the years immediately after the War, the over-representation of clerical work has created an office occupation structure which is at variance with regional or national trends in which occupations other than clerical grades are expanding most rapidly. The contraction of port-related services combined with rationalization of clerical work as a result of improved office machine technology has nevertheless contributed to a decline of 3 per cent in the number of clerical workers in the conurbation between 1966 and 1971 (Daniels, 1977). This was the largest decline for any of the British conurbations. Administrative and professional occupations effectively counterbalanced this decline by increasing in absolute terms by some 11 per cent, but this was slower than in the other conurbations and particularly for Manchester where the growth was almost 16 per cent in five years. Merseyside cannot afford to lose office jobs which are desperately needed to counter job losses in other sectors of its economy.

Liverpool was the location of several headquarters of major companies and national organizations during the early 1960s but many of them have subsequently moved to other places in the North-West or to other parts of the country. Some of the most important examples, because of the number of office jobs that they represent, are the Cunard Company, Merseyside and North Wales Electricity Board, Silcock and Lever, and various government offices and smaller organizations. Merseyside also has a substantially lower proportion of civil service office jobs than expected from its share of the total national population (City of Liverpool, 1973). In view of Merseyside's position in the metropolitan hierarchy it should have rather more office jobs than the national average since it has been shown that office occupations are disproportionately concentrated in Britain's major cities (Daniels, 1975). In practice, Merseyside has between 5 to 10,000 fewer office jobs than expected. There can be little doubt that this level of under-representation is not just the result of out-migration by headquarters offices but is also a product of the degree to which Manchester has diverted service and office jobs away from Merseyside. Since 1961 Manchester has established itself as the regional capital and many regional offices of central government such as the Department of the Environment, Department of Transport, or Department of Trade and Industry, are located there along with the regional headquarters of nationalized industries and commercial companies, some of which have moved from Merseyside. Many of these are also producer

Table 10.6. *Distribution of service industry employment by district, Merseyside 1973.*

	Manufacturing		*Services*[1]		*Total*	
District	*M.*	*F.*	*M.*	*F.*	*M.*	*F.*
Knowsley	15·1	15·1	4·7	6·9	9·5	9·1
Liverpool	44·9	48·6	60·3	53·2	51·9	51·8
St Helens	17·8	14·0	7·0	7·8	13·0	9·5
Sefton	7·1	4·8	14·2	15·1	11·2	13·5
Wirral	14·6	13·2	13·6	17·3	14·3	16·0
	(100)	(100)	(100)	(100)	(100)	(100)
Merseyside (absolute totals)	157,224	71,431	191,533	197,859	391,447	272,374

1. Excluding construction.
Source: Department of Employment.

services and their presence as a group in Manchester is conducive to the further attraction of similar or related service industries which benefit from the information and contact-rich environment which exists. The absence of such growth in Merseyside has not provided conditions conducive to the growth of indigenous service/office activities or the attraction on a significant scale of such activities from outside.

The discussion so far has concentrated on the inherent structural weaknesses in the Merseyside service economy and its consequences for office employment in the context of trends in other cities and regions in Britain. These problems also manifest themselves as spatial variations within Merseyside and these must also be taken into account when trying to identify appropriate strategies for the future.

It cannot be expected that service employment will be evenly distributed throughout a city for two reasons; firstly, the distinction between producer and consumer services dictates that activities in the latter category will need to be located as near to their markets as possible i.e. their distribution is determined by the distribution of the city's population (retail employment is a good example), and secondly, many of the producer services are large-scale sources of office work and, until recently, this kind of activity has sought the most accessible locations in the centre of cities (insurance or shipping company offices are good examples). It is to be expected therefore that within Merseyside, Liverpool will have the largest share of service employment, rather more than expected from its share of total employment (table 10.6). The discrepancy is revealed most clearly for male workers of whom 60 per cent of the total employed in services in Merseyside are located in Liverpool which only has 52 per cent of all the jobs. Sefton also has rather more service jobs than expected and this probably reflects the expansion of office activities in the Borough, almost exclusively in Bootle, during the late 1960s and early 1970s prior to local government reorganization. Similar discrepancies for Liverpool and Sefton also apply to female workers in service employment although the differences compared with total employment for females in each area are much narrower than for males. A possible explanation for this is that female office workers, and probably other female workers, usually travel much shorter distances to work than males (Daniels, 1980) so that there is less opportunity for labour movement between the districts within Merseyside. In addition, this is reinforced by the fact that many of the jobs in the distributive trades are occupied by female workers. Nevertheless, there are rather fewer female workers than expected employed by service industries in Knowsley, St Helens, and Wirral, and this is not necessarily because these areas are under-serviced, but because they are dormitory areas for workers in office occupations or in port-related services who must travel to central Liverpool for employment.

It should already be evident that the uneven distribution of service employment and activity on Merseyside is connected with the distribution of office employment, much of which is generated by the producer and mixed services. Unfortunately, office employment has been declining in Merseyside as a whole but that which remains continues to be highly centralized in the centre of Liverpool. Thus, almost 30 per cent of the clerical workers employed in the Merseyside conurbation in 1971 (97,800) were employed in the city centre along with almost 23 per cent of the administrators and managers (Office of Population Censuses and Surveys, 1975). The degree of concentration in the office-dominated insurance, banking, and finance industry is even more marked with 42 per cent of those employed at workplaces in the conurbation working in Liverpool city centre (10,210); equivalent figures for transport and communications are 30 per cent and for local and central government offices, 28 per cent.

In common with most other British conurbation centres, Merseyside has been losing employment both in general and specifically connected with services and offices. This in itself should not be a matter for undue concern since decentralization of employment from city centres is a well established phenomenon in large cities but, almost characteristically, the rate of job loss from Liverpool city centre has been higher than for any other British city of comparable size. This is a matter of great concern because the decline may be undermining the functional diversity conducive to the attraction of replacement office and service activities from elsewhere in the country or the expansion of established (or indigenous) activities. Total employment in the city centre decreased by 35 per cent between 1966 and 1971 (table 10.7). Fortunately, office employment declined at a slower rate (20 per cent) so that whereas office occupations

Table 10.7. *Changes in the level of total and office employment in Merseyside conurbation centre, 1966–71.*

Employment (000's)[1]	*Year* *1966*	*1971*	*% Change* *1966–71*
Total employment	139	92	– 34·7
Office employment[2]	58	46	– 19·9
Clerical workers	40	28	– 29·3
Administrators and managers	6	4	– 24·2
Professional workers[3]	12	14	13·9
Great Britain (office)	5,484	5,998	9·3
Great Britain (total)	24,855	25,020	0·7

1. Office occupations by workplace as defined by the office of Population Censuses and Surveys, 1970.
2. The number of jobs has been rounded to the nearest thousand but the percentage change is based on the absolute figure for each year.
3. Includes a small number of sales, and transportation and communication workers.

Source: Census of Population, 1966 and 1971, *Economic Activity, County Leaflets.*

accounted for 42 per cent of city centre jobs in 1966, they had increased their share to 50 per cent in 1971. It is likely that this proportion has increased further since 1971, perhaps to 52 or 53 per cent as the overall decline of employment in the city centre continues. An increase in the proportion of city centre jobs in offices has been accompanied by important structural changes in the kinds of office occupations located there. Those office jobs which most depend on contact, often on a face-to-face basis and at frequent intervals, have been declining much more slowly and indeed, in the case of professional workers the numbers have increased by 14 per cent. Clerical workers, mainly engaged in routine work, in the city centre decreased by 30 per cent, however, along with a decline in the number of administrators and managers. These changes clearly show that the most specialized service and office jobs are attempting to remain in the most accessible, central part of the Merseyside conurbation but this trend towards locational and functional specialization is occurring against a background of deteriorating infrastructural diversity.

The loss of office jobs from the city centre does not mean that they are lost to Merseyside; some have been redistributed to suburban areas of the County, others have relocated to places beyond, and a third group comprise 'deaths' as a result of labour force contraction or closure of organizations in the city centre. Ideally, the reduction of city centre office employment would be balanced by an equivalent increase in the suburban areas. But on Merseyside many of the office jobs have been lost to places outside the County (perhaps 25 per cent) and therefore there is an imbalance between population and employment in office establishments as well as in service industries. Some success in retaining office employment outside the city centre has been achieved through large-scale office development at Bootle when, prior to local government reorganization, the County Borough was an active competitor for office space with central Liverpool. The former's more flexible planning criteria, readily available and cheaper sites, and very active promotion were important ingredients in its success at attracting office development and related employment (City of Liverpool, 1973). Most of the office space generated by this expansion has been occupied by central government departments, the most notable being the National Giro which brought a large number of clerical as well as some higher level posts to Merseyside. Given the current demise of the city centre it is perhaps worth pondering whether the expansion of Bootle has served the best long-term interests of Merseyside's service economy in that it has diverted valuable additional jobs and organizations from a more functionally diverse area which could have remained above the threshold of attraction for more office and related employment (for a fuller discussion see Daniels, 1977).

III

The ability of Merseyside's economy to adjust to the substantial economic and social changes since 1945 has been curtailed by inherited structural imbalances in its service industries, unfavourable conditions for the expansion of office employment, and a combination of environmental/image attributes which are considered detrimental to the attraction of new economic activity. Both national and local government agencies have been aware of these problems, particularly since the early 1960s in the case of services and office activities. The national interest stemmed from the over-concentration and high growth-rates of office activities in London and the South-East to the detriment of housing, transport, and related costs such as congestion. This prompted efforts to induce re-distribution of office establishments beginning with the creation of the Location of Offices Bureau (LOB) in 1963 and followed in 1965 by the introduction of office development permits (ODPs) which restricted the size and number of applications for new office development in London, the South-East and, for a time, the Midlands. It was hoped that the LOB through publicity and persuasion (it had no statutory powers) combined with the inability to expand or obtain space, especially in central London, would encourage organizations to move at least some of their office functions to regions such as the North-West or to problem areas such as Merseyside where office employment was badly under-represented.

The volume of relocation to Merseyside consequent upon such policies has been disappointing; LOB records show that between

1963 and mid-1977 twelve offices moved to Merseyside and provided 1167 jobs (Location of Offices Bureau, 1978). The majority of these jobs have been filled by workers from the local labour pool since long distance moves from London rarely attract more than ten per cent of the London office staff affected. Over half the moves (involving 1023 jobs) were to locations in Liverpool, principally the city centre, with the remainder moving to St Helens (64 jobs) and Southport (80 jobs). In relation to the employment decline already outlined the contribution of in-migrant private sector office to employment growth has clearly been negligible and Merseyside has largely relied on relocation or the creation of new offices by central government. Up to 1973 almost 2000 out of 9785 non-industrial civil service jobs in Liverpool (defined for this purpose as including Birkenhead, Bootle, Crosby, Litherland, and Wallasey) were the result of dispersal from London or new office work. Under the Hardman proposals (Civil Service Department, 1973) a further 1850 civil service jobs were to be dispersed from London to Merseyside beginning with the Ministry of Agriculture, Fisheries, and Food (1250 jobs) in 1980–1 and be accommodated in a new building to be constructed in Liverpool city centre on the site of the former Exchange Station. It was hoped that would be followed by the Foreign and Commonwealth Office (850 jobs) at a date yet to be fixed but recently announced cutbacks in public expenditure by the new Conservative government have put the dispersal programme in jeopardy and Merseyside may not receive all the jobs planned.

Large-scale relocations of this kind stimulate short-term demand for the output of other service industries, particularly construction, although this effect should not be exaggerated because other services such as building design, interior office organization, is often undertaken centrally and does not represent a gain to Merseyside (Yannopoulos, 1973; Civil Service Department, 1973). In the medium- and longer-term these offices create demand for additional office labour, particularly clerical workers, much of which can be undertaken by female office staff. While this may help to relieve some local unemployment it is now considered desirable that expansion of office activities in an area like Merseyside should include as large a component as possible of administrative and professional occupations since it is these executive and decision-making functions which provide the diversity necessary for a dynamic office and service economy which generates additional demand for labour and is attractive to organizations pondering alternative locations in the provinces.

Taken together, the combined contribution of commercial and government sector relocation of office employment has not been adequate to meet Merseyside's requirements. Up until mid-1973 this problem was aggravated by the absence of government incentives for service industries; most of the incentives have been directed at manufacturing industry and although it has clearly been necessary to try to attract such activities to Merseyside, this has overlooked the structural weaknesses in the service sector. Some scope for remedying this was provided by the introduction in 1973 of incentives specifically directed towards service industries. Some producer services might be attracted by the prospect of assistance with removal costs, a grant for each employee moved with his work, and up to five years rent-free accommodation or equivalent assistance if a building is purpose built by the occupier rather than leased. It is unnecessary to give the details of the original scheme except to say that the incentives did not appear to be adequate. Very few service firms took advantage of the scheme and, although precise figures are difficult to obtain, it is likely that only two or three office-based services used the incentives to come to Merseyside. Indeed, it has been suggested that, for operational reasons, these firms would have moved to the area whether or not grants were available.

The lack of interest in the service industry incentives has perhaps stemmed from the fact that compared to those available for manufacturing industry they are very limited; the availability of the assistance over 5–7 years is too long a period, and they have only favoured mobile service industries with a genuine choice of location between the assisted areas and elsewhere. Hence, at the end of March 1979 service industry grants were increased with the maximum grants for the creation of new jobs in the special development areas such as Merseyside increased to £6000. The grant for assisting the relocation of essential staff moving with their work has been increased to £1500 for each individual up to a maximum of 50 per cent of the total jobs offered in the assisted area. Two other important changes have been made; firstly, the grants are available to new projects and expansion of service industries already in Merseyside, for the ancillary offices of manufacturing industries, and for the administrative offices of nationalized industries. It has therefore been recognized, not before time as far as Merseyside is concerned, that indigenous companies need encouragement to remain where they are and assistance to expand and take on additional labour where possible. By providing assistance for ancillary offices in manufacturing it is hoped that this will discourage centralization of office functions (often in other parts of the country such as the South-East) or conversely decentralization because manufacturing companies often own land adjacent to their plants which may be cheaper to develop for office purposes than renting or constructing office space at similar sites in the South-East. There is at least one major company on Merseyside which has provided additional office work in this way in its national computer headquarters, although this took place before the service industry grants were introduced.

The second change has been a reduction in the period over which the grants are spread from up to seven years down to two years and this should be a major attraction. The only other change which may be helpful in the future is a building relief grant of 20–25 per cent of the cost of capital development which will stimulate office development on Merseyside where the asking rents at present costs may be too high to attract clients while others may be discouraged because there is no new vacant space immediately available.

In circumstances where Merseyside is dependent upon externally provided and controlled incentives to provide badly needed service or office employment its success depends upon its ability to compete with other provincial cities which can expect to benefit from the same provisions. A significant factor in this exercise may be the degree to which self-help is used to supplement the regional incentives and as a way of providing the conditions which will cause the decline of the service and office sectors to be halted and reversed into a growth situation. Since much of the recent growth in these sectors has mainly been undertaken by indigenous firms, self-help may also benefit them. It is now recognized that this source of growth is probably to be the major source of future expansion in Merseyside and other provincial areas (Department of the Environment, 1976).

Liverpool City Council has been most involved in trying to identify ways of stimulating office and service activities to expand or locate in the city centre. It is perhaps curious to find that despite the loss of office jobs in recent years the city centre has a very low vacancy rate for office premises; lower indeed than is normally considered acceptable for the operation of a 'healthy' office market. A recent survey (University of Liverpool, 1979) has shown that less than 500,000 sq. ft. (about 3 to 4 per cent) of the city centre office floorspace was vacant and this is a level very similar to that found in an identical exercise two years earlier. The true position is even more serious, however, because over 50 per cent of the vacant premises are in buildings which date before 1914 which are much more difficult to let and only seven per cent of the vacancies were found in buildings completed since 1970. Hence, only 22 per cent (18) of the 82 premises found to be vacant could be classified as in good condition with almost 39 per cent (32) decaying and probably difficult to let. A further important characteristic of the vacant space is that it is almost exclusively in units of less than 10,000 sq. ft. and this is inadequate to meet the requirements of office users looking for accommodation in Liverpool who, in recent years, have been looking for units between 10,000 and 30,000 sq. ft. The absence of new and larger units of office floorspace seems to indicate a lack of confidence on the part of development companies and investors on Merseyside and in the city centre. Yet the City of Liverpool promulgates the view that if office space of the right size in the right location was provided, demand would be forthcoming. The 'right' office expansion area is the Moorfields/Old Hall Street area and the appropriate size of development is considered to be that which can be let in units of 10 to 40,000 sq. ft. (City of Liverpool, 1978). If this is the case, surely the developers would have appreciated the scope for additional office space especially as medium-sized developments considered to be in demand involve fewer financial risks than larger developments which may still prove difficult to let. Even if some of the latent demand can be met in this way, there is also scope for more rehabilitation of existing office premises in order to improve the offices used by smaller enterprises which, in absolute terms, are far more numerous than large employers in the city centre. The problems which confront attempts to attract office development and employers to the city centre are a microcosm of the situation on Merseyside as a whole, particularly when the effect of two long-term factors which are the County's image and its environment are included.

There seems to be little doubt that both these variables require improvement but, at best, this can only be a gradual process over several years. The image of Merseyside commonly portrayed in the media seems to be a disincentive to developers and investors even though many would agree that the picture presented is invariably very selective and never counterbalanced by a view of the positive qualities of the area. It seems that when the private sector considers the possibility of providing office floorspace in the city centre, for example, it includes in its estimates of the capital value of the proposed development an allowance for the poor image of Merseyside. These include the threat of industrial stoppages in the construction industry; pessimistic forecasts of the future prospects for the region; and pessimistic forecasts therefore of the demand for office space (City of Liverpool, 1978). It is difficult to know how the imageability of Merseyside can be changed except through positive efforts by local agencies to modify, through publicity and other mechanisms, the image of the County. The environmental factor includes planning blight and vacant, often derelict, land in the city centre and elsewhere, particularly the inner city areas where the delayed plans for the Inner Ring Road have blighted large areas. An air of decay or stagnation in site and property development hardly indicates a dynamic urban economy and the city centre in particular would benefit from completion of some schemes such as the Central Station site, the cleaning-up, seeding, or enclosure of existing vacant sites, and attempts to minimize the amount of planning blight.

A 'cosmetic' package may reap returns but will do little to resolve short-term problems; local authorities will need to take more positive initiatives in this respect and one of the principal possibilities is for the local authority to engage in some kind of partnership in the office development process to produce 'advanced offices' akin to the advanced factories made available to manufacturing industry. This was suggested in 1977 by the National Enterprise Board on the basis that the local authority would not levy rates on an office building until a tenant takes possession. Rates are levied on empty office buildings in most cities and this is considered another major disincentive to office development in Merseyside. Other possibilities in partnership are rent-sharing schemes, rent guarantees for fixed periods, leaseback arrangements, or the formation of a development company in which public and private enterprises are brought together in a way which allows the local authorities to raise funds on the private market and the development companies to utilize their skills in providing new office development (City of Liverpool, 1978). An example of this arrangement is the Manchester Mortgage Corporation which successfully financed the development of the Arndale Shopping Centre in central Manchester. Finally, it has also been considered necessary to seek permission from the Department of the Environment for 125 year rather than 99 year leases. It seems that if the freehold of a site cannot be obtained developers are discouraged by 99 year leases which, assuming a 60 year building life, only allows enough time for one building to occupy a site. A more financially viable investment is possible if there is the likelihood of two buildings occupying a site during a 125 year lease.

It remains to be seen whether these and related initiatives will produce the desired effect when they are implemented. There are advantages and disadvantages attached to all the alternatives, not least the need for approval from central government or the effect of the proposal on local financial resources. Whatever the outcome it is only likely to satisfy the demand for immediately available good quality office space in substantial volume. But there is also scope for encouraging more rehabilitation of existing small office premises. Redevelopment in the city centre or other centres in Merseyside usually involves replacing smaller structures with larger ones for which the rents may be higher and the developers unwilling to lease the space in small units because of the increase in administrative overheads. Rehabilitation in selected parts of the city centre such as the lower part of Mount Pleasant or the east side of Bold Street upgrades the environment, provides accommodation which may be especially attractive to small indigenous office enterprises, and may in turn encourage other activities to move to or rehabilitate office premises in the same area.

IV

Service industries have played an above-average role in Merseyside's economy during the twentieth century. But as our national economy becomes increasingly dominated by the service sector as a source of employment and income, Merseyside enters the 1980s with a range of office and service industry problems which belie its traditional role as a major national centre for service industries. It would be wrong to suggest that these problems can easily be traced to the structural and functional deficiencies evident during the 1930s but the die was cast by the time the Second World War had come to an end. Circumstances on Merseyside since 1945 have worked against the re-orientation of the service and office economy in order that it can play its proper part in the life of a large provincial city during the last quarter of the twentieth century. This does not just involve adequate provision of consumer services but a range of producer services which are a major source of office employment as well as being vital cogs in the post-industrial economy of cities. They service the diverse and increasingly specialized needs of manufacturing and other service industries and generate a business and economic environment which boosts confidence in the merits of office and other development. Merseyside's problem is how to break out of the spiral of cumulative decline in office and service activities which acts as a barrier against the attraction of new or replacement activities. National policies for regional development have been singularly unsuccessful in this respect and it seems vital that Merseyside should help itself as far as resources and other limitations permit.

Much of the discussion in this paper has focused on the office sector within services but many of the comments are pertinent to services in general. The city centre has also been given considerable attention and this bias reflects its key role in any successful effort to maintain the stability of the present service economy of Merseyside as a whole. There are of course other issues relating to the spatial distribution of office and service employment in an area as large as Merseyside; should a more dispersed pattern be encouraged in order to ensure a better balance between the distribution of population and employment; should this pattern incorporate a small number of centres which are complementary to or compete with the city centre; should office or science parks be promoted at locations on the edge of Merseyside where the environmental and working conditions would be attractive to high technology migrant service industries? These are only a few of the possible questions for which an answer has not been attempted here. In many ways these questions are of secondary importance, for Merseyside, along with its constituent local authorities and agencies, must first find the right blend of image rectification and incentives to attract investment before it can worry about where these activities should be located. It may even be unrealistic to search for growth of services and office activities on Merseyside for the rest of the century, rather it will be enough if the *status quo* or stability of the present service economy, however imperfect, can be retained at present levels.

BIBLIOGRAPHY

D. Bell, *The Coming of Post-Industrial Society*, London (1974).

Central Statistical Office, *Social Trends*, London (1978).

City of Liverpool, *Office Development in Liverpool City Centre*, Liverpool, City Planning Department (1973).

——, *City Centre Statement: Second Progress Report*, Liverpool, City Planning Department (1978).

Civil Service Department, *The Dispersal of Government Work from London*, London (1973).

R. E. Crum and G. Gudgin, *Non-production Activities in UK Manufacturing Industry*, Brussels, Commission of the European Communities, Regional Policy Series No. 3 (1977).

P. W. Daniels, *Office Location: An Urban and Regional Study*, London 1975).

——, 'Office location in the British conurbations: trends and strategies', *Urban Studies*, **14** (1977).

——, 'Service sector office employment and regional imbalance in Britain, 1966–71', *Tijdschrift voor economische en sociale geographie*, **69** (1978).

——, *Office Location and the Journey to Work*, Farnborough (1980).

Department of Economic Affairs, *The Problems of Merseyside* (An Appendix to *The North West: A Regional Study*), London (1965).

Department of the Environment, *Office Location Review*, London, Department of the Environment (1976).

V. R. Fuchs, *The Service Economy*, New York, Bureau of Economic Research (1968).

J. I. Gershuny, *After Industrial Society*, London (1978).

J. B. Goddard, 'Office development and urban and regional development in Britain', in P. W. Daniels (ed.), *Spatial Patterns of Office Growth and Location*, Chichester (1979), pp. 29–60.

J. T. Hughes and E. Thorne, *Service Industries in Metropolitan Areas* (mimeo), University of Glasgow, Department of Economic and Social Research (1975).

Location of Offices Bureau, *Decentralization from London by LOB Clients* (mimeo), London, Location of Offices Bureau (1978).

J. Marquand, *The Role of the Tertiary Sector in Regional Policy: Comparative Report* (Second Draft), Brussels, EEC Commission (1978).

Merseyside County Council, *Merseyside Structure Plan: Draft Report of Survey, Economic*, Liverpool, County Planning Department (1975).

D. Morris, 'Trends in office employment: are planners initiating the right strategies?', *The Planner*, **64** (1978), pp. 106–7.

Office of Population Censuses and Surveys, *Population Census 1971: Workplace and Transport Tables (Part I)*, London (1975).
D. E. Reeve, 'Service employment trends in the North West, 1971–76', *Working Paper No. 9*, Manchester, North West Industry Research Unit (1979).
W. Rostow, *The Process of Economic Growth*, Oxford (1960).
A. D. Smith, *The Measurement and Interpretation of Service Output Changes*, London, National Economic Development Office (1972).
W. Smith, *The Distribution of Population and the Location of Industry on Merseyside*, Liverpool (1942).
University of Liverpool, *An Industrial Survey of Merseyside* (1932).
——, Survey of vacant office premises in central Liverpool by Department of Geography undergraduates, March 1979.
G. Yannopoulos, *The Local Impact of Decentralized Offices*, London, Location of Office Bureau, Research Paper No. 7 (1973).
Report of the Royal Commission on the Distribution of the Industrial Population, London (1940).

INDEX